Laura S. Scherling (ed.)
Digital Transformation in Design

Design | Volume 63

Laura S. Scherling (Ed.D.) is a designer, researcher, and author. She is a director and faculty at Columbia University, where she also completed her doctorate. Her research foci are emerging technologies, design, media, and sustainability topics.

Laura S. Scherling (ed.)
Digital Transformation in Design
Processes and Practices

[transcript]

Bibliographic information published by the Deutsche Nationalbibliothek
The Deutsche Nationalbibliothek lists this publication in the Deutsche Nationalbibliografie; detailed bibliographic data are available in the Internet at https://dnb.dnb.de/

This work is licensed under the Creative Commons Attribution 4.0 (BY) license, which means that the text may be remixed, transformed and built upon and be copied and redistributed in any medium or format even commercially, provided credit is given to the author.
https://creativecommons.org/licenses/by/4.0/
Creative Commons license terms for re-use do not apply to any content (such as graphs, figures, photos, excerpts, etc.) not original to the Open Access publication and further permission may be required from the rights holder. The obligation to research and clear permission lies solely with the party re-using the material.

First published in 2024 by transcript Verlag, Bielefeld
© **Laura S. Scherling (ed.)**

Cover layout: Maria Arndt, Bielefeld
Printed by: Majuskel Medienproduktion GmbH, Wetzlar
https://doi.org/10.14361/9783839471425
Print-ISBN: 978-3-8376-7142-1
PDF-ISBN: 978-3-8394-7142-5
ISSN of series: 2702-8801
eISSN of series: 2702-881X

Printed on permanent acid-free text paper.

Contents

Acknowledgements 9

Making Sense of the Digital Transformation in Design
An Introduction
Laura Scherling 11

Part 1: Essays on Equitable Processes and Practices

Digital Design for Trust and Trustworthiness
Jeffrey Chan 19

Delegated Power
The Ethics of Nudging in Building More Equitable Product Experiences
Timothy Bardlavens 35

DialecTikTok
The Dynamic Semiotics of Amateur Visual Trends on TikTok
Sarah Edmands Martin 55

Equality of Fit in Digital Typography
Thomas Jockin 65

Equitable Digital Access in an Era of Uncertainty
Laura Scherling 79

Learning from FemTech to Inform the Design of Healthcare Technologies
Catalina Alzate 97

NFTs between Art and Design
A Story of Digital Transformation
Lucilla Grossi and Luca Guerrini 113

Design of Virtual Worlds
Zhenzhen Qi 133

Crafted Identities
Technological Transformations in Textile Design
Nishra Ranpura 149

Part 2: Case Studies and Interviews on Educational Processes and Practices

Design for Future Skills
Three Case Studies on the Role of Design in Shaping the Narrative
of Technology Education
Serena Cangiano 169

Reflections on Digital Transformation in Design
An Interview with John Maeda
Laura Scherling 187

No Back to Normal: Studio Forward at California College of the Arts
An Interview with Cristina Gaitán and Juan Carlos Rodriguez Rivera
Rachel Berger 195

An Archaeology of Digital Architecture
Kai Franz 211

Designing Games for Social Change
An Interview with Colleen Macklin
Laura Scherling 229

Digital Transformation and Service Design Practice in Public Sector
Sahar Nikzad and Paulina Porten 241

In Support of Design Students
An Interview with Ellen Lupton
Laura Scherling 255

Designing and Digital Storytelling for Climate Change Education
Gege Dong, Mir Sana Ullah Khan, and Andrea Orellana 261

Navigating the Transformative Potential of Technologies in Design
A Conclusion
Laura Scherling 277

Contributing Authors 283

Selected Readings 289

Acknowledgements

This book involved a group of multidisciplinary designers, researchers, educators, creative technologists, and computer scientists from varied backgrounds in product design, design research, interaction design, service design, game design, architecture, graphic design, and creative technologies. They work in universities such as California College of Arts, Columbia University Teachers College, Köln International School of Design, Parsons School of Design, Singapore University of Technology and Design, Rhode Island School of Design, University of Applied Sciences and Arts of Southern Switzerland, University of Notre Dame, and at organizations like Microsoft, Adobe, and The Ethafa project.

Thank you to the authors for taking part in an open-source book project. This project was inspired by my doctoral research at Teachers College Columbia University. I would also like to thank my partner Dr. Laurence Wilse-Samson for his research and editing support.

Many book chapters contain excerpts from interviewees and artistic contributions by close collaborators of the authors. We would like to thank them for their generous contributions. These outstanding individuals and organizations include: Dr. John Maeda, Colleen Macklin, Ellen Lupton, Raul Enriquez and Community Tech New York, Essie Workie and the Migration Policy Institute, Cristina Gaitán, Juan Carlos Rodríguez Rivera, Ian Cheng, Gen Ramírez, Renée Steven, Mandy Michael, Nicholas Lea Bruno, Kate Yang, Morgan Wash, Claudia Cossu Fomiatti, Tim Pulver, and Oliver Brückner.

Making Sense of the Digital Transformation in Design
An Introduction

Laura Scherling

This edited collection of essays, case studies, and interviews critically examines digital transformation in design. By "digital transformation" is meant the set of transformations that occur as organizations learn to adopt and integrate digital technologies into their processes and practices, which often involves the design of new products and services. It is a significant organizational and cultural shift to embrace emerging technologies, which at a minimum can mean keeping up with new tools and techniques, but also means fostering innovation and economic growth. These organizational "shifts" to engage with emerging technologies can simultaneously expose social inequities, biases, and unethical use.

People are naturally consumers of design. Without much deliberation, they embrace digital tools, social media, websites, apps, smart devices, digital art, video games. As technologies are adopted, designs are invented, redesigned, and modified. These transformations are now familiar. Yet as our "human-technology entanglement" grows, considerations about the ethical, economic, and social outcomes of product transformations, digitization, and "algorithmization" become more urgent.[1] Satish Nambisan, Mike Wright, and Maryann Feldman pointed out that in order to use digital technologies to solve "societal challenges," underlying tensions must be explored.[2] Amarolinda Zanela Klein argued that it is essential to consider how exactly technologies

---

1   Amarolinda Zanela Klein, "Ethical Issues of Digital Transformation," *Organizações & Sociedade* 29 (2022), 444.
2   Nambisan, Satish, Mike Wright, and Maryann Feldman, "The digital transformation of innovation and entrepreneurship: Progress, challenges and key themes." *Research Policy* 48, no. 8 (2019): 103773.

are used to ensure the creation of designs that consider social justice, sustainability, "human dignity," and trust. Seeking to fill this gap, the authors in this collection investigate some of the issues that emerge in the adoption of digital technologies in design.

The chapters in this collection gather leading designers, researchers, and educators who come from the United States, China, Colombia, Germany, India, Iran, Italy, Pakistan, Singapore, and Switzerland. The authors' ideas and expertise come from varied design disciplines. Their essays, interviews, and case studies paint a layered and diverse picture of what digital transformation in design can look like.

This collection is divided into two parts. Part 1, "Digital Transformation: Essays on Equitable Processes and Practices," examines the varied ways in which designs can empower or impede the digital transformation process. Part 2, *"Digital Transformation:* Case Studies and Interviews on Educational Processes and Practices" considers the pedagogical practices and insights that have supported those pursuing design and technology-driven work, recognizing that educators and their students, in particular, have undertaken the tremendous task of preparing to work in technology-focused industries.

Part 1 provides an overarching investigation of some of the critical issues pertaining to digital transformation in design. Dr. Jeffrey Chan's chapter considers the increasing interactions between people and intelligent machines, highlighting the need for trust and trustworthy attributes in digital design. Chan explores examples like blockchain technologies and autonomous digital design. Challenging sensibilities around race, power, and privilege, Timothy Bardlavens examines the intersection between behavioral public policy ethical frameworks (BPP) and design, demonstrating that designers and organizations have the ability to "nudge" users towards certain behaviors. Examining some of these manifestations in social media, Sarah Edmands Martin questions how major platforms like TikTok can disrupt and reinvent user experience and visual semantics. Thomas Jockin considers ways to better engage people through designing and developing digital typography models that are more sensitive to users' needs. Dr. Laura Scherling next considers interventions that have been designed to address digital divide and digital access issues.

Chapters 6-9 more examine technology trends related to digital transformation in design, including digital health, the use of blockchain-based technologies, immersive design, and textile design. Catalina Alzate advocates for designers to engage with digital health technologies for women,

"FemTech," in a way that prioritizes health equity and social justice. Looking at developments in another emerging area of study, Lucilla Grossi and Luca Guerrini study how non-fungible tokens (NFTs) have transformed the art market, while also offering a new field for experimentation for designers and artists. Also considering some of the tensions between traditional and contemporary interactive and experiential design, Zhenzhen Qi investigates the agent-world entanglement and related dilemmas in contemporary gaming environments, taking into account historical events and case studies. Part 1 concludes with Nishra Ranpura looking into how the work of textile designers is simultaneously advanced and disrupted by digital transformation, questioning what it means to preserve traditional identities in textile design as digital simulations promote ease of production.

While Part 1 provides an exhaustive snapshot of digital transformation in design, Part 2 provides inspiring research on educational processes and practices. These chapters on the relationships between digital transformation, design, and education are explored through a series of case studies and interviews that provide practical examples and frameworks. Some of the themes in these chapters include design and experimentation, civic engagement research and experiences engaging with the local communities, and what it has meant to deal with digital learning during the Covid-19 pandemic.

Part 2 begins with a case study by Dr. Serena Cangiano on humanist approaches to designing inclusive interfaces. Cangiano observes that while narratives on digital transformation in education are often focused on one's coding ability, it is rarely considered how new technologies can also reinforce social inequity. Like Cangiano, Dr. John Maeda contemplates some of the inadvertent fallouts that can take place in regard to working with new technologies. In an interview with Maeda, he explores the meaning of digital transformation, considering technology use for social innovation, while describing ways in which unintended consequences of technology use can be better mediated in educational and work spaces. Chapters 12 through 14, foreground "curiosity" and "speculation" as a means to contend with digital transformation. In an interview and conversation between Rachel Berger, Juan Carlos Rodriguez Rivera, and Cristina Gaitán, Berger investigates how multi-disciplinary teams of design students can imagine design futures and address the problem of "poverty-of-the-imagination" through speculation, worldbuilding, and storytelling. Kai Franz builds on these imaginative approaches to thinking about technology by critically interrogating how the use of computer-aided design and 3D-printed artifacts can help designers to reflect on technological determinism. He shares his ideas through his body of work and research in architecture, computational design, and art. Colleen Macklin, in an interview, shares insights into how game design and play-based interventions can support socially innovative practices to help address issues like environmental sustainability. These explorations of design pedagogy are followed by a short interview and provocation with Ellen Lupton, describing some of the contemporary issues that designers, particularly design students and young professionals, must navigate today, including epidemic levels of mental health distress. In the concluding chapters, Sahar Nikzad and Paulina Porten research how service design can promote citizen participation in light of the worldwide trend toward the creation of e-governance and Gege Dong, Mir Sana Ullah Khan, and Andrea Orellana look at how design and digital technology has transformed the way we share stories and how digital storytelling can be used for climate change education.

There is no doubt that digital technologies will continue to play a major role in society, work, and education. We envision that this edited collection will serve as a resource for designers and creative professionals across many design, technology, and research disciplines. As organizations, schools, and individuals embrace cultures of digital design, coding, research, and artificial intelligence, the broad appeal of design will only continue to grow and flourish. To date, there continues to be a limited number of publications on the topic of digital transformation in design, with a majority of digital transformation-focused literature grounded in business and economic studies,[3] or in the digital humanities and social sciences.[4] The designer's voice is frequently absent from discussions about the impacts of digital transformation. The insights of designers are an important feature of this collection because these

---

3 See Mark Baker, *Digital Transformation*, 2nd ed. (Buckingham: CreateSpace Independent Publishing Platform, 2014); Neil Perkin and Peter Abraham, *Building the Agile Business through Digital Transformation* (Kogan Page, 2017); David L. Rogers, *The Digital Transformation Playbook: Rethink Your Business for the Digital Age* (New York: Columbia Business School Publishing, 2016); Kader Sakkaria, Imran Karbhari, and Trevor Macomber, *Chaos by Design: Tales of Empowerment on the Path to Digital Transformation* (California: Leaders Press, 2021).

4 e.g., Katherine Hayles, *How We Think: Digital Media and Contemporary Technogenesis* (Chicago: University of Chicago Press, 2012); Howard Gardner and Katie Davis, *The App Generation: How Today's Youth Navigate Identity, Intimacy, and Imagination in a Digital World* (New Haven, CT: Yale University Press, 2013).

perspectives help us better understand how digital transformation elevates design and renders them obsolete.

Much technology- and design-focused research continues to be lacking in diversity and it is important to create more comprehensive educational resources that support "a more diverse audience of design students, practitioners, managers, thinkers, enthusiasts, clients, consumers, and policy makers."[5] There have been some recent notable scholarly developments, as seen with research by Jacinda Walker and Ksenija Berk, and the growth of global collectives and organizations dedicated to diversity and inclusion initiatives such as Decolonising Design, and the Design Justice Network. Nevertheless, progress toward this goal has been relatively slow. As a research limitation, this book cannot be fully representative of all ethnicities, identities, and belief systems, however we aim to expand the voices that you will hear from on this important topic of digital transformation in design.

At the heart of contemporary change are the many creative professionals and educators who play central roles in digital transformations processes and practices and are also uniquely placed to interpret it. Their views are critical to understanding technology change. Collectively, these chapters address work being done across the design disciplines to address digital transformation, document what progress has been made so far, and explain what ideologies, priorities, and agendas are necessary to see more ethical processes and practices implemented.

---

5 AIGA National Committees & Task Forces, "Diversity, Equity, & Inclusion," https://www.aiga.org/membership-community/diversity-equity-inclusion.

Part 1: Essays on Equitable Processes and Practices

Digital Design for Trust and Trustworthiness

Jeffrey Chan[1]

Digitalization in design is likely to mean that people are increasingly interacting with machines—especially intelligent machines that can learn from and respond to human behaviors. Trusting these intelligent machines will be critical to their successful deployment. However, what does trust in intelligent machines mean? The trust observed in cooperative and sustained human relationships at least relies on (i) encapsulated (shared) interest (i.e., A trusts B because B's interest encapsulates A's), or (ii) a moral commitment for trustworthiness, or (iii) strong psychological disposition to be trustworthy. At least for the immediate future, intelligent machines can only demonstrate reliable and robust functioning for building trust. Although reliable functioning is a necessary attribute, it is insufficient because people tend to trust intelligent machines when they also know, inter alia, why these machines make a particular decision or prediction. To cement trust between people and intelligent machines, there should be formative conditions for trust and trustworthy attributes embodied by intelligent machines—conditions and attributes that can come about through design. This chapter discusses different theories of trust and then explains why they are limited when applied to the context of interacting with intelligent machines. This knowledge gap suggests the need to consider how to design conditions for trust and attributes of trustworthiness in artificial artifacts, processes, and systems. In sum, this chapter aims to highlight the emerging gap between digital design and artificial intelligence, and demonstrate why the design of trust and trustworthiness will be vital to bridging this gap.
— Dr. Jeffrey Chan, Singapore

---

[1] Singapore University of Technology and Design, Singapore.

Digitization can be defined as a shift, either in part or in full, from what once required in-situ human interaction with physical artifacts to virtual, automated, or even autonomous machine interaction. Consider a visit to the bank. Customers used to enter a lofty-looking building, were greeted by a bank-teller, attended to their transactions, and when in doubt, queried the teller. Even in the span of this brief visit, customers were able to gauge many things for trusting the bank with their transactions: for instance, knowing something about the reputation of the bank before the visit, observing its physical upkeep, noting the countenance of the bank-teller, and perhaps, evaluating if their complaints had been empathetically addressed. Uncertainty and vulnerability may be the core elements of trust relations;[2] but trust only begins when the apprehension of uncertainty and vulnerability is somewhat assuaged—for instance, when customers' expectations and their experiences of in-person banking align, reinforcing the bank's real or perceived trustworthiness.

But digital banking has upended conventional conduits of building trust. Through a digitized assemblage consisting of information storage, transmission, networking, processing hardware and associated software and interface capabilities—presented via a virtual banking platform—a customer now interacts with a set of prefigured choices on the screen while being assisted by a disembodied bot.[3] This customer can no longer observe the bank's upkeep, verify a query, or gauge the helpfulness of tellers. Complaints to customer service are often directed to an automated system, where replies are all but uncertain. Yet a customer is nevertheless asked to trust the bank. The intangibility of digitization clouds judgment and phishing scams lure even savvy customers to surrender their banking credentials on fake bank websites where vast sums of money are lost and where mistrusting scammers for the bank has escalated into open distrust of digital banking and even reputable banks.[4]

---

2 Carol A. Heimer, "Solving the Problem of Trust," in *Trust in Society*, ed. Karen S. Cook (Russell Sage Foundation, 2001), 43.
3 William J. J. Mitchell, *E-Topia* (Cambridge: The MIT Press, 1999), 71–72.
4 Bryan Tan, "Commentary: Banking Scams and Phishing Attacks – New Measures Should Apply to Other Business Sectors," *ChannelnewsAsia*, January 27, 2022, https://www.channelnewsasia.com/commentary/ocbc-phishing-banking-scams-digitalisation-monetary-authority-singapore-cybersecurity-2459961.

This example highlights how digitization can often diminish, if not directly, undermine trust. Instead of designing for trust, digital designers promise even more sophisticated (cyber-)protection or impregnable security architectures. The distributive networked technology of blockchain has been described as an ironic architecture of "trustless trust"—an example of how digital design sidesteps the many vulnerabilities of trust.[5] Blockchain technology shares information among parties that may not necessarily trust one another, but nevertheless generates an output that can be considered trustworthy.[6] Yet the blockchain, while guaranteeing greater security, cannot enjoy the many pleasures of trust that generate benefits for social life.[7] A bank receives the benefit of a good reputation from the lavished trust of its customers, just as customers who are trusted by a reputable bank can access greater credit than those who are not. Subsequently, a trusted bank is incentivized to do better, which benefits shareholders and customers, and by extension, also the community. Conversely, trusted customers can afford to invest in new businesses, creating jobs that in turn empower individuals and their communities. This "regard-seeking" element of trust may appear trivial but when compounded, provides regenerative civic possibilities.[8] The alternative "trustless trust" architecture of blockchain has perhaps taken away far more than it gives.

Gaps and Key Questions

How digital designs are shaped can moderate trust—with significant technical, social, political, and ethical consequences. Even so, focused discussions on trust remain anemic in design studies.[9] Questions of trust

---

5   Kevin Werbach, *The Blockchain and the New Architecture of Trust* (Cambridge, MA: The MIT Press, 2018), 246.
6   Werbach, 7, 96–98.
7   Philip Pettit, "The Cunning of Trust," *Philosophy & Public Affairs* 24, no. 3 (1995), 218, https://doi.org/10.1111/j.1088-4963.1995.tb00029.x.
8   Pettit, 222.
9   Notable exceptions are: Pieter E. Vermaas et al., "Designing for Trust: A Case of Value-Sensitive Design," *Knowledge, Technology & Policy* 23, no. 3 (December 1, 2010): 491–505, https://doi.org/10.1007/s12130-010-9130-8; Philip J. Nickel, "Design for the Value of Trust," in *Handbook of Ethics, Values, and Technological Design*, ed. Jeroen van den Hoven, Pieter E. Vermaas, and Ibo van de Poel (New York: Springer, 2015), 551–67,

have regularly surfaced with the rise of Information and Communication Technologies (ICT).[10] Early consolidation in this direction has culminated in the notion of e-trust, which is trust developed in digital contexts and/or involves artificial agents. An example of e-trust is found in the practice of commercial content moderation. Can users trust a social media platform to protect them from traumatizing materials uploaded by other users of this platform? Without e-trust, users will be disinclined to use this platform. The path-breaking work of e-trust has sketched out four key vectors, namely: (i) the distinctive aspects of e-trust; (ii) the relation between trust and e-trust; (iii) how e-trust may emerge; and (iv) the extent to which artificial agents are involved in an e-trust relationship.[11] Debates on how e-trust may be similar or different from interpersonal trust persist.[12] Discussions of e-trust with autonomous artificial agents now span disciplines of AI, robotics, and ethics.[13]

These philosophical analyses and reflections cover important ground. However, they have largely sidestepped the design questions of trust and trustworthiness. Designers are increasingly tasked to reinforce trust relations rendered vulnerable by digitization. But how should trust be designed into digital systems?[14] Are greater regulations and more securitized features the answer? Or are there other approaches, by design, that can also build trust? To be certain, digital systems that lean heavily on security features will

---

    https://link.springer.com/book/10.1007/978-94-007-6970-0; Melvin Chen, "Trust and Trust-Engineering in Artificial Intelligence Research: Theory and Praxis," *Philosophy & Technology* 34, no. 4 (December 1, 2021): 1429–47, https://doi.org/10.1007/s13347-021-0 0465-4.

10   Batya Friedman, Peter H. Khan, and Daniel C. Howe, "Trust Online," *Communications of the ACM* 43, no. 12 (December 1, 2000), 34–40, https://doi.org/10.1145/355112.355120.

11   Mariarosaria Taddeo and Luciano Floridi, "The Case for E-Trust," *Ethics and Information Technology* 13, no. 1 (March 1, 2011), 1–3, https://doi.org/10.1007/s10676-010-9263-1.

12   Jonathan Tallant, "You Can Trust the Ladder, But You Shouldn't," *Theoria* 85, no. 2 (2019): 102–18, https://doi.org/10.1111/theo.12177.

13   Helga Nowotny, *In AI We Trust: Power, Illusion and Control of Predictive Algorithms* (Medford, MA: Polity, 2021); Marcello Pelillo and Teresa Scantamburlo, eds., *Machines We Trust: Perspectives on Dependable AI* (Cambridge, MA: MIT Press, 2021), 2; Claudia Hauer, "Should We Trust Robots? The Ethical Perspective," in *Trust in Human-Robot Interaction*, ed. Chang S. Nam and Joseph B. Lyons (London: Academic Press, 2021), 531–33.

14   See, for example, James Clayton and Jasmin Dyer, "Roblox: The Children's Game with a Sex Problem," *BBC News*, February 15, 2022, https://www.bbc.com/news/technology-6 0314572.

drastically differ from others characterized by fostering trust relations.[15] Furthermore, building trust often requires counter-intuitive approaches; for instance, the design of constructive d istrust.[16] Here, conflicts are intentionally designed into digital systems to provoke active questioning and critique.[17] Constructive distrust prevents individuals from relying on institutions or systems that would abuse them if they had acted as though they trusted them.[18] Drawing on the earlier example of phishing scams again, an example of constructive distrust is to remind users that all digital messages claiming to be legitimate should be distrusted until further authenticated.[19] This approach of deliberately interleaving d istrust for trust in digital design remains under-explored.

On the other hand, the sporadic literature that foregrounds design for trust has significantly advanced conceptual and practical knowledge of the intersection between trust and design. Nearly all are built on the important framework of value-sensitive design, where trust is defined as a key human value.[20] Nevertheless, differences also abound. In reviewing the trust that exists between organizations, Pieter Vermaas and his collaborators highlight how different types of trust—calculus-based trust, knowledge-based trust, identification-based trust—call for different design considerations.[21] On the other hand, Philip Nickel draws out key factors when designing for the value of trust.[22] Among many, salient factors include first, providing evidence that meets acceptable standards of trust to people, and second, building in social

---

15   Batya Friedman and Peter H. Kahn, "Human Values, Ethics, and Design," in *The Human-Computer Interaction Handbook: Fundamentals, Evolving Technologies and Emerging Applications*, ed. Julie A. Jacko and Andrew Sears (New York: Lawrence Erlbaum Associates Inc., 2002), 1183.
16   Mireille Hildebrandt, "Privacy as Protection of the Incomputable Self: From Agnostic to Agonistic Machine Learning," *Theoretical Inquiries in Law* 20, no. 1 (March 16, 2019): 83–121, https://doi.org/10.1515/til-2019-0004.
17   Carl Disalvo, *Adversarial Design* (Cambridge, MA: The MIT Press, 2012), 4–7.
18   Karen S. Cook, Russell Hardin, and Margaret Levi, *Cooperation Without Trust?* (New York: Russell Sage Foundation, 2005), 62.
19   Rei Kurohi, "4 Common Types of Scams and How to Recognise Them," *The Straits Times*, January 20, 2022, https://www.straitstimes.com/singapore/courts-crime/4-common-t ypes-of-scams-and-how-to-recognise-them.
20   Batya Friedman and David G. Hendry, *Value Sensitive Design: Shaping Technology with Moral Imagination*, (Cambridge, MA: The MIT Press, 2019).
21   Vermaas et al., "Designing for Trust."
22   Nickel, "Design for the Value of Trust," 564.

and linguistic attributes that invite interpersonal trust. Other works focus on how to build trust in socially inclusive and democratic co-design processes.[23] These studies all underscore that trust is a value and relation amenable to design interventions.

Nevertheless, trust is also a value with ethical import.[24] Rightly, Nickel acknowledges that trust is not always good; instead, it is also a psychological state that represents the trusted as trustworthy.[25] Trust renders the trustor vulnerable, who can be made substantially worse off if they trust a scammer.[26] Designing for trust when the trusted entity is in fact untrustworthy is unethical. How should designers justify the design of trust relations? What are the assurances provided as a warrant to trust? Influencing or persuading individuals to trust through design is a moral matter.[27] The need to secure users' scarce attention to increase profits has been normalized in digital design.[28] All things equal, attention is lavished on platforms that invite trust, and these platforms are more frequently used. However, advertisers can also exploit this trust for objectives that do not always align with users' best interests. Where then is the redline beyond which building trust on digital platforms by design becomes patently unethical? Digitization has rendered the perplexing ethics of "design for trust" palpable.

The subsequent discussions will address these identified gaps through the following three clusters of questions. First, what is trust in digital design? What are other concepts closely associated with trust? Second, why is trust important, and how is it relevant to what designers do? Third, what are the considerations in the design of trust and trustworthiness—and how are they different? And beyond design considerations, what are preliminary ethical considerations of designing trust and trustworthiness? Working answers to these questions provide a primer to the examination of trust in digital design.

---

23 Ezio Manzini, *Design, When Everybody Designs: An Introduction to Design for Social Innovation*, trans. Rachel Coad (Cambridge, MA: The MIT Press, 2015).
24 Friedman and Hendry, *Value Sensitive Design*, 28.
25 Nickel, "Design for the Value of Trust," 552.
26 Russell Hardin, *Trust and Trustworthiness* (New York: Russell Sage Foundation, 2004), 37.
27 James Williams, "Persuasive technology," in *Future Morality*, ed. David Edmonds (Oxford: Oxford University Press, 2021), 137.
28 Williams, 137.

What is trust—in digital design?

Reliability and confidence are concepts that bear a close resemblance to trust. Yet, neither is trust, even though each overlaps trust in important ways. The following discussion serves to highlight key distinctions and, through them, elicit the notion of trust.

First, a reliable thing is competent in performing a particular task, and in everyday parlance, people are said to trust reliable things. Yet, to count on a reliable thing to do something is different from trusting a person to do something.[29] To trust a person to do something is not only to count on this individual's competency for a certain task but also on their motivation when performing this task. This is a categorically different matter from merely expecting an outcome from a reliable artifact. Insofar as a person is concerned, competency alone is necessary but not sufficient for trust: after all, it is possible to rely on a highly competent or intelligent person to perform a specific task without trusting them. To trust a person, in other words, is to accept the vulnerability of being exposed to the power of this trusted individual.[30]

In the context of design, a reliable artifact can only be interpreted as *functionally trustworthy*. But it is not necessarily trustable.[31] This is because users may not completely understand the working of this artifact or the motivations driving its design.[32] For example, users of a reliable online search engine are quick to discover that it is functionally trustworthy for showing a robust range of results, but they become quickly apprehensive when they discover certain results tend to be prioritized before others.[33] Similarly, deep learning systems can produce accurate and reliable results, but their opacity precludes straightforward explanations that can aid trustability.[34] These examples demonstrate that the functionally trustworthy artifact is

---

29   Richard Holton, "Deciding to Trust, Coming to Believe," *Australasian Journal of Philosophy* 72, no. 1 (March 1, 1994): 63–76, https://doi.org/10.1080/00048409412345881.
30   Annette Baier, "Trust and Antitrust," Ethics 96, no. 2 (January 1986): 231–60, https://doi.org/10.1086/292745.
31   John D. Lee and Katrina A. See, "Trust in Automation: Designing for Appropriate Reliance," Human Factors 46, no. 1 (March 1, 2004): 50–80, https://doi.org/10.1518/hfes.46.1.50_30392.
32   Frank Pasquale, *The Black Box Society: The Secret Algorithms That Control Money and Information* (Cambridge, MA: Harvard University Press, 2016), 7.
33   Pasquale, 66, 75.
34   Mark Coeckelbergh, *AI Ethics* (Cambridge, MA: The MIT Press, 2020), 115.

merely the first step toward trust. Ideally, the goal is to attain high functional trustworthiness alongside high trustability. But there are often design trade-offs between functional trustworthiness and trustability.[35] For example, one way to improve trustability in artificial intelligence (AI) systems is to ensure as little bias as possible in their computations. Yet reducing bias in certain cases is likely to mean compromising accuracy, which in turn reduces reliability or functional trustworthiness.[36]

The second concept is confidence.[37] Positioned more strongly, confidence is akin to faith. Faith is usually one-sided and is maintained by the trustor independent of the actual trustworthiness of what is being trusted. An individual that professes faith in something or someone does not necessarily require reasons that can explain their trust—if only because trust at the level of faith is unverifiable even when it can be unreservedly accepted as true and real.[38] In faith, one simply trusts.[39] In this way, faith can be distinguished from trust because the latter usually requires some degree of rational assessment on why trust is warranted even when both presume some vulnerability on the trustor's part.[40] According to Hardin, trust should be defined as a three-part relation: A trusts B to do X, and B's (the trustee) interest is encapsulated in A's (the trustor) interest on task X.[41] Furthermore, A is able to explain why B can be trusted on task X. To render this relation in a concrete example, I can trust my neighbor's daughter Sally to babysit my toddler James, because I have observed their interactions in the past year and concluded that Sally really has the best interest of James at heart, which encapsulates my own interest for James. In contrast, faith is mostly a two-part relation, where A simply trusts B.

Is there any room for faith in design? The emergence of critical design theory can be interpreted as a deliberate attempt to question the inbuilt optimism of design action, tantamount to a kind of unquestioned faith in

---

35 Lee and See, "Trust in Automation," 74–75.
36 Michael Kearns and Aaron Roth, *The Ethical Algorithm: The Science of Socially Aware Algorithm Design* (New York, NY: Oxford University Press, 2019), 19.
37 Vermaas et al., "Designing for Trust," 497.
38 Josef Pieper, *Faith, Hope, Love* (San Francisco, CA: Ignatius Press, 1997), 15.
39 Russell Hardin, "Conceptions and Explanations of Trust," in *Trust in Society*, ed. Karen S. Cook (New York: Russell Sage Foundation, 2001), 13.
40 Hardin, 12.
41 Hardin, 4–6.

design for solving wicked problems.[42] On the contrary, democratic design institutions require not faith but trust-building exercises experienced through participatory and inclusive co-design processes.[43] Trust is cultivated through the germinating conditions of mutual respect, publicity, transparency, and autonomy. Under these conditions in participatory processes, designers and stakeholders can repeatedly encounter one another, find opportunities for cooperation, and discover reasons to trust one another.[44] Design for trust should at least provide cues and evidence that can allow users to ground their trust.[45]

The Importance of Trust in Digital Design

Trust is important in digital design for two primary reasons. First, trust can mitigate concerns about risks, especially when users are adopting a new design.[46] Maintaining some constructive distrust when encountering a novel platform or digital artifact is prudent. For instance, over-trusting the Autopilot in one's automobile, even when this self-driving technology is incomplete, could be fatal.[47] Yet, under-trusting can lead to an overestimation of risk, resulting in premature disuse. Increasing autonomous digital designs require locating that sweet spot between over-trusting and under-trusting. Second, recognizing the integral roles of trust in digital design can enable designers to avoid designing artifacts, institutions, or systems that will reduce trust, or else

---

42 Anthony Dunne and Fiona Raby, *Speculative Everything: Design, Fiction, and Social Dreaming* (Cambridge, MA: The MIT Press, 2013), 2.
43 Manzini, *Design, When Everybody Designs*, 173–75.
44 Manzini, 175.
45 Nickel, "Design for the Value of Trust," 556.
46 Ahmed Shuhaiber and Ibrahim Mashal, "Understanding Users' Acceptance of Smart Homes," *Technology in Society* 58 (August 1, 2019): 101110, https://doi.org/10.1016/j.techsoc.2019.01.003.
47 Faiz Siddiqui, "Tesla Driver Faces Felony Charges in Fatal Crash Involving Autopilot," *Washington Post*, January 20, 2022, https://www.washingtonpost.com/technology/2022/01/20/tesla-autopilot-charges.

drive trust out completely.[48] The practice of sharing users' data, for instance, has reduced trust and renders the task of rebuilding users' trust arduous.[49]

Trust is also connected to digital design in the following three broad ways.

First, there are artifacts, institutions, and systems that are designed with trust as one of their primary goals. Where uncertainty is present, trust as a design goal is paramount. As discussed, blockchain technology has been designed, for instance, to resist censorship or tampering by any one party using this system.[50] This feature aims to build trust, even though it is an ironic form of "trustless trust." Here, consider the case of Singapore's TraceTogether app. This app was designed for contact tracing during the COVID-19 pandemic. At the time of writing, this app has become a "catch-all" official platform for contact tracing, demonstrating proof of vaccination, and the portal to all pandemic-related protocols. Designers recognized early that to get as many people as possible habituated to this new app, its design had to "gain the trust of the people."[51] Among the different design considerations for building trust are assuring users that this app does not track their movement and location, using neutral white and teal color to indicate unvaccinated and vaccinated status, respectively, instead of the more common symbolic red colors to avoid discrimination (because everyone has their personal reason for or against vaccination), and the use of a swimming otter animation as a distinguishing mark of legitimate vaccination credentials.

Second, there are artifacts that mediate trust between people. Designs that specify how users encounter or interact with one another can bring people closer together, which can popularize the use of a certain artifact, or else render indifference and push users apart over time, leading to technological disuse and abandonment. For example, consider the reputation system for online transactions.[52] A clear and transparent reputation rating system on an

---

48   Pettit, "The Cunning of Trust," 202.
49   Elizabeth Schulze, "Facebook Says It Got Users' Permission to Share Data. Those Users Might Say Differently," *CNBC*, December 20, 2018, https://www.cnbc.com/2018/12/20/facebook-data-sharing-with-amazon-microsoft-netflix.html.
50   Werbach, *The Blockchain and the New Architecture of Trust*, 47.
51   Clement Yong, "Designer behind Otter on TraceTogether Check-in Page Wanted It to Dance," *The Straits Times*, https://www.straitstimes.com/singapore/designer-behind-otter-on-tracetogether-check-in-page-wanted-it-to-dance.
52   Paul Resnick and Richard Zeckhauser, "Trust among Strangers in Internet Transactions: Empirical Analysis of EBay's Reputation System," in *The Economics of the Internet and E-Commerce*, ed. Michael R. Baye, vol. 11, Advances in Applied Microeconomics

e-commerce platform, where sellers or buyers who have either been praised or criticized can respond, is instrumental for cementing a three-way trust: between users, the user and the platform, and a community of users and this digital platform. The greater the trust engendered by this reputation system, the more trustworthy the platform will be, and more users will want to use it.

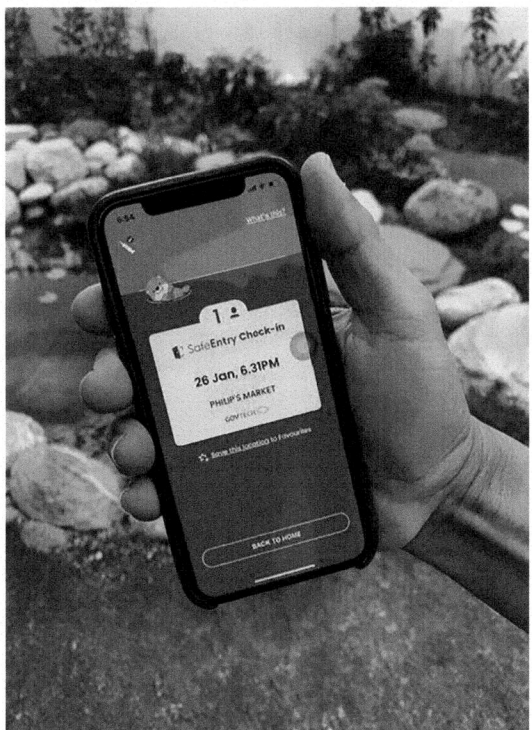

The TraceTogether App in Singapore.[53]

(Emerald Group Publishing Limited, 2002), 127–57, https://doi.org/10.1016/S0278-098 4(02)11030-3.

53 Jeffrey Chan, Photograph, 2021.

There are also more tangible examples. For instance, users of the BlueSG electric shared car in Singapore must ensure that after their use, the shared car is properly plugged into the charging station so that the next user will find this car fully charged and ready to use.[54] Unless the shared car is returned and properly plugged into the charging station, the user's credit card charges will not terminate. By constraining prior users to be responsible, subsequent users can be guaranteed a fully charged car ready to be driven. Through this design that mediates how strangers encounter each other in the BlueSG system, users can be said to trust one another on the matter of a fully charged car.

Third, an entirely novel category of autonomous artifacts and systems now requires trust. People depend on things to do something, yet increasingly, things are also deciding what to do and when to do it.[55] Trust is required when it is no longer possible for users to completely predict or control autonomous technologies. From autonomous vehicles and urban robots to the "Just Walk Out" automated stores, the effectiveness of these AI-powered artifacts depends on users trusting them. Users of future autonomous vehicles must trust them enough not to intervene at every conceivable opportunity during fast-moving traffic. Likewise, individuals who interact with urban robots and use "Just Walk Out" automated stores such as Amazon Go must sufficiently trust automated processes in these artifacts not to infringe their privacy, collect confidential data, and influence their behaviors without consent.[56] Failure to offer sufficient warrant for trust either in the autonomous vehicle or the "Just Walk Out" stores is likely to precipitate an escalation of distrust, which is penultimate to disuse and abandonment. Stated plainly, autonomous systems that are not trusted will not be used.[57]

---

54 "How It Works," BlueSG, September 20, 2017, https://www.bluesg.com.sg/how-it-works.

55 Rachel Botsman, *Who Can You Trust?: How Technology Brought Us Together and Why It Might Drive Us Apart* (New York: PublicAffairs, 2017), 319.

56 Shoshana Zuboff, *The Age of Surveillance Capitalism: The Fight for a Human Future at the New Frontier of Power* (New York: PublicAffairs, 2019), 7–8.

57 Kristin E. Schaefer et al., "A Meta-Analysis of Factors Influencing the Development of Trust in Automation: Implications for Understanding Autonomy in Future Systems," *Human Factors* 58, no. 3 (May 1, 2016): 377–400, https://doi.org/10.1177/0018720816634228.

Design and Ethical Considerations of Trust and Trustworthiness

The primary task in design for trust is to transform trust as a human value into socio-technical design requirements.[58] This is a three-part process where the key value is first identified (i.e., trust), followed by explicating the norms or conditions that can support trust. These conditions can be made explicit by asking the following question, "under what norms or conditions is trust enabled and sustained?" Finally, these norms or conditions are further specified into various socio-technical requirements that are amenable to design. In turn, this produces a socio-technical feature, attribute, or artifact. This three-part process not only comprises different stakeholders' participation but is also iterative and integrative. This framework recalls the tripartite iterative methodology of value-sensitive design, which integrates conceptual, empirical, and technical investigations.[59] Nevertheless, this framework assumes that trust is good or desirable, and does not question why trust should be designed in the first place.

Consider Singapore's TraceTogether app again. Applying the three-part design method retroactively to this case, it may be possible to see how trust could be designed. Trust was likely first identified as an important goal of this app. As aforementioned, users that trust this app are more likely to use it; a higher usage leads to greater protection of public health. This was then followed by defining the conditions under which trust can be sustained. One defining condition for trusting this app is integrity. Integrity must be satisfied from at least two directions. On the one hand, officers performing gatekeeping functions outside of restaurants, shops, and offices must be able to ascertain that the individual requesting access has a legitimate vaccination certification. On the other hand, patrons of these venues must be reassured that the people they meet there have legitimate vaccination status. Therefore, no one should be able to access these venues using illegitimate credentials, for instance, in the form of a static screenshot of vaccine certifications borrowed from elsewhere. To counter this illicit use of a static screenshot, an animation of a swimming otter was programmed as the distinguishing feature of legitimate vaccination status.[60] A dynamic animation is far harder to counterfeit than a

---

58 Evgeni Aizenberg and Jeroen van den Hoven, "Designing for Human Rights in AI," *Big Data & Society* 7, no. 2 (July 1, 2020): 1–14, https://doi.org/10.1177/2053951720949566.
59 Friedman and Hendry, *Value Sensitive Design*, 32.
60 Yong, "Designer behind Otter on TraceTogether Check-in Page Wanted It to Dance."

static screenshot. This moving animation of a swimming otter gliding back and forth across the smartphone screen presents a hard-to-replicate sociotechnical artifact that can secure integrity. The preservation of integrity, in turn, builds trust.

If this is a snapshot for the design of trust, what about the design of trustworthiness? Trust has been defined as a psychological disposition primarily consisting of people's expectations, whereas trustworthiness is a quality of a person, system, or artifact.[61] A reliable artifact is at least functionally trustworthy; an autonomous vehicle that is not only reliable but can further explain its decision to take a lengthier route exhibits an attribute of trustworthiness that one may accord to another human being. Yet, the design of trustworthy attributes in artifacts and systems is necessary but not sufficient for trust relations. For example, the city of San Francisco, California, has banned the use of facial recognition technology (FRT) by the police and other public agencies.[62] But this ban on FRT as a trustworthy attribute of a publicly accountable AI on its own does not mean that people now trust law enforcement agencies. Social norms and other political and cultural factors impinge on the perception of trustworthiness. In other words, it may be important to establish preconditions of social trust before directly designing trustworthy features.

Even so, trustworthiness must remain the kernel of trust relations. Acting on trust in the absence of trustworthiness can bring harm.[63] In philosophy and political theory, trustworthiness has been assessed as a moral matter.[64] Sociotechnical artifacts are primarily designed with functional trustworthiness in mind (i.e., they perform a certain function reliably). Yet, they are increasingly also expected to meet the standards of moral trustworthiness—for instance, integrity, fairness, honesty, autonomy, and nonmaleficence. Nevertheless, the simultaneous fulfillment of functional and moral trustworthiness can be "tricky."[65] For example, the Apple AirTag trackers appear to have satisfied

---

61   Nickel, "Design for the Value of Trust," 559.
62   Kate Conger, Richard Fausset, and Serge F. Kovaleski, "San Francisco Bans Facial Recognition Technology," *The New York Times*, May 14, 2019, https:// www.nytimes.co m/2019/05/14/us/facial-recognition-ban-san-francisco.html.
63   Hardin, *Trust and Trustworthiness*, 30.
64   Hardin, 36.
65   Tom Fisher and Lorraine Gamman, "Introduction: Ways of thinking tricky design," in *Tricky design: The ethics of things*, ed. Tom Fisher and Lorraine Gamman (New York: Bloomsbury, 2019), 2.

all performance criteria of functional trustworthiness. However, anti-social use of AirTags can violate privacy, which conflicts with values integral to moral trustworthiness.[66] Should designers now consider every way that a device could be used? Or should designers preempt paternalistic features that automatically report anti-social uses to the law enforcement agencies? If the former quickly becomes intractable, then the latter easily corrodes trustability. At the very least, designers should have considered a counterfactual scenario that the AirTag could be used to infringe privacy, and then equipped this device with an alerting feature that reminds users of unwanted AirTags in their vicinity. Designing this feature into the AirTag before it was introduced might have been a more responsible strategy than introducing a privacy update after public furor following privacy violations.

Toward an Interdisciplinary Research of Trust

As social relations are increasingly mediated by digital design, the design of trust and trustworthiness has become salient and urgent. But an efficacious and ethical design of trust and trustworthiness is hardly straightforward. Nevertheless, this chapter demonstrates that designing for trust is not only possible but there are also different design choices for building trust. One may opt for more securitized architecture, for instance, observed in blockchain technologies. Conversely, one can also consider morally trustworthy attributes that can result in a more trustable artifact. However, one thing is clear: interdisciplinary research intersecting digital design, artificial intelligence, and ethics on trust and trustworthiness has only just begun. The discussion in this chapter offers a primer for further work in this important area.

---

66 See Brett Molina, "Apple AirTag Trackers to Receive Privacy Update amid Stalking Concerns," *USA TODAY*, February 10, 2022, https://www.usatoday.com/story/tech/2022/02/10/apple-airtags-privacy-update-stalking/6738071001.

Delegated Power
The Ethics of Nudging in Building More Equitable Product Experiences

Timothy Bardlavens[1]

The ethics of design and technology have been discussed for years, yet digital products can still create harm and negatively impact marginalized and underinvested communities. As the world recently woke up to the existence of racism, "equitable product development" became the new trend; but what does it mean? Is it possible to build equitable products while still questioning the ethics of products? By interrogating how the industry has framed ethics through the lens of digital products, an interesting intersection between behavioral public policy (BPP) ethical frameworks and digital design emerges. In tech, the goal is to solve human needs. In reality, however, designers create digital pathways for people to follow, making critical decisions about their mental and physical health, financial wellbeing, or social interactions. In BPP, this is referred to as nudging—"any aspect of the choice architecture that alters people's behavior in a predictable way."[2] Nudges in digital design are products, design systems, patterns, and more. Digital designers nudge in directions they believe are "best for the user" to complete a task, reach a goal, or find fulfillment. These digital nudges are sanctioned through explicitly and implicitly gained power delegated by the people for whom (not with whom) digital designers create. Centered in this is the understanding of how power and its delegation play a critical role in designers' everyday decisions. By challenging their sensibilities around power and its privileges, designers can move beyond building reactive digital products—created after harm has been caused—to building proactive or even transformative, equitable products. The "Challenge": How is it possible to leverage BPP ethical frameworks as mechanisms to reposition the view

---

1 Adobe, US.
2 Richard H. Thaler and Cass R. Sunstein, *Nudge: Improving Decisions about Health, Wealth, and Happiness*, Revised & Expanded edition (New York: Penguin Books, 2009), 8.

of ethics and show designers how to leverage (or share) delegated power to create products with more equitable outcomes?
— *Timothy Bardlavens, US*

Over the past decade, my vocabulary on whiteness has evolved. What began as an awareness of my personal experience with micro- and macro-traumas has expanded to include an understanding of systems and how they were designed to be the conduits, purveyors, and protectors of whiteness.

Now, "Whiteness" refers to how white people, their customs, culture, and beliefs operate as the standard by which all other groups are compared. But it also surfaces in the systems navigated to articulate "good design," accessibility, and, yes, ethics. These systems are layers of interlocking tendrils built from centuries of sociopolitical decisions. They are traditions, reactions, protections, and causes meant to create the perception of order, morality, and rightness. Systems themselves are the societal fabric connecting policy, economics, and justice. These systems are complex and overwhelming, but by beginning to understand them, you start the root cause analysis work to more clearly see the world we all navigate.

In thinking about navigating whiteness through the lens of product design, inevitably, the notion of the "ethics of design" emerges. These ethical exercises are meant to reduce harm to the people who use our products, yet we continue to cause it—especially to those most historically excluded.

When discussing the ethics of anything, one must also come to terms with **power**. Who has the power to impose a set of ethics or morals within a space or community? Are the ethics or morals culturally representative and expandable? Do they impose undue expectations or restrictions on those who lack the resources or language? Many of the people we lean on to speak about the ethics of design or artificial intelligence in the US are white men, frequently based out of Silicon Valley, Seattle, or New York. They are privileged individuals with limited lived experiences related to the impact of unethical, inequitable products and have enough financial or institutional capital to have been given the space and platform to pontificate on such matters. They are our moral white saviors.

Yet, those whom we should lean on, who have the lived and acquired experience, are institutionally abused, ignored, tokenized, and fired for their efforts,[3] or are exhausted and jaded by the emotional and psychological toll they experienced for daring to consider the muddied, bloodied experiences of the oppressed, marginalized and underinvested. Thus, the ouroboros of whiteness continues.

So, where do we begin? How do we think about building more equitable products? Over the past few years, I have been increasingly intrigued by the field of behavioral science and the intersection of sociology and anthropology as it relates to society, culture, social organizations, and inequality. Through this intersection, I stumbled across frameworks from behavioral public policy (BPP)—the study of human behaviors as it relates to policy and policymakers. BPP offers the concept of "nudging."

Nudging is defined as "any aspect of the choice architecture that alters people's behavior in a predictable way without forbidding any options or significantly changing their economic incentives."[4] Policymakers, leaders, and people in power design nudges to predictably steer people in specific directions. At its core, this is product design—jobs to nudge people into certain directions. "Nudges" can be products, experiences, design systems and patterns, experience paths, and more. As designers, we nudge people in directions we believe are best for them to complete a task, reach a goal, or find fulfillment. This is referred to as "digital nudging" where the use of user-interface design elements to guide people's behavior in digital choice environments.[5] To further understand the correlation between the two disciplines, let us examine the MINDSPACE and EAST frameworks.

In 2010, the Institute for Government, in the United Kingdom (UK), was commissioned to study the implications of behavioral theory for policy-making. In doing so, a team of researchers identified nine non-coercive influences on human behavior. MINDSPACE was created as a checklist of those influences to aid policymakers in effectively implementing policies. This acronym breaks down into:[6]

---

3   Karen Hao, "We Read the Paper That Forced Timnit Gebru out of Google. Here's What It Says," *MIT Technology Review*, December 4, 2020, https://www.technologyreview.com/2020/12/04/1013294/google-ai-ethics-research-paper-forced-out-timnit-gebru.
4   Andreas T. Schmidt and Bart Engelen, "The Ethics of Nudging: An Overview," *Philosophy Compass* 15, no. 4 (2020): e12658, https://doi.org/10.1111/phc3.12658.
5   Markus Weinmann, Christoph Schneider, and Jan vom Brocke, "Digital Nudging," *Business & Information Systems Engineering* 58 (2016), 433–436.
6   Paul Dolan, Michael Hallsworth, David Halpern, Dominic King and Ivo Vlaev, "MINDSPACE: Influencing behaviour through public policy," *Institute for Government*,

Messenger: we are heavily influenced by who communicates information
Incentives: our responses to incentives are shaped by predictable mental shortcuts such as strongly avoiding losses
Norms: we are strongly influenced by what others do
Defaults: we "go with the flow" of pre-set options
Salience: our attention is drawn to what is novel and seems relevant to us
Priming: our acts are often influenced by subconscious cues
Affect: our emotional associations can powerfully shape our actions
Commitments: we seek to be consistent with our public promises and reciprocate acts
Ego: we act in ways that make us feel better about ourselves

The year following the development of MINDSPACE, the Behavioural Insights Team was formed to spread the understanding of behavioral approaches across the UK's policy community. In doing so, they had the challenge of MINDSPACE being too complicated, so they sought to develop a framework that was easier to understand. Thus, in 2012, the EAST framework was developed with the assertion, "if you want to encourage a behavior, make it Easy, Attractive, Social, and Timely."[7] The Behavioural Insights Team went on to develop a method for developing a project with four main stages: 1) Define the outcome, 2) Understand the context, 3) Build your intervention, 4) Test, learn, and adapt. It sounds hauntingly similar to what we define as effective product design and development—1) Defining the problem to solve, 2) Developing user understanding 3) Designing and iterating 4) Testing and learning.

The problem with both MINDSPACE and EAST frameworks is that they inform policy makers on *how* to nudge, but neither whether or not they *should* nudge or whether or not it is accessible, inclusive, and equitable. Much like design, some of these nudges have different or opposing effects on various people, cultures, and classes.

As a result, Leonhard K. Lades and Liam Delaney penned a paper entitled *Nudge FORGOOD* to address this absence. FORGOOD is an acronym for

---

2010, https://www.instituteforgovernment.org.uk/sites/default/files/publications/MI NDSPACE.pdf.

7   Owain Service, Michael Hallsworth, David Halpern, Felicity Algate, Rory Gallagher, Sam Nguyen, Simon Ruda, Michael Sanders with Marcos Pelenur, Alex Gyani, Hugo Harper, Joanne Reinhard & Elspeth Kirkman, "EAST: Four Simple Ways to Apply Behavioural Insights," *Behavioural Insights Team*, April 11, 2014, https://www.bi.team/p ublications/east-four-simple-ways-to-apply-behavioural-insights.

Fairness, Openness, Respect, Goals, Options, Opinions, and Delegation.[8] This framework connects to a series of questions centered on policy, but it is observable that we can replace "behavioral policy" with "product," and the questions are still relevant in understanding the impact of the products built.

Fairness

"Fairness" questions whether a product has undesired redistributive effects. In essence, fairness assesses whether or not a nudge will have a disparate impact on other groups. This typically occurs when we assume a specific path is right for everyone. These assumptions are reinforced through user research that unintentionally prioritizes whiteness, then accepts that as the general case for all people. Consider the launch of Bank of America's "Keep the Change" program,[9] where they automatically rounded up purchases to the nearest dollar and transferred that change into your savings. This program was great for those with plenty of "cushion" in their bank account, but for many lower-income families, this meant that their bank accounts were consistently overdrawn. In fact, a 2016 *Pew Charitable Trusts* study on "Heavy Overdrafters"[10] showed that most low-income bank account holders, particularly Black and Latinx, know exactly how much money they have in the bank and typically spend based on that amount. Thus, having just enough money for a purchase plus the rounded-up amount would result in a negative balance and a $35 fee. While this nudge might lead to "optimal behavior" (saving), it ultimately resulted in a negative consequence for those not considered or prioritized. For a product to be "Fair," it must be able to measure the effects on *all* the people using it. When considering the "Fairness" dimension, the questions to consider are:[11]

- Does the product focus too much on one group and neglect another group that is in more need of the product?

---

8 Leonhard K. Lades and Liam Delaney, "Nudge FORGOOD," *Behavioural Public Policy* 6, no. 1 (January 2022): 75–94, https://doi.org/10.1017/bpp.2019.53.
9 Bank of America, "Keep the Change® Savings Program from Bank of America: How It Works," accessed June 27, 2022, www.bankofamerica.com/deposits/keep-the-change.
10 The Pew Charitable Trusts, "Heavy Overdrafters: A Financial Profile," April 20, 2016, www.pewtrusts.org/-/media/assets/2016/04/heavyoverdrafters.pdf.
11 Lades and Delaney, "Nudge FORGOOD," 75–94.

- Does the product lead a subset of the population to behave against their preferences and best interests?
- Does the product lead to a reallocation of resources (positively or negatively)?

Understanding the fairness of a product or product experience requires a realistic understanding of its impact on those who use or are prevented from using it. Altruistic intentions are no substitute for unfair harms.

Openness

Following "Fairness" is "Openness," which delves into whether a product is overt and transparent or covert and manipulative. For example, how often have you gotten a "free" subscription that ultimately charged you? Or agreed to allow an app to gain access to your information only to learn through other sources it is being used in ways you agreed to only by the extension of it being buried in a user agreement? Continuing on the financial sector theme, consider a scenario where a small business owner is a first-time popular invoice-processing company, for the first time. Because there was no clear indication of fees, I thought it would be an easy tool to keep track of my business finances.[12] It was not until the full amount was deposited into my account and a subsequent charge labeled "fee" was taken out, that I realized it was not a free tool that came with my subscription to the platform. While I have some level of financial stability, imagine a small business that cannot afford a 3 percent fee. For some, it is nominal, but for others, it is the ability to ultimately pay the mortgage or rent.

For a product to be "open," key features, costs, and implications of usage must be communicated clearly and be easily acknowledged by people using the platform. When considering the Openness dimension, the questions to consider are:[13]

- Does the product have the potential to be manipulative?

---

12 Arvind Narayanan, Arunesh Mathur, Marshini Chetty, and Mihir Kshirsagar, "Dark Patterns: Past, Present, and Future: The Evolution of Tricky User Interfaces," *Queue* 18, no. 2 (2020), 67–92.

13 Lades and Delaney, "Nudge FORGOOD," 75–94.

- Does the public have the chance to scrutinize the product?
- Is it possible for the person who is influenced by the product to identify its influence and impact?

Openness is a critical factor in digital nudging as it highlights the potential for digital manipulation, regardless of altruistic intent. In this, respect for human autonomy and consent is key as it provides users of our products with the opportunity to opt-out of experiences misaligned with their needs, values or expectations.

Respect

Respect is arguably one of the most interesting FORGOOD dimensions. It questions if the product respects people's autonomy, dignity, freedom of choice, and privacy. Today, so many tech companies are reckoning with this topic in needing to define and ban misinformation,[14] develop the implementation of privacy transparency, and more.[15] The Respect dimension is minor as downloading an app and having the ability to skip a tutorial or onboarding experience because *we know how apps work* (autonomy), or as big as perpetually wading through racist tropes being blasted across a platform, all for the sake of "free speech" and "open discourse"[16] (dignity).

Freedom of choice is unique as it encompasses a person's right to privacy and control over their personal data, as well as the ability to navigate a space the way you want regardless of what others may see as the optimal path (fairness). If we go back to the Bank of America example, upon roll-out, the bank defaulted people into the "Keep the Change" program, forcing account holders to opt out. This is a compounding problem of not considering the distributive effects of a product (fairness), not communicating clearly what the impact would

---

14   Shannon Bond, "Facebook Widens Ban On COVID-19 Vaccine Misinformation In Push To Boost Confidence," *NPR*, February 8, 2021, https://www.npr.org/2021/02/08/965390755/facebook-widens-ban-on-covid-19-misinformation-in-push-to-boost-confiden.

15   Apple Newsroom, "Data Privacy Day at Apple: Improving Transparency and Empowering Users," January 27, 2021, https://www.apple.com/newsroom/2021/01/data-privacy-day-at-apple-improving-transparency-and-empowering-users.

16   Colby M. Everett, "Free speech on privately-owned fora: a discussion on speech freedoms and policy for social media," *Kan. JL & Pub. Pol'y* 28 (2018): 113.

be (openness) and not giving an option to opt in vs. forcing people to opt out (respect).[17] When considering the "Respect" dimension, the questions to consider are:[18]

- Does the product respect people's autonomy?
- Does the product respect people's dignity?
- Does the product respect people's freedom to choose?
- Does the product respect people's privacy?

In many ways the "Respect" dimension connects well with pre-existing ethical frameworks which question the degree to which a product or service adheres to well-defined ethical guidelines regarding fundamental values, such as individual rights, privacy, non-discrimination, and non-manipulation. It is through policy interrogation, rigorous user research and usability testing that a product team can best understand how respectful their products are and what the impact of a lack of respect can have on the person using their product.

Goals and Options

The "Goals and Options" dimensions are quite simple: does the product serve good, legitimate goals, and do people have an option regarding how they navigate the space? "Goals" question if there is a purpose for the work you do, or is it merely for metric gain or to beat the competition? Are you making product decisions for a "quick win" to hit an arbitrary metric created for the illusion of progress over real and clear human needs? The "Goals" dimension forces us to take a critical look at our motivations and intent while also requiring us to clearly define expected outcomes. This gives us a success criteria while also gauging whether or not we have met the needs of "the lowest common denominator" or the worst-case scenario.

Quite plainly, the "Options" dimension questions whether or not the person has options regarding how they navigate a space or if they must follow

---

17   Yee-Lin Lai and Kai-Lung Hui, "Internet opt-in and opt-out: investigating the roles of frames, defaults and privacy concerns," Proceedings of *The 2006 ACM Sigmis Conference On Computer Personnel Research: Forty Four Years Of Computer Personnel Research: Achievements, Challenges & The Future* (2006), 253–263.

18   Lades and Delaney, "Nudge FORGOOD," 75–94.

a predefined path—likely to meet our internal goals of metric gains vs. their goal of accomplishing a particular task.[19] This is okay for *some* experiences where following a set of key actions is imperative compared to the success of a particular task. However, in other ways, we as designers use this form of forced syntax—or an imposed system that does not allow people to navigate experiences in a manner natural to them—to push people through a path we have defined as "optimal."

I pair these two dimensions together because they both force us to think beyond ourselves, understand our goals, and be realistic about whether they are legitimate or simply corporate fluff, while also deeply considering the needs and pathways of individuals who will have the *worst* time navigating the space and creating for them *first*.[20] When considering the "Goals and Options" dimension, the questions to consider are:[21]

- Does the product serve ethically acceptable goals?
- For products that aim to improve people's lives, do these products really make people better off? How do you know, and how is this "better off" defined?
- Are there other pathing or experience options?
- Is one path the best amongst all of the options? Why?
- Does the experience divert attention away from better experiences?

The "Goals and Options" dimensions can be interpreted as accountability measures. Their intent is to not only to define desired outcomes, but to interrogate whether those outcomes are, or can be achieved. Product designers and developers must consistently ask themselves, are we accomplishing what we intended and do we have mechanisms to see the tangible impact?

Opinions

"Opinions" question if people accept the means and the ends of the product. In other words, do they accept both the intent and the impact of a product? Too

---

19   Debbie Stone, Caroline Jarrett, Mark Woodroffe, and Shailey Minocha, *User Interface Design and Evaluation*, (San Francisco, CA: Elsevier, 2005).
20   John A. Powell, "Post-Racialism Or Targeted Universalism," *Denv. UL Rev.* 86 (2008), 785.
21   Lades and Delaney, "Nudge FORGOOD," 75–94.

often, we center our work in whiteness (the majority), get our hands slapped, and then beg the world to consider our intent regardless of the impact. For example, Twitter's algorithm prioritized white faces when selecting images.[22] The communication surrounding this was that it was not the platform's intent, regardless of the feature's impact—therefore ignoring the opinions of the public, and those who must experience the product.

That said, with the advent of Twitter Spaces,[23] X (formerly known as Twitter) has also begun efforts to create collective awareness of and gather feedback regarding their new products. This is important because the "Opinions" dimension challenges product designers to create systematic ways to identify public opinion.[24] More concisely, "Opinions" are most satisfied when the product development process is co-creative. It resists the notion that innovation is created in a silo by a few, but is rather a collection of many to ensure broad, diverse needs are being met. When considering the "Opinions" dimension, questions to consider are:[25]

- What is the public opinion about the product?
- How does the public view the goals of the product?
- How does the public view the means used by the product?

At its core, equitable product development requires co-creation, which takes form through investing in understanding the needs and expectations of historically underinvested and ignored communities. In doing this, product teams can more consistently identify novel product solutions or opportunities, drive stronger product implementation, and expect deeper market penetration.

---

22   Abeba Birhane, Vinay Uday Prabhu, and John Whaley, "Auditing saliency cropping algorithms," *Proceedings of the IEEE/CVF Winter Conference on Applications of Computer Vision*, (2022), 4051–4059.
23   Twitter, "About Twitter Spaces," accessed June 27, 2022, https://help.twitter.com/en/using-twitter/spaces.
24   Karl, Lang, Richard Shang, and Roumen Vragov, "Consumer co-creation of digital culture products: business threat or new opportunity?," *Journal of the Association for Information Systems* 16, no. 9 (2015), 3.
25   Lades and Delaney, "Nudge FORGOOD," 75–94.

Delegation

The "Delegation" dimension is unique because it does not question the product but the product designer and broader development team. It is a question of power. As designers, we have the power to create for the world, and as Lades and Delaney point out, that power does not come from the ether. Power is consciously and unconsciously delegated to us by the people for whom we create. Do the product designers and developers have the right and ability to nudge using the power delegated to them? This actually goes back to the example of Twitter Spaces. The product team identified the importance of creating community experiences; they do not have all of the right inputs, people, or lived experiences to leverage the power delegated to them, so they shifted to a co-creative process in which the public can provide insight into products being built for them (opinions). To understand our own power, we must also question: Do we have the right competency? Do we come with any level of cognitive bias, and how does it show up? What are our organizational biases, and how have or will they harm people? We must assess products on a case-by-case basis and, in doing so, always self-reflect on our power and its impact on people.[26] When considering the Delegation dimension, the questions to consider are:[27]

- Do the product designers/developers have biases or conflicts of interest?
- Do the product designers/developers have the competency to design, implement, and evaluate the product?
- How do those potential biases or conflicts of interest and lack of competency influence the assessment of a product?

Delegation centers on reflection of self and team, it is likely the most difficult of dimensions as it requires introspective analysis of our biases, interrogation of our approaches and an understanding of our power. None of which are achievable without maturity and humility. While that may seem overwhelming, the FORGOOD framework is just one of many approaches to thinking about ethical design practices, but how does that lead to more equitable products and outcomes?

---

26 Tania Anaissie, Victor Cary, David Clifford, Tom Malarkey, and Susie Wise, "Liberatory design: Mindsets and modes to design for equity," *Liberatory Design*, 2021.
27 Lades and Delaney, "Nudge FORGOOD," 75–94.

First, there is no agreed-upon definition for an "equitable product." Is it one that is made with everyone considered in the product development process? Or at least the most marginalized? An equitable product is one that reduces harm, increases access, and is co-created to first meet the needs of the historically excluded, then augmented to meet the broader population's needs. That said, the lack of definition and examples often results in designers relying more on their own moral intuition than on a widely-accepted theory or set of best practices.

I define equitable products, more specifically *product equity*, as the state in which every person, regardless of human difference, can access and harness the full power of digital products, without bias, harm or limitation. In this view, product equity is both a practice and an outcome. As a practice, product equity considers all forms of human diversity and difference throughout the product design and development process, acknowledges systemic inequities that limit or prevent equal access and value to digital products, and solves for those imbalances; resulting in products that first meet the needs of historically underinvested and ignored, and also creates more fair outcomes.

There are very few examples of proactive, or transformative, equitable products—products built with historically excluded social identities in mind. These are different from reactively equitable products that were augmented after causing harm to a specific group. There are many reasons why there are so few examples, but a dearth of frameworks to propel more equitable design is not one of them. With frameworks like Creative Reaction Lab's *Equity Centered Community Design* pioneered by Antionette Carroll,[28] or equityXdesign[29] developed by Caroline Hill, Michelle Molitor, Christine Ortiz —and so many more, the options and opportunities are endless.

That said, people continue searching for ethical and equitable frameworks without addressing their own core sensibilities. Understanding how we navigate whiteness within systems and using equitable design frameworks are important, but they do not make the crux of the work the design community needs to do. Seeing systems helps designers to understand the context of their work, while equitable design frameworks offer mechanisms to guide

---

28   Antionette D. Carroll, "Equity-Centered Community Design," *Slow Factory*, accessed June 27, 2022, https://slowfactory.earth/courses/equity-centered-community-design.

29   Andrew Plemmons Pratt, "Designing for Race Equity: Now Is the Time," *NGLC* (May 15, 2020), https://www.nextgenlearning.org/articles/designing-for-race-equity-now-is-the-time.

the inception, production, completion, and implementation of product work. However, the underlying systems and frameworks are our preconceptions, and addressing whiteness in products means addressing the internalized sensibilities of whiteness we see as normal. So, how do we begin addressing internalized whiteness in ourselves, our disciplines, and our organizations?

Bias as Our Default

All people have biases, and most people exhibit it unconsciously. While not intentional, bias enforces and promulgates existing stereotypes. Even if we want to do the right thing, we might not recognize our own biases. By the same token, teams must also recognize that bias exists "as our default" within the products that are made and shipped globally. This means that we have sometimes failed to represent users equitably within our products, with launches that did not focus enough on underinvested groups.

"Bias as our default" means digital product teams expect every part of their process and products to contain some potential to create or exacerbate harm. By assuming all products are biased from their inception means teams must establish bias mitigation strategies to reduce bias. This begins with having an open and honest culture in which individuals in teams can document and discuss their bias, in addition to creating mechanisms to identify bias—whether it's homogenous search results, an inaccessible user experience, or a subscription model that lacks socioeconomic context. This becomes even more difficult with some technologies, like machine learning and artificial intelligence, where data sets are so expansive that a human's ability to accurately and impartially review all data is nearly impossible. In these scenarios, technologists must question, "how can we do more good than harm?" and "what processes do we need to implement to review, diagnose and remedy problems in an ongoing manner?"

Managing bias is a distinctly different set of actions to promote user trust and safety. It is consistent work to interrogate and address our thoughts, actions, and approaches to building products. This internal work is never complete—it is lifelong and uncomfortable.

Rejecting the "Right to Comfort"

Second, we must accept that dismantling unjust systems is uncomfortable, especially to those who benefit from them most. If you are to develop or adapt to more equitable systems, you cannot protect your comfort. In the equitable design world, we call this resistance "the right to comfort."

The right to comfort appears in design through the oversimplification of work. For example, in many cases, making products more accessible, inclusive, and equitable means relegating essential framing to checklists, which we use to make work simpler and more efficient. We see this in the accessibility space: Web Content Accessibility Guidelines (WCAG) checklists abound, and while the strides that the World Wide Web Consortium has made in building the WCAG guidelines to help designers make more accessible products is appreciable, there is a long way to go in terms of connecting what is on these checklists to designers' understanding of their guidance. Accessibility checklists can dehumanize the process of understanding human needs as it relates to those living with disabilities or who are neurodivergent; they replace understanding with rules for type, size, color, and alt-text—much of which only scratch at the surface of a person's need to navigate physical and digital space comfortably.

A checklist is, among other things, a mechanism of comfort. Checklists make whiteness feel at ease while offering a sense of accomplishment for "being the ally" in doing the minimum work with little or no understanding of the work.

When considering how to address equity in products, the prioritization of white comfort also dictates who, how, and why these efforts should exist. I have seen senior product engineering and design leaders prioritize engineering costs or metric gains over improving the quality of our products and, by extension, the quality of people's lives. Demma Rosa Rodriguez, Senior Anti-Discrimination & Equity Modeling Lead at Airbnb, said, "At its core, this is a quality problem. When we build products that are inaccessible and inequitable, they are of low quality; they do not meet the bar for shipping."[30] Through this lens, how many products exist today that are of low quality?

---

30   Demma Rodriguez, "Engineering for Equity," O'Reilly, accessed April 16, 2023, https://www.oreilly.com/library/view/software-engineering-at/9781492082781/ch04.html.

Vivianne Castillo, Founder of HmntyCntrd, sums up the need to change our sensibilities about comfort by asking: "are you willing to suffer?"[31] Black, Latinx, and Indigenous designers have disproportionately suffered and experienced organizational trauma in driving towards more equitable cultures, systems, and products—it would be nice if others shared the load.

Step Outside Yourself

Be thoughtful and get out of the way. Step outside of yourself, your experiences, and your biases and truly, deeply learn about, absorb, and consistently consider the human condition of the most ignored, traumatized, and marginalized. This is bigger than empathy; it is humility. In her talk, "Design No Harm: Why Humility is Essential in the Journey Toward Equity," Antionette Carroll described "empathy without humility often shows up as judgment... if empathy does not have humility, it is still about you."[32] She goes on to quote Emily Rowe Underwood, Community Initiatives Specialist at the Missouri Historical Society who described that, "Humility asks us to step outside of ourselves, listen and absorb someone else's truth, even if it makes us feel defensive."[33] This means identifying and addressing the internalized whiteness we all have absorbed simply by living in a commercial, capitalistic society.

In developing digital products, "stepping out of yourself" typically arises in four key areas: 1) participant recruiting phase of research, 2) insights interpretation, 3) strategic development and 4) the design phase. Each of these areas may be highly dependent on a person's role as to how much control they have over the outcomes. In recruiting for research, it is imperative for researchers to ensure that participant selection is over indexed on racial/ethnic, gender, age, ability status and geographic diversity.

The interpretation of insights is a multidimensional challenge in which researchers create themes based on their understanding of participant feedback. These insights are then passed to product owners and designers who further filter participant goals, experiences and challenges through their own interpretations, typically anchoring on data that is seen as achievable,

---

31   HmntyCntrd, "What We Do," accessed June 28, 2022, https://hmntycntrd.com.
32   Antionette D. Carroll, Design No Harm: Why Humility Is Essential in the Journey Toward Equity, In/Visible Talks 2020, 2020, https://vimeo.com/389018075.
33   Rodriguez, "Engineering for Equity."

desirable, or favorable to predetermined outcomes. While many of these individual disciplines' jobs are to interpret data to create solutions and strategies, "gut check" mechanisms must be put in place with living experts, for instance, people who have lived experience of a particular problem or scenario, to ensure product outcomes actually align with human need—beginning with those who are historically underrepresented and marginalized. In developing product strategy, it is imperative product owners to balance qualitative and quantitative data, to highlight the outlier and opportunity as opposed to only focusing on "the majority."

In the design phase, designers must seek out ways to co-create experiences with real people, and this can be done in partnership with research. All too often, designers make assumptions about how people approach product experiences based on their own rationalizations, then test those assumptions through usability testing, thus resulting in a confirmation bias. Designers must first work with living experts on whether the solution a design presents is actually solving the core problem, and then work towards whether the product is usable for people living with disabilities and other limitations (financial, geographic and otherwise).

Stepping outside of yourself is a call to step outside of your comfort, to interrogate your approach and, in doing so, interrogating the system in which digital products are developed.

Question the "Master Approach"

Different products require different considerations and ask as often as possible how product designers can take a more nuanced, case-by-case approach to researching, planning, designing, launching, and assessing products. Because many of us work in for-profit companies, efficiency has a significant hand in crystallizing our approaches into repeatable "mechanisms," but there is no singular, master approach that will meet the needs of every person or product.

For example, can we free ourselves to question the use of "people problems" or problem statements as mechanisms for identifying the gap between a person's current and desired experience or to clearly articulate a person's unmet needs? These mechanisms oversimplify human needs and do not consider the implications of age, gender identity, race/ethnicity, ability, health, and socioeconomic status on people's experience of products. Persona-based design can be effective, but it must take into account social identities and context as a part of the overall user journey and narrative.[34] This is not a new idea, of course, but one many before me have said.[35]

Reassess Innovation

We should reassess our definition of "Innovation." Consider product development wholly for a moment. The past several decades of product development has largely remained the same. A select few people identify gaps in the market, they create "a thing" to fill that gap, over time they add new features and capabilities based on a vocal majority, and a competitive advantage. A company's desire to be innovative leads to a culture of secrecy, a rush to be first to market, and the "big reveal". This sense of urgency, paternalism, and individualism inevitably leads to the needs and perspectives of those who make the products trampling on those who may use or want to use them. Innovation means nothing if it causes harm, ignores whole populations, or negates the experiences of the historically excluded and marginalized.

Reassessing innovation means to interrogate the process in which digital products are developed. To not only see gaps in an industry or specific behavioral patterns, but to understand the context of those inputs and the system which creates them. True innovation can be achieved through understanding and integrating the experiences of those who can't fully access digital products—financially, geographically, mentally, physically or emotionally—into product solutions. This is a co-creative process in which organizations do not hide their digital products, but create openness, access and mechanisms for feedback; where outlier feedback is respected as equally as majority feedback and investigated to understand its root cause.

Reducing whiteness in products begins and ends with redefining innovation to be co-creative, accessible, and equitable. It is our job to redistribute power back to communities and not only include them in the

---

34 Saul McLeod, "Social Identity Theory," *Simply Psychology*, October 24, 2019, https://www.simplypsychology.org/social-identity-theory.html.

35 Also see Yashasri Sadagopan, "How To: Make the Persona Work," *Medium*, November 8, 2019, https://uxdesign.cc/how-to-make-the-persona-work-5cd636cd1db7; Patricia Rodriguez, "How to Reduce Bias in Your UX Practice with Persona Scenarios," *Kalamuna*, July 17, 2019, https://www.kalamuna.com/blog/how-reduce-bias-your-ux-practice-persona-scenarios.

product design and development process, but also ensure they are heard, respected, and paid.

Reassess Success

Last, let us open up to different ways of measuring progress. In for-profit companies, such things as metric gain, more customers, and higher revenue are prized. But if we are to do the hard work of designing for everyone, we cannot chase those carrots alone.

The reassessment of success is also a conversation about power, power to influence policies, metrics, goals and outcomes. It's a question of, "are we willing to feel the pain?" This pain is metaphorical, but it's a provocation to interrogate leaders' ability to articulate what guardrails exist, to be clear about the amount of risk they're willing to take when balancing potential metric loss for societal gain. Metric loss is not always the outcome of more equitable practices, but it is typically the fear. This fear is inextricably connected to a business culture focused on short-term gains and market wins over long-term impact. When considering the long-term impact of these approaches, leadership must consider benefits such as an increase in brand trust and legitimacy, increased market penetration, new market segments, as well as efficiency and cost reduction. While these are not easily or quickly quantifiable, each are direct results of focusing on previously ignored communities and building digital products with those communities in mind and within the process.

A Provocation, not a Panacea

This chapter addressed complicated topics, and many of us have fallen into the trap of seeking out the simplest of solutions. Systems are broad and deep, with tendrils stretching back hundreds of years.

Frameworks are general and flexible tools meant to create a foundation for navigating your work. You can understand the systems and leverage the frameworks, but without understanding how your sensibilities connect to the micro- and macro-systems and how they can influence frameworks, you run the risk of causing harm.

Checklists and boxes will not work here. A two-hour inclusivity workshop or a book on white fragility is not enough. Commitment to removing whiteness from the products we build is ongoing work for the rest of our natural lives—and for generations to come.

Acknowledging that we all navigate—or make space for—whiteness within larger systems necessarily means acknowledging the problem's scale, and hopefully provoking us all to question the efficacy of quick performative fixes (i.e., adding more skin colors choices for emojis, creating profile stickers, etc.). Such band-aid solutions are trivial in the face of the real work required to drive more equitable outcomes through digital products. It would also be remiss not to say that this is big talk coming from a person working in "big tech." This is a provocation for us internally and externally—we are all accountable.

Progress is comfortable, and change is uncomfortable—you better get comfortable with being uncomfortable.

DialecTikTok
The Dynamic Semiotics of Amateur Visual Trends on TikTok

Sarah Edmands Martin[1]

This chapter explores in some detail the design elements of TikTok's specific user interface features which distinguish it from other social media platforms in important ways, and create a mesmeric user experience. Special attention is paid to the dialectical relationship between these features and the user experience; the "prosumer" phenomenon is taken to the extreme so that engagement with the app itself creates new and ever-changing alphabets, vocabularies, and "trends" that subvert, obfuscate, and liberate in equal measure, and constantly encourage more disruption. It concludes with some notes of caution about this mode of engagement.

The signs and symbols developed by users on the social networking platform TikTok mutate in a flash. The visual gags, memes, hashtags, and "trends," as the company calls them, usher forth alphabets of inventive text, emojis, symbols, graphics, closed captions, and sound, all encoded with meaning. Unlike the other social media giants (Twitter, Instagram, etc.), the tools to design one's own media-rich communications are built natively into the interface. Like a cacophony of stimulus, it shatters user experience (UX) and user interface (UI) standards. Additionally, the authorship of this fast-paced and digital semantic is being transformed by a young and amateur design demographic: in the United States, 60% of users are between the ages of thirteen and twenty-four.[2] This new kind of public square virtually simulates ancient Greek forums in their social heterogeneity.

---

1   University of Notre Dame, US.
2   Raymond Zhong and Sheera Frenkel, "A Third of TikTok's U.S. Users May Be 14 or Under, Raising Safety Questions," *The New York Times*, August 14, 2020, www.nytimes.com/20 20/08/14/technology/tiktok-underage-users-ftc.html.

Compound this multifariousness by the addictive pace at which TikTok's visual semantics evolve and the app becomes a resplendent (if sometimes nauseating) petri dish of new visual codes and cues. This chapter reflects on the platform as a design environment, in general, while cataloging and examining the semiotics of its more popular amateur "trend" languages, both typographic, graphic, and auditory. Embedded in contemporary culture like a hornet's nest just out of reach, the hum of dialogue on TikTok has incited protests, counter-protests, solved murders, whistleblowing racists, witnessed atrocities, promoted hate speech, and even provoked a presidential executive order. Former United States President Donald Trump unsuccessfully tried to ban the app in August 2020.[3] It also reinforces echo chambers of information and misinformation. Even as the platform tightens its censorship of critical voices, often African American and queer voices, these "shadow banned" users nimbly evolve. In response, they develop new "leetspeak" homophones. Leetspeak, or "1337," adopts early internet substitutions of numbers with letters (as in the cases of "n00b," "@$$," and "c3n50red") in order to bypass text filters. TikTok users deploy 1337, double entendre visuals, silenced sounds, and witty graphics in order to share ideas that might normally be suppressed. This blend of type and image has always been at the core of design.

The outbreak of COVID-19 was disruptive. It wrenched people from the normalcy of their respective routines while simultaneously rending new spaces for unexpected experiences. In particular, the pandemic supercharged digital communications. It is within this context that TikTok, with its novel, short video-sharing format design, peaked in the US. Early TikTok content was a mixture of dance moves and humorous clips, similar to the much-loved Vine app.[4] As its popularity grew, the variety of content on TikTok also exploded. This included vegan recipes, riot footage, sexually enticing posts that ensnare viewers called "thirst traps," pranks, conspiracy theories, "canceling" or online shaming, and the paresthesia of autonomous sensory meridian response or ASMR.

---

3   Naomi Xu Elegant, "TikTok Banned Trump before Trump Could Ban TikTok," *Fortune*, January 11, 2021, https://fortune.com/2021/01/11/tiktok-bans-trump-before-trump-bans-tiktok.

4   John Herrman, "Vine Changed the Internet Forever. How Much Does the Internet Miss It?," *The New York Times*, February 24, 2020, https://www.nytimes.com/2020/02/22/style/byte-vine-short-video-apps.html.

The wave of engagement might have been due, in part, to TikTok's newness. While established platforms like Twitter, Facebook, Instagram, and YouTube were embroiled in things like Congressional hearings, the banning of U.S. Presidents, and pedophilic content controversies, TikTok was a brand-new bastion of silly, harmless fun.[5] Another factor could be that the design and content creation tools native to its UX/UI gave a younger audience more creative freedom to play with digital content creation.

Like a pair of spectacles, the UI is designed to be transparent. A clear apparatus, it works by clarifying the images passing before the eyes, capturing a viewer's minimal interactions in order to show them ever more clearly what (it thinks) they want.[6] The main interface is an endless vertical scroll of singular short videos, one right after another. The videos completely fill the phone's screen and the user's attention with only a simple sidebar of sticky white icons on the right and a three-button navigation on the bottom, all of which remain unchanged no matter what video plays. This minimal UI allows the design of whatever a user has created to take center stage. A user may like, follow, share, and comment. Yet, even while the text-heavy comment section is open, the ever-looping video content is never fully obscured, and one-fifth of the background video is still visible. The pair of spectacles metaphor becomes a pair of bifocals, where the viewer is expected to focus on the text only briefly, their vision compelled back to the moving pageantry above.

Just like other titans in the panoply of social media apps, TikTok affords its user the opportunity to be both content creators and content consumers, fostering what philosopher Byung-Chul Han describes as "communicative reflux" wherein respect hierarchies are destabilized into carousels of impetuous destruction.[7] On TikTok, switching from viewer to creator is effortless. Tapping the large call-to-action (CTA) "+" button at the bottom center converts the screen to creation mode. By default, the front-facing camera activates, and a smorgasbord of built-in design, video, and sound editing icons populate to the right. Filters, speed adjustments, video effects, voiceover, automatic captioning, emojis, typography, and more appear at the tip of a finger. Viewers and users can also "stitch" one another, creating

---

5   Sarah Perez, "It's Time to Pay Serious Attention to TikTok," *TechCrunch*, January 30, 2019, https://techcrunch.com/2019/01/29/its-time-to-pay-serious-attention-to-tiktok.

6   Patrick Gamez, text conversation with author, May 5, 2022.

7   Byung-Chul Han, *In the Swarm: Digital Prospects*, trans. Erik Butler (Cambridge, MA: The MIT Press, 2017), 3.

immediate video reactions that duet alongside the original video in a split-screen design. Dialogue expands into stunted "Parts," or 150-character comment threads.

However, unlike other social media platforms, experiencing content on TikTok is immediate and hyper focused. The alluring promise of the next, upcoming video, divorced from any decision-making exertion, is part of what makes TikTok so addictive. Only one video may be viewed at a time, with no choice in what video might come next. It is the social media manifestation of Hick's Law: decreasing the number of choices means a user will make decisions easier.[8] It also keeps the effort of the viewer's actions to a minimum while streamlining data input for the algorithm. Additionally, before a major update in late 2019, no videos on TikTok had timestamps.[9] It was a realm outside of time. Users could never be sure when a post had been uploaded (or re-uploaded), and content flowed in an endless evergreen succession, like what George Bataille describes as "one wave lost in a multitude of waves."[10] This was all intentionally designed to keep users trapped in TikTok's thrall.

Behind this front-end UI lies the powerful but occulted algorithm of TikTok: an artificial intelligence system that determines what posts get the widest audience. Having a large following does not guarantee that one's videos are seen, as the long-scrolling main page of the app is a uniquely generated page for each unique user. Posts that end up on this page are determined by the algorithm. Like Plato's parapet of puppeteers in his *Allegory of the Cave*, the algorithm determines what shadows are cast on the wall, with a user's interactions and content being the fire that feeds it. The algorithm shapes what is seen in the false reality of cascading videos. The algorithm will factor a video's number of likes, shares, comments, watch duration, video duration, music/sound popularity, and hashtag popularity, and blend it all with a unique set of predictive programming. According to leaked documents, TikTok's algorithm curates content that is optimized to keep you hooked to its infinite

---

8   Luca Rosati, "How to Design Interfaces for Choice: Hick-Hyman Law and Classification for Information Architecture," in *Proceedings of the International UDC Seminar* (Classification And Visualization: Interfaces To Knowledge, The Hague, 2013), 125–38.

9   Louise Matsakis, "On TikTok, There Is No Time," *Wired*, June 13, 2022, https://www.wired.com/story/tiktok-time.

10 Mark Featherstone, "The Eye of War: Images of Destruction in Virilio and Bataille," *Journal for Cultural Research* 7, no. 4 (October 1, 2003): 433–47, https://doi.org/10.1080/1479758032000165066.

scroll for as long as possible.[11] Thus, users typically seek to tailor their content to accommodate the algorithm's metric. A number of implications can be drawn from this, but this chapter will focus on the typographic, semiotic, and graphic decisions users make to appease this algorithm.

While TikTok is not the first app to embed design tools into its user interface, it has the most extensive array for native content creation and editing among the highest-downloaded apps: Instagram, Facebook, Snapchat, and YouTube. TikTok was the No. 1 most-downloaded app of the year on iOS and was one of the most downloaded across iOS and Android combined, suggesting that download trends parallel users' interests in shaping typographic, design, moving-image communication.[12]

It is not just that the means of production are in the hands of young people with a low threshold for design skills. The content that is being produced is further influencing new alphabets. Emerging from TikTok is a fascinating mashup of visual trends and memes that blend sonic, typographic, graphic, and motion design.

Audio has always been a primary component of TikTok. The bottom right-hand (right-thumb) corner features a rotating record icon indicating the sound file associated with each video. Some of these are unique sounds recorded by the creator while some are samples of pre-recorded, copyrighted music. A classic example is the clip featuring The Shangri-Las 1964 hit "Remember (Walking in the Sand)," written by George "Shadow" Morton. Colloquially known as the "Oh No" sound, the setup is 12 seconds of foreboding crooning, "Whatever happened to/The boy that I once knew?/The boy who said he'd be true." This resolves in the music equivalent of a record scratch: "Oh, no/Oh, no/ Oh, no, no, no, no, no!"[13] The videos that utilize this sound typically showcase what philosopher Thomas Hobbes describes in *Human Nature and De Corpore Politico* as "the passion of laughter [that] is nothing else but a sudden glory arising from sudden conception of some eminency in ourselves, by comparison

---

11   The two metrics that TikTok's leaked internal document tailors the algorithm toward are "retention" — that is, whether a user comes back—and "time spent." See Ben Smith, "How TikTok Reads Your Mind," *The New York Times*, December 6, 2021, https://www.nytimes.com/2021/12/05/business/media/tiktok-algorithm.html.

12   Both App Annie and Sensor Tower agree that TikTok scored the No. 3 position for most installs among all apps worldwide in 2018. Perez, "It's Time to Pay Serious Attention to TikTok."

13   The Shangri-Las, *Remember (Walking in the Sand)*, Audio Recording, The Best of the Shangri-Las (Mercury Records, 1964).

with the infirmities of others, or with our own formerly."[14] A cat attempts ambitious acrobatics across water only to fall immediately in, a horrifying homemade Easter bunny costume trundles closer to two traumatized toddlers, a teen attempts to open a 50 ML mini bottle of vodka with her teeth only for her tooth to chip in half. Equivalently, just as TikTok creators have recontextualized the meaning of a 1960's Billboard hit via cultural osmosis, so too has the construction of the meme also broadened. Advancing beyond slapstick or schadenfreude, the "Oh No" sample has also been overlaid on critiques of social, professional, and political red flags. This reframing, produced at the lightspeed of TikTok's design engine, fosters entire galaxies of new meaning and coded signification.

Tapping the spinning record icon reveals that sample's entire library of uses, including the designated "Original" or first upload. This index provides an important function in the "meme-ification" of sounds on TikTok: the sonic lexicon is open-source and available for plumbing. A user can scroll through and witness all the combinations of how a sample has been applied previously. It is also an archive of the sample's own communicative entropy.

The swirling maelstrom of creative invention also affects the deployment of language, typography, and symbols. One example of evolving semantics is "algospeak:"[15] Gen Z's Aesopian language strategy to avoid sanction from the algorithm. Like the allegorical double-speak of 19th-century Russian satirists before them, creators on TikTok swap in code words for taboo topics. For example, the profession of "accountant" does not actually refer to someone preparing and maintaining important financial reports. On TikTok, an "accountant" is code for someone working in the sex industry. This arguably originated with user Rocky Panterra's video "I am an Accountant," in which Rocky sings, "If I am asked by a stranger what I do, I'd rather smile and simply state that I have a full-time job—as an accountant. Nobody asks you questions when you say you are an accountant." [16] Panterra's video was quickly co-opted by adult content creators to speak openly about their livelihood online, with

---

14   Thomas Hobbes, *The English Works of Thomas Hobbes of Malmesbury*, ed. Sir William Molseworth, vol. 3 (London: Bohn, IX, 1839).
15   Taylor Lorenz, "Internet 'Algospeak' Is Changing Our Language in Real Time, from 'Nip Nops' to 'Le Dollar Bean,'" *Washington Post*, April 8, 2022, https://www.washingtonpost.com/technology/2022/04/08/algospeak-tiktok-le-dollar-bean.
16   Austin Morris, "NSFW: Sex, Humor, and Risk in Social Media," *Velvet Light Trap*. Austin: University of Texas at Austin (University of Texas Press, 2021), https://doi.org/10.7560/VLT8809.

the connecting inference perhaps being that both careers can deal out a lot of money.

Also called "Voldemorting,"[17] as coined by Emily van der Nagel in her paper entitled "Networks that Work Too Well: Intervening in Algorithmic Connections," these popular algospeaks include replacements such as: "unaliving" = "suicide," "swimmers" = "vaccinated people," "panini" = "the pandemic," "cheetoh" = "Donald Trump," and "le dollar bean" = "lesbians."[18] In addition to simply replacing words or phrases with innuendo, some users opt for "lexical variants" in order to thwart censorship. A research paper on eating disorder groups on the app found that "one popular technique used by the community is adopting non-standard linguistic variants of moderated tags. These variants include adding or deleting characters in tags ("anorexiaa"), substituting letters ("thynsporation"), or deliberate misspellings ("anarexic") but keeping the semantics of the tag consistent."[19] Unlike the leetspeak of the 1980s which simply swapped numbers with letters while still maintaining the original word, the linguistic metamorphosis on TikTok is a radical alteration. It leaves outsiders in the dust. Moreover, this transformation of language only augments the remixing of TikTok's sonic and visual communications.

The design environment on TikTok affords users a relatively unique opportunity to synthesize type, graphics, moving-image, and sound to shape new meanings. Creators play with emojis and symbols—freely replacing letters and whole words in a text, or simply overlaying floating symbols atop moving-image content—to encode layers of significance into a post. One such example is the corn emoji which, when used on TikTok, almost always signifies "porn" (an alteration of this is the corn emoji followed immediately by the star emoji) and may accompany sex-worker-positive videos that clarify the experiences of those within that community. Alternatively, bookending words between a set of sparkle emojis adds dramatic emphasis and sometimes is used ironically to indicate the overuse and occasional misuse of symbols, for example: "it

---

17   Emily van der Nagel, "Networks That Work Too Well," Intervening in Algorithmic Connections," *Media International Australia* 168, no. 1 (August 1, 2018), 81–92, https://doi.org/10.1177/1329878X18783002.

18   Lorenz, "Internet 'Algospeak' Is Changing Our Language in Real Time, from 'Nip Nops' to 'Le Dollar Bean.'"

19   Stevie Chancellor, Jessica Annette Pater, Trustin Clear, Eric Gilbert, and Munmun De Choudhury, "# thyghgapp: Instagram content moderation and lexical variation in pro-eating disorder communities," In *Proceedings of the 19th ACM conference on computer-supported cooperative work & social computing*, (2016), 1201.

is almost *Virgo* season." The app also comes with a series of derivative, default fonts: "Classic," "Typewriter," "Handwriting," "NEON," and "Serif," that each connote a flexible array of implied meaning depending on how they are deployed. Users make design decisions determining scale, rotation, alignment, and color of type with the tap or pinch of their fingers.

Trends on TikTok influence the use of video editing techniques like montage, cuts, filters, and other video effects in conjunction with typography, graphics, and music to generate even more novel connotations. The "Slipping Through My Fingers" trend from late 2021, for example, featured montages of a user's own home-videos, typically of a sibling growing up over a significant number of years, which accompanies the matching, nostalgic 2008 *Mamma Mia!* track of the same name.[20] Text overlays state "POV: You are _____," with the blank filled with a narrative the similar to "watching your brother grow up," or "watching your sister become an NYC fashion model," with subsequent text message screenshots or video montage in line with this point of view.

If, on its surface, these design trends appear juvenile, it's likely because most of the app's users in the United States are Gen Z.[21] Thus, the design tastes that succeed are molded mostly by young hands (or fingers). The impact of amateur, impetuous, fear of missing out or #fomo-driven "communicative reflux" is not clear. One thing is certain, though, the churning hum of TikTok can produce incredible experiences, both wondrous and terrible. In Byung-Chul Han's *In the Swarm: Digital Prospects*, the philosopher provides an acoustic metaphor for how overwhelming TikTok can be, describing that, "the choices effected by the intendent of power are followed silently, as it were, by the subjects of power. Sound, or noise, provides an acoustic cue that power is faltering."[22] TikTok is a cacophony of loud, reactionary commotion. What users on the app might describe as punching up towards axes of power and institutional oppressions can also be described as "a society without mutual respect" or as an outrage society. From 2019 to the writing of this chapter, TikTok has been the digital exhibition platform for protests, war, witnessing

---

20   Amanda Seyfried and Meryl Streep, *Slipping through My Fingers*, 'Mamma Mia!' The Original Motion Picture Soundtrack (Polydor Records, 2008).
21   Zhong and Frenkel, "A Third of TikTok's U.S. Users May Be 14 or Under, Raising Safety Questions."
22   Han, *In the Swarm*, 4.

atrocity, presidential bans, censorship,[23] harassment, doxxing, hate speech, witch hunts, murder, crime sleuthing, and misinformation campaigns—just to name a few. One well-documented example involved a young woman named Gabby Petito, whose disappearance (and later, murder) generated unending speculative content from would-be detectives on TikTok. For weeks, creators debated all possible perspectives on the case, exploiting the murder of a young woman for engagement, popularity, and money. On the other hand, it was a TikTok couple that helped lead authorities to Petito's remains.[24] The disproportionate focus on Petito's story, that of a white, affluent, and able-bodied cis-woman, also helped expose the disparity of news coverage not brought to missing brown and black bodies in the United States.[25] TikTok has a dual-edge; one embodies possibility, connection, and hope, while the other is a vapid, degrading catastrophe.

Effective design requires space for reflection, a slowness that TikTok may not be able to accommodate as a social media platform. In his book called *Lateral Thinking*,[26] philosopher Edward de Bono described a process akin to TikTok's algorithmic mashings that can be utilized to generate ideas. de Bono suggested ideating one particular object by considering a completely random object as a point of departure. He advised bringing both disparate items close together while trying to make the ideas fit together. This process, like the racking of a kaleidoscope where each idea is a random bit of colored glass, aims to couple as many "points of departure" next to one another as possible. Innovative ideas sprout from these unexpected connections. However, de Bono's creative method is just one stage of the design process, and the speed at which TikTok hurtles through topics, trends, and content certainly does not feel right for a flexible, speculative, or meditative design practice.

---

23   Lily Kuo, "TikTok 'Makeup Tutorial' Goes Viral with Call to Action on China's Treatment of Uighurs," *The Guardian*, November 27, 2019, https://www.theguardian.com/technology/2019/nov/27/tiktok-makeup-tutorial-conceals-call-to-action-on-chinas-treatment-of-uighurs.
24   Jesus Jiménez, "Gabby Petito's Death Ruled a Homicide, F.B.I. Confirms," *The New York Times*, September 21, 2021, https://www.nytimes.com/2021/09/21/us/gabby-petito-homicide.html.
25   Katherine Rosman, "How the Case of Gabrielle Petito Galvanized the Internet," *The New York Times*, September 21, 2021, https://www.nytimes.com/2021/09/20/style/gabby-petito-case-tiktok-social-media.html.
26   Edward de Bono, *Lateral Thinking: A Textbook of Creativity*, (Penguin, 2010).

The agoras, or public squares, of pre-Platonic Athens were physical gathering spaces to share social, political, and philosophical ideas among most members of the public. If social media platforms of the 21st century, such as TikTok, have become the virtual public square, what does it mean that the various communication methods in that square evolve so quickly? On the one hand, this might give more agency to users, as they actively shape the linguistic vehicle of discourse. Alternatively, meme scholar Jamie Cohen ponders the implications of this accelerated change, stating that "on one hand, this may increase our ability to read Internet content better, but on the other, it severs and fractures our ability to communicate collectively."[27] If design communication is about the health and care of people, then perhaps more oversight on the set of machines and algorithms in our virtual agoras would produce a kinder social media experience.

---

27   Jamie Cohen, "Why We're Creating Language to Hide from Tech's Censorship Systems," *OneZero*, April 12, 2022, https://onezero.medium.com/why-were-creating-language-to-hide-from-tech-s-censorship-systems-ad024f083c89.

Equality of Fit in Digital Typography

Thomas Jockin[1]

> Responsive typography according to cognition could provide a more humane access to knowledge and experience previously blocked to many readers. However, such a potential requires deliberation on when and how much this capacity should be implemented. The implementation of Internet of Things and machine learning into typography will, if only imperceptibly, nudge the outcome for our civil society in the 21st century.
> — *Thomas Jockin, US*

The essential difference between digital typography and all other kinds of typography is its capacity to respond to data. Data can be the device the user is using, the lighting conditions in the room, or even the attention of the reader. This essay has a three-part structure: first, we will trace a genealogy of responsive typography on the web; second, is a literature review on reading and eye-tracking research; and third, a summary of the ethical and moral implications of using algorithms that direct the individual visual presentation of text. It is the hope of the author that web-design practitioners consider how currently available technology allows typography to have the same degree of responsiveness to individual user cognition as is currently applied to external environments and devices. For thought leaders and educators, the author hopes this chapter will aid the reader to articulate a more nuanced understanding about how technology may engender equity in design.

Responsiveness to Devices

As the adoption of mobile phone devices allowed Internet access growth in the 2000s, both web designers and technologists required an efficient

---

[1] University of North Georgia, US.

method to support the presentation of website content on a wide range of screen sizes. Ethan Marcotte coined the web design term "Responsive Design" in 2010 to describe a particular application of the Cascade Style Sheet (CSS) that streamlined website content presentation on both desktop and mobile devices.[2] Marcotte explained that using relative units of sizing and media queries in CSS allows a website to accommodate various screen sizes while maintaining usability and consistency. Media queries within the CSS document instruct the web browser to ping a user's screen for specific properties and return that information to the browser. If the user's configuration meets specific conditioned rules described in the CSS document, the browser is instructed to change the visual presentation of the web page according to those conditioned rules.

For example, the CSS media query would first check to determine the width of the user's browser. If the web page is being viewed at a width of 1400 pixels or more, the CSS could specify that the body text should be displayed at 18 pixels. If the webpage is being viewed at a width of less than 1400 pixels, the CSS could specify that the body text should be only 12 pixels. Along with media queries, the introduction of relative unit values within web design has allowed for proportion-based typographic control for screen widths and resolutions not explicitly declared in the CSS document. When relative units are used, a change in the base font size, triggered by an instruction, would result in all other text elements scaling proportionally to the browser and change the other text elements accordingly.[3] Fixed font sizes are not responsive to the change in base font size.[4] For example, when a media query detects that the browser window size is 1400 pixels, following the rule set by a designer, the font-size attribute in the HTML tag is set to 24 pixels. Then, the web browser sets the font-size of a header by multiplying the base font size by 3.4 rems. The explicit pixel size of the header in the document is calculated by multiplying the document root font size of 24 pixels by the specified rems unit 3.4, which would approximate 81.6 pixels. The decision of what font size to set the typography is left to this simple algorithm in the CSS document. Rather than follow an

---

2   MDN, "Responsive Design — Learn Web Development," accessed June 28, 2022, https://developer.mozilla.org/en-US/docs/Learn/CSS/CSS_layout/Responsive_Design.
3   MDN, "Learn to Style HTML Using CSS – Learn Web Development," accessed June 28, 2022, https://developer.mozilla.org/en-US/docs/Learn/CSS.
4   MDN, "CSS Values and Units — Learn Web Development," June 28, 2022, https://developer.mozilla.org/en-US/docs/Learn/CSS/Building_blocks/Values_and_units.

explicit instruction by the designer, the font-size of the document is set by an indirect parametric provided by the designer. Such relative parameters allow for more flexible response to diverse devices and reader preference.

Responsiveness to Physical Spaces

The first treatment of responsive typography responds to the device used to access content. A second treatment of digital typography responds to data from the physical space. The legibility of typography is related to the luminosity in the environment the reader finds themselves within.

Sensor APIs allow the typography in a document to respond to the room's luminosity, 2019.[5]

---

5   Mandy Michael, *Light It Up*, YouTube Video, 2019, https://www.youtube.com/watch?v=ivz1hdAhJmE.

Studies as far back as 1934 confirmed the design intuition that a dim environment diminishes the legibility of text, especially at smaller font sizes.[6] Mandy Michael, a front-end developer and designer who spoke at the community-run conference DDD Perth in 2019, explained how sensor application programming interfaces (APIs) allow the typography in a document to respond to the room's luminosity. Light sensors come prepackaged in digital devices and detect ambient light present in the environment. Illuminance returns the current light level measured in lux units. To give a sense of the scale of lux units: a family living room would have 50 lux units, office lighting could range from 320 to 500 lux units, and direct sunlight starts at 32,000 lux units. In her conference talk, Michael provided an example of a font consisting of dots that increase in size as the brightness of the room increases and, likewise, decrease in size if the room is dim. She also suggested that such a response to lighting conditions could be applied to increasing font weight as the ambient light decreases.[7] Integrating lux values into the rule-based CSS declarations would allow typography to respond both to diverse devices as well as the environmental lighting conditions the reader finds themselves reading text.

Along with luminance, typography may be responsive to the physical distance of the reader. Reneé Steven's project, TagAR, incorporates augmented reality technology to position nametags of conference attendees above the heads of users. The tag font size responds to the distance of the smartphone user and the other persons in the room. The closer the person is to the user, the larger the font and the farther away the person is from the user, the smaller the font.[8] Gen Ramírez's thesis project at Koninklijke Academie van Beeldende Kunsten (KABK), Entorno, explores how typography can account for distance and perspective distortion. Entorno is a variable typeface family that interacts with physical and virtual spaces. Of particular interest is the subfamily Entorno Roadmark. Entorno Roadmark distorts the letterforms according to the viewer's distance from the text object on the ground, like roadway lettering. The variation 0 m is normal in appearance, whereas the other master,

---

6   M. A. Tinker, "Experimental Study of Reading," *Psychological Bulletin* 31, no. 2 (1934): 101, https://doi.org/10.1037/h0074040.

7   Mandy Michael, "Fun with Browser and Sensor APIs," DDD Perth Conference, Perth WA, Australia, August 2019, https://noti.st/mandy/HBCdTl.

8   Renée Stevens, *Never Forget A Name Again*, TED Talk, 2019, https://www.ted.com/talks/renee_stevens_never_forget_a_name_again.

30 m, has significant vertical distortion that appears completely normal at 30 meters away.⁹ When we consider both Entorno Roadmark and TagAR, digital typography has the potential to incorporate environmental distance and perspective in the rule-based CSS declarations of digital typography. Many wayfinding use cases could benefit from such a distance-based typography. The use of such distance data allows for typography that better orients the reader in the environment.

TagAR, a social app designed to provide visual name tags in an "augmented view."[10]

---

9 Gen Ramírez, "Entorno," TypeMedia 2018, https://www.typemedia2018.com/gen.
10 Reneé Steven, "TagAR," interactive, augmented reality, and motion design studio, 2019, http://reneestevens.design/tagar.

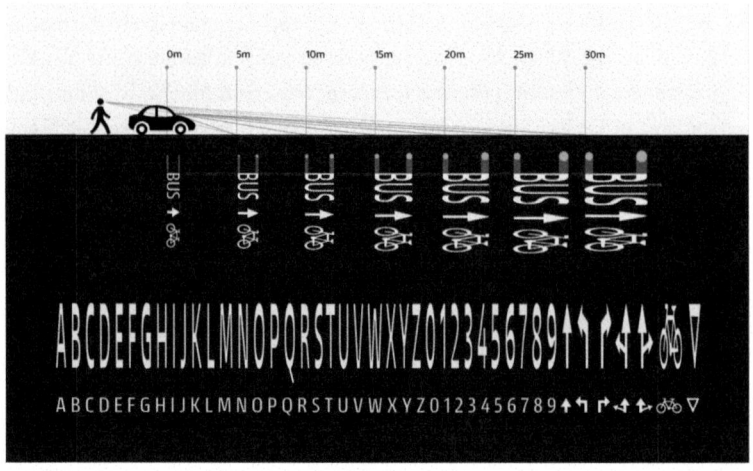

The typeface Entorno by Gen Ramírez, 2018.

Responsiveness to Cognition

So far, we reviewed data according to the device and the physical space of the device. Next, we explore the cognition of the reader holding these devices. For example, Word Lens allowed Google Glass users to automatically translate signage, packing, and other environmental graphics into the user's native language with the typography matching the size, width, and colors of the original language. In this example, the native language of the reader is considered to orient themselves in an environment where their native language is absent.

Development of Measurement Instruments

Researchers have explored the relationship between eye movement and reading since 1879. However, significant innovations in the measurement devices for such research to be practical were required. Initial instruments for measurement were quite intrusive, with some studies conducted with a search coil attached to the eye like a contact lens. Current methods use less invasive and accessible means of measurement such as video-based pupil monitoring.[11] With the advent of open-source computer vision libraries, standard web cameras can detect a user's pupil position automatically.

In eye-movement research, eye-movements are divided into two broad categories; fixations and saccades. A saccade is when the pupil of a reader is in motion: fixation is when the pupil of the reader is at rest. When the saccade movement is backward rather than forward, it is called regression. Saccade distance is measured in degree units. Fixation is measured in milliseconds. Fixation time and saccade length are related to aspects of the text currently being read.

There are significant differences in eye movement measures between skilled and struggling readers. Skilled readers make shorter fixations, longer saccades, and fewer regressions than struggling readers. On the other hand, poor readers make longer fixations, shorter saccades, more fixations, and more regressions than regular readers. Likewise, bilingual readers make shorter fixations, longer saccades, and fewer regressions in their primary language.[12] A 2019 paper from Stony Brook University developed a classifier that accurately predicted reading or skimming behavior of readers. Individuals who were reading encompassed wide horizontal saccade distances with small vertical saccades, whereas persons who were skimming encompassed narrow horizontal saccade movements with large vertical saccades.[13] Eye-tracking research on reading suggests differences in kinds of readers and reading behavior is measurable. Once reading status and behavior are measured, typographic properties may change just as CSS media queries direct changes based on device viewport, lux level, or object distance. With this review of responsive digital typography and eye-tracking research, it is important to consider if the typography of diverse reading statuses and behaviors ought to be the same.

---

11 Keith Rayner, "Eye Movements in Reading and Information Processing: 20 Years of Research," *Psychological Bulletin* 124, no. 3 (November 1998), 372, https://doi.org/10.10 37/0033-2909.124.3.372.

12 Rayner, 392.

13 Conor Kelton, Zijun Wei, Seoyoung Ahn, Aruna Balasubramanian, Samir R. Das, Dimitris Samaras, and Gregory Zelinsky, "Reading Detection in Real-Time," in *Proceedings of the 11th ACM Symposium on Eye Tracking Research & Applications*, vol. 43 (The 11th ACM Symposium, 2019), 2, https://doi.org/10.1145/3314111.3319916.

Is One-Size-Fits-All Digital Typography Valid?

Typography within the graphic design discipline continues to live in the shadow of Modernism. A hallmark of Modernism was the search for typography stripped of variation to an essential simple form. Herbert Bayer's influential essay "Towards A Universal Type" is typical of such a viewpoint. Bayer is concerned primarily with the cultural dimension of design artifacts such as buildings, transportation, dress, and, of course, typography; he juxtaposes historical type specimens with gothic cathedrals, horseback riding, and Victorian dress against skyscrapers, automobiles, and 1920s dress. These pairings are meant to justify the need for typography that embodies the cultural moment of Modernism and breaks away from—in Bayer's words—the oppression of tradition. At the heart of Bayer's argument for a geometric sans serif design is the claim that reading is most legible when the glyph shapes of a script are uniform.[14] Even the variation between uppercase and lowercase ought to be stripped away for the sake of efficiency. Such uniform typography and script would be optimal for the diverse applications of both encoding, such as printing and handwriting, and decoding, such as reading books and signage.

Research since the time of Bayer's essay has offered a contrary account of legibility in typography. Readers who are neurodiverse, older in age, or with low vision tend to need typography set differently than typical readers. While dyslexic individuals have a phonetic processing deficit, dramatically increased spacing between character glyphs improved reading fluency for readers with dyslexia.[15] For readers with low vision, one study found the variation to their font is required, and such variation is significant among the forty elderly readers with low vision.[16] In the study, patients were permitted to adjust font attributes until the modified font met the same legibility as the control in the study. The attributes available to manipulate were spacing, stroke width, serif

---

14   Herbert Bayer, "Towards a Universal Type," *Industrial Arts*, 1936, 78.

15   Marco Zorzi, Chiara Barbiero, Andrea Facoetti, Isabella Lonciar, Marco Carrozzi, Marcella Montico, Laura Bravar, Florence George, Catherine ech-Georgel, and Johannes C. Ziegler, "Extra-Large Letter Spacing Improves Reading in Dyslexia," *Proceedings of the National Academy of Sciences of the United States of America* 109, no. 28 (July 10, 2012): 11457, https://doi.org/10.1073/pnas.1205566109.

16   Aries Arditi, "Adjustable Typography: An Approach to Enhancing Low Vision Text Accessibility," *Ergonomics* 47, no. 5 (April 15, 2004): 476, https://doi.org/10.1080/001401 3031000085680.

size, and x-height. The adjusted font spacing was between 5 and 70 percent relative to the cap height of the font. Likewise, x-height was adjusted between 60 and 100 percent relative to the cap height of the font. In another study, a team of researchers, including well-known typeface designer Nadine Chahine, deployed a methodology where subjects were randomly exposed to either a real word or a pseudo-word. The exposure started at a time duration of 500 milliseconds. As the subject correctly answered a prompt after each word exposure ("Was that a word?") the time duration of the next word stimulus was decreased in a 3-steps-forward-1-step-back staircase progression. This progression continued until the subject repeatedly failed to correctly answer the "Was that a word" prompt due to the time duration being too short. The more legible the font was, the more a subject could correctly answer the prompt in the shorter time duration.[17] The results of the research established that an increase in the tracking of letterforms improves response rate thresholds within subjects. The paper hypothesizes that the less-legible square sans serif could be brought up to the same legibility performance as a humanist sans serif by increasing the intra-spacing of the letterforms within the font design.

Ultimately, research shows that typography is not one-size-fits-all. While the idea of an average that works for most readers is a reasonable position when physical materials require printing and distribution, typography is responsive to data in the digital era. Now with non-intrusive eye-tracking technology, typography change for sensitive readers is as feasible as adjusting typography based on device size, lighting conditions or object distance. The technology to enable typography to respond to the individual reader is already here; we just need to shift our mental model for typography. In most studies, typography has been found to have no impact on reading performance between subjects. However, typography does impact reading performance within-subjects, especially older subjects or those with reading difficulties.[18] The belief in the uniformity of typographic properties for all readers comes from averages generated from between-subjects. The level of measurement for reading needs to shift from between-subjects to within-subject. What has prevented more use of within-subject averages is not efficacy, but technological constraints and

---

17 Jonathan Dobres, Nadine Chahine, Bryan Reimer, David Gould, Bruce Mehler, and Joseph F. Coughlin, "Utilising Psychophysical Techniques to Investigate the Effects of Age, Typeface Design, Size and Display Polarity on Glance Legibility," *Ergonomics* 59, no. 10 (October 2016): 1379, https://doi.org/10.1080/00140139.2015.1137637.
18 Dobres et al., 1383.

expense—collecting individualized data is expensive and time-consuming. Such limitations for individuated data are removed thanks to open-source Computer Vision (CV) libraries such as TensorFlow.

The shift to an equal fit of typography for individual readers, rather than the prior notion of the same typography for all readers, requires we consider what one means by equality. Aristotle knew the difference between the mean for the object and the subject as he wrote *The Nicomachean Ethics*. The mean for an object was the same for all persons, but the mean for an individual subject will vary. Aristotle uses the example of athletic training. The mean between 10 and 2 pounds of weight is 6 pounds. However, it does not follow that 6 pounds are fitting for different athletes. For the developed athlete, 6 pounds is too little, whereas, for the beginner, 6 pounds is too much. The trainer needs to find the intermediate, not in the weight, but for the athlete. Finding such an intermediate for the person and not in the object is the equitable.

Aristotle continued this approach with his commentary on equity. Equity, for Aristotle, is the correction of error when a universal rule is applied to a particular case.[19] In the example, he provided a flexible ruler, in contrast to a rigid linear ruler, that adapted itself to the shape of a statue. One can take this explanation as finding the ideal for the subject rather than in the universal object; The trainer who considers the right number of weights according to the athlete's ability is an equitable trainer. This is the opposite of the procrustean bed—the Greek myth of a storekeeper who allowed travelers to rest at his residence but either stretched the limbs of the traveler if they were too short for the bed or cut off their limbs if they were too tall for the bed.[20] A procrustean bed is a metaphor for removing outliers that do not fit the idealized model.

Our current method of responsive typography, in the context of the reader's cognition, is a procrustean bed. Media queries, at best, respond to different devices accessing digital content. An assumed ideal for what constitutes legible and accessible typography and what outliers may exist are either trimmed away or stretched into prepacked accessibility guidelines. Applying this notion of equity to responsive typography would mean developing a rule that can adapt to the particular reader encountering a digital document. Machine learning (ML) could provide fertile ground to develop such a rule-set. The next section

---

19 Aristotle, *Aristotle, XIX, Nicomachean Ethics*, trans. H. Rackham, 2nd edition (Cambridge, MA: Harvard University Press, 1934).
20 Britannica, "Procrustes: Greek Mythological Figure," accessed June 28, 2022, https://www.britannica.com/topic/Procrustes.

of this chapter provides an overview of Machine Learning and its application to responsive typography.

Applying Machine Learning to Typography

While the concept of delegating design decision-making to artificial intelligence may seem alien to designers, the historical development of typography on the web reviewed at the start of this chapter displays a trend away from explicit instruction to conditional rules in typography attributes. First, precise units of measurement such as pixels were replaced with relative proportionate units of measure like em. Then, media queries directed the typography of a document to respond differently to devices and viewports. As Tim Brown, Head of Typography at Adobe Systems, states in an *A List Apart* article, this shift from explicit visual presentation to implicit rules and instructions points to the potential for typography to fit everyone perfectly. In Brown's words, "In theory, at least, the web is universal."[21] Machine learning continues this trend of implicit rule-making as the designer's activity by permitting designers to specify conditional rules not just to viewports but also to indicators of cognition. For example, a webpage's typography or design elements could respond either to rapid scrolling actions or prolonged reading of a particular passage of text,[22] quantifying the effectiveness of such interventions according to key performance indicators and adjusting the conditional typography rules. Handing such a decision feedback loop to an algorithm introduces the need to consider the ethics of such a procedure.

Regarding benefits and risks, it is one thing to affect the presentation of text based on a user's device compared to affecting typography based on the user's cognition. While typography responding to the reader's cognition is an exciting possibility, the time at which a design algorithm should intervene in users' intentions is a living question within design ethics. Competing incentives between profit, autonomy, privacy, and authorship need to be placed

---

21 Tim Brown, "Typography & Web Fonts," A List Apart, accessed June 28, 2022, https://alistapart.com/blog/topic/typography-web-fonts.
22 Sian Gooding, Yevgeni Berzak, Tony Mak, and Matt Sharifi, "Predicting Text Readability from Scrolling Interactions," in *Proceedings of the 25th Conference on Computational Natural Language Learning* (CoNLL-EMNLP 2021, Online: Association for Computational Linguistics, 2021), 380–90, https://doi.org/10.18653/v1/2021.conll-1.30.

into harmony and context, acknowledging that such diverse incentives may be adverse. The next section of this chapter maps out the social ethic paradigm.

Implication for Design Ethics

While ethics are embedded in the design process, design requires an understanding of ethics different from those traditionally studied in classrooms.[23] Traditional ethics is concerned with individuals who act and cause consequences, but social ethics moves the concern of ethics to norms, trends, and policies, both explicit and implicit, that shape decision-making. Such a shift in ethics is required in design because design is a collaborative activity with many individuals contributing to the end product. These individuals come from different departments and disciplines with various incentives. Likewise, the consequences of design also affect large sections of society and individuals. One author goes as far as stating that design is a mode of social experimentation without control samples.[24] As design activities obfuscate our traditional senses of responsibility for undesirable and unseen consequences, a social ethics framework promises a better understanding of the implications of algorithm-guided design decision making.

Decision-Making in Design

The act of decision-making in design includes three major elements. The first is the requirements and criteria of success for the design.[25] The second is the potential risks and secondary effects of an act, and the last is balancing success criteria with acknowledged risks called trade-offs. Mostly, this decision process is implicit in the design process, usually guided by norms and trends within the organization and best practices of the disciplines involved in the design process. Research finds that moral problems in design are not singular and deliberate immoral choices but rather a multitude of questionable choices repeated over a long period of time. The possibility that individuals may wish

---

23 Richard Devon, "Design Ethics: The Social Ethics Paradigm," *International Journal of Engineering Education* 20, no. 3 (2004): 461.
24 Devon, 467.
25 Devon, 466.

to be ethical yet organizations make unethical acts is described by one writer as organizational deviance—decisions that seem fine on the inside appear deviant to outsiders looking in should give pause to the notion that decision-making should be left to the organizations which produce design artifacts.

Consequences of Algorithms in Design

In one sense, the kind of machine learning-guided responsive typography proposed throughout this essay would circumvent the traditional pitfalls of design decision-making—no individual, or even organization, is deciding the best trade-off between success and risks. Instead, the algorithm is making the decision. Such an algorithm, if given access to biomarkers that indicate cognition of the reader, would be able to find the optimal fit of typographic properties to aid that individual reader without causing a significant cost to the organization. This optimism needs to be countered against what are the criteria of success and what are the risks to be balanced is still very much a human endeavor, incentivized by priorities that may not be in the best interest of readers. The same technology that would allow text to respond to eye-fatigue or difficulty understanding a passage could be used to manipulate information in such a manner to best achieve a key performance indicator such as the purchase of products. Considering corporations—and their officers—have a legal obligation to pursue profit, such a dystopian outlook is very likely. These kinds of concerns mean informed consent for users to opt in to such advanced application of computer vision technology to track and respond to the cognition of the individual reader is necessary—but not sufficient—to address the potential ethical consequences of such a technology.

About three-in-ten U.S. adults say they are "almost constantly" online.[26] Overall, 85 percent of Americans say they go online on a daily basis. Yet, half of US adults read at a 6th-grade level or lower.[27] Considering the trend of

---

26   Brooke Auxier and Monica Anderson, "Social Media Use in 2021," *Pew Research Center: Internet, Science & Tech*, April 7, 2021, https://www.pewresearch.org/internet/2021/04/07/social-media-use-in-2021.

27   Mary E. Hanly, "Adult Literacy and Lifeskills Survey (ALL) U.S. 2003 Restricted Use File (RUF) with Rescaled Literacy and Numeracy Scores for Trend with the Program for the International Assessment of Adult Competencies (PIAAC)," National Center for Education Statistics, January 31, 2022, https://nces.ed.gov/pubsearch/pubsinfo.asp?pubid=2022007.

technology, it is inevitable that digital spaces—meditated by typography—will be the public space for commerce, discourse, and community. These digital spaces will bore the consequences of decision-making around priorities directed by AI. Will such AI-directed decision-making result in a techno-optimism where text fits transparently to the needs of each particular reader, like prescribed eyeglasses for cognition? Or will AI-directed decision-making emerge to manipulate consumer preference, information, and association for the sake of quantified metrics?

While Herbert Bayer was wrong in his legibility arguments for a singular and simplified geometric sans serif design, his argument for a kind of authenticity between technology, artifacts, and culture rings true. Typography, as a digital artifact, is placed in a new cultural and technological context with IoT powered artifacts, yet the essence of digital typography has yet to be expressed. Responsive typography for the individual reader in terms of device, environment, and cognition is both theoretically and technically possible today. The kind of typography described in this chapter could provide a more humane access to knowledge and experience previously blocked to many readers. However, such a potential requires deliberation on when and how much this capacity should be implemented. In the personal opinion of the author, rules and regulations alone cannot address the complexity and obfuscation of ML-guided design introduced into ethics. Our discipline will also need to consider normative exemplars that may direct how to use the artifacts that shape our lives. The implementation of IoT and ML into design and typography will, if only imperceptibly, nudge the outcome for our civil society in the 21st century.

I would like to thank Laura Scherling, Erin McLaughlin, Micah Rich, and Alec Gilfillan for their feedback on early drafts of this essay.

Equitable Digital Access in an Era of Uncertainty

Laura Scherling[1]

It is now hard to fathom a world without the Internet and the wide range of digital products and services to which we have become accustomed. As digital technologies have become fundamental, those without reliable digital access live in a precarious situation. In 2021, as many as 2.9 billion people were still living without a reliable Internet connection.[2] As described by Essie Workie, the Director of Human Services Initiatives for the Migration Policy Institute, "the same way that education is a doorway to economic opportunity," today, "digital transformation [...] unlocks opportunity in the modern world."[3] Without digital transformation, there is a serious risk of a deepening bifurcation between those living with digital resources and those struggling to secure them. To genuinely understand this divide, known as the "digital divide," it is important for communities to grasp its complexity. This inequitable situation is not merely about hardware and infrastructure. It is also about user experience design, visual communication, and having the skills and digital literacies to compete in a digitizing world, and about having access to employment, social networks, healthcare, and education-related platforms and services.
— Dr. Laura Scherling, US

1   Columbia University, US.
2   International Telecommunication Union, "Measuring Digital Development: Facts and Figures 2021," ITU, accessed June 25, 2022, https://www.itu.int:443/en/ITU-D/Statistics/Pages/facts/default.aspx.
3   Essie Workie, Migration Policy Institute, interview by author, online, April 12, 2022.

In imagining a just and well-designed society, it is now hard to imagine a life without being digitally connected. The ability or inability to access and use digital products and services is frequently thought of as an infrastructure or information technology (IT) failure or expense, but should also be acknowledged for its nuanced socioeconomic reasons and digital literacy barriers. User experience and user interface design are important to addressing these barriers, and designers can play a more integral role in helping address "digital exclusion." In order to explore contemporary challenges related to digital access, this chapter examines several organizations, policies, and projects working to improve equitable digital access.

Digital Divide Challenges and Misconceptions

In 1995, approximately "42 percent of American adults said they had never heard of the Internet."[4] By 2021 the Organisation for Economic Co-operation and Development (OECD) estimated that South Korea had household Internet access rates above 99% and that by 2022 Norway had also reached 99%, accounting for some of the highest percentages in the world.[5,6] In 2021 it was estimated that about 82% of US households had Internet access, and by comparison in the same year (among OECD member countries), Colombia saw household access at around 60.2% and Mexico at around 66%. These indicators speak to the ongoing effort toward being digitally connected, while at the same time a great deal of variance in terms of access exists. Many people have benefited from consistent access to Internet-connected devices, and others still live without reliable connections to fundamental technologies. These statistics only highlight part of a complex and evolving situation.

Many people now rely on online news sources, e-commerce "giants" like Amazon, digital payments, and platforms to access healthcare, educational

---

[4] The Pew Charitable Trusts, "Internet & Tech," accessed on April 4, 2023, https://www.pewtrusts.org/en/topics/internet-and-tech.

[5] OECD (2023), "Internet access (Indicator)," accessed on April 7 2023, https://doi.org/10.1787/69c2b997-en.

[6] In the OECD's definition access is through a personal computer using ADSL, dial-up, or cable broadband access.

materials, and job prospects.[7] Uneven access to information—described as a "digital divide"—is now especially devastating to those living without dependable services. In decades, the importance of being digitally connected has become urgent. To get access to the best quality information, platforms, and social networks it is the expectation, at a bare minimum, to have a reliable Internet connection. Around the start of the COVID-19 pandemic, Anne-Marie Grey, executive director for the United Nations High Commissioner for Refugees (UNHCR), declared that "digital connectivity should be a human right" as it "enables access to information, education and opportunity."[8] Yet to be an empowered participant in the digital economy often requires more than a working connection, however, this is the baseline. It also means fostering "digital literacies," which can be a combination of technical or design-focused competencies along with the ability to be critically discerning of information presented online.[9]

Technical and design-focused digital literacies can include specific competencies such as understanding website navigation. This benefit would enable the designing and editing of original content found in photography, videos, and graphics which are intended for websites and social media. It can also include developing advanced skills in coding, data wrangling, and the flexibility to learn and adapt to use ever-emerging technologies. Discerning information online can mean developing the critical thinking skills needed to evaluate information sources as reputable or not, ensure e-safety, and understand others' social and emotional behavior online. It can also mean being sufficiently keyed into economic, social, and political events.[10] To be fully confident in digital spaces is like being a "digital citizen." Beth A. Buchholz, et

---

7   Carlo Combi, Gabriele Pozzani, and Giuseppe Pozzi, "Telemedicine for Developing Countries. A Survey and Some Design Issues," *Applied Clinical Informatics* 7, no. 4 (November 2, 2016), 1025–50, https://doi.org/10.4338/ACI-2016-06-R-0089.
8   Anne-Marie Grey, "The Case for Connectivity, the New Human Right," United Nations, December 10, 2020, https://www.un.org/en/un-chronicle/case-connectivity-new-human-right.
9   David Bawden, "Origins and Concepts of Digital Literacy," ed. Colin Lankshear and Michele Knobel, *Digital Literacies: Concepts, Policies and Practices* 30, no. 2008 (2008), 17–32.
10 Carole L. Jurkiewicz, "Big Data, Big Concerns: Ethics in the Digital Age," *Public Integrity* 20, no. sup1 (January 18, 2018), 46–59, https://doi.org/10.1080/10999922.2018.1448218

al. argued that a full-fledged "netizen"[11] is in the position to engage in Internet-based civic discourse, act as a decision maker in digital spheres, and participate in creating more equitable communities online.[12] Exemplary "netizens," for example, could be defined as those who have donated their time to Wikipedia authorship,[13] monitored chat rooms,[14] shared open source code on GitHub, or contributed to building an online community as well as using a fundraising platform for a charitable cause.

Nevertheless, a large part of the world remains offline and are unable to build critical, digital competencies. Researchers Franz Drees-Gross and Pepe Zhang estimated that less than 50% of the Latin American and Caribbean (LAC) population has "fixed broadband connectivity, and only 9.9% have high-quality fiber connectivity at home."[15] In an International Telecommunication Union (ITU) report "Facts and Figures 2021," they estimated that only about 33 percent of people in Africa have reliable Internet access.[16] In another ITU report on "measuring digital development"[17] it was estimated that about 4.9 billion people were using the Internet in 2021 globally, while another 2.9 billion are still without reliable Internet use. The ITU described:

> The statistics reveal a connectivity 'grand canyon' separating the digitally empowered from the digitally excluded. This is exemplified through data indicating that 96 percent of the 2.9 billion living in the developing world are still offline. Location plays a big part: our figures reveal that the share of Internet users in urban areas is twice as high as in rural areas.

---

11   Internet theorist Michael Hauben is widely credited with popularizing the term "netizen", a conglomerate word for a citizen of the Internet.

12   Beth A. Buchholz, Jason DeHart, and Gary Moorman, "Digital Citizenship During a Global Pandemic: Moving Beyond Digital Literacy," *Journal of Adolescent & Adult Literacy* 64, no. 1 (2020), 11–17, https://doi.org/10.1002/jaal.1076.

13   Hoda Baytiyeh and Jay Pfaffman, "Volunteers in Wikipedia: Why the Community Matters," *Journal of Educational Technology & Society* 13, no. 2 (2010): 128–40.

14   See Hector Postigo, "America Online Volunteers: Lessons from an Early Co-Production Community," *International Journal of Cultural Studies* 12, no. 5 (September 1, 2009): 451–69, https://doi.org/10.1177/1367877909337858.

15   Franz Drees-Gross and Pepe Zhang, "Poor Digital Access Is Holding Latin America and the Caribbean Back. Here's How to Change It," *World Bank Blogs*, August 12, 2021, https://blogs.worldbank.org/latinamerica/poor-digital-access-holding-latin-america-and-caribbean-back-heres-how-change-it.

16   International Telecommunication Union, "Measuring Digital Development."

17   International Telecommunication Union.

While the ITU's assessment included a large share of offline users who were living in rural or developing areas, these statistics include people living in high-income countries. In 2021, researcher Emily A. Vogels reported that approximately a quarter of American adults with household incomes below $30,000 "do not have home broadband services (43%) or a desktop or laptop computer (41%)," with these households relying more heavily on smartphones.[18] By comparison, the share of households with Internet access across the European Union "crossed the 90 percent milestone" in 2021.[19] Even so, as many as 20 percent of children in the United Kingdom, for example, did not consistently have access to "a device for online learning." The pandemic lockdowns pointed to how precarious the connectivity situation, often defined as the "digital divide," can be.[20]

Historically, the term "digital divide" has been described by the Organisation for Economic Co-operation and Development (OECD) as "the gap between individuals, households, businesses and geographic areas at different socio-economic levels with regard to both their opportunities to access information and communication technologies (ICTs) and to their use of the Internet for a wide variety of activities."[21] Before the digital divide was more widely measured and addressed in forums such as the UN, ITU, and the OECD, author Don Tapscott, wrote that while widespread digitization would reshape our lives, networked intelligence could also result in "differential access" issues, employment displacement, and play a significant role in economic inequality.[22] In 2015 Laura Robinson, et al. observed that "the relationship between digital inequalities and other forms of inequality"

---

18 International Telecommunication Union; Emily A. Vogels, "Digital Divide Persists Even as Americans with Lower Incomes Make Gains in Tech Adoption," *Pew Research Center* (blog), June 22, 2021, https://www.pewresearch.org/fact-tank/2021/06/22/digital-divi de-persists-even-as-americans-with-lower-incomes-make-gains-in-tech-adoption.

19 Joseph Johnson, "Number of Internet Users in EU Countries as of December 2020," *Statista*, July 21, 2021, https://www.statista.com/statistics/252753/number-of-internet -users-eu-countries/.

20 Zoe Kleinman, "Internet Access: 1.5m UK Homes Still Offline, Ofcom Finds," *BBC News*, April 28, 2021, sec. Technology, https://www.bbc.com/news/technology-56906654.

21 OECD, "Understanding the Digital Divide" (Paris: OECD, January 1, 2001), 5, https://do i.org/10.1787/236405667766.

22 Don Tapscott, *The Digital Economy: Promise and Peril In The Age of Networked Intelligence* (New York: McGraw-Hill, 1997).

was still largely unappreciated, finding that "digital exclusion" impacts underrepresented groups and those with economic disadvantages.[23]

Given these facts, it is easy to be drawn in by digital divide misconceptions.[24] One misconception is toward narrowly defining the *digital divide* itself, that it is merely a "problem of access to IT."[25] Author and professor, Lisa Servon, argued that it is a tripartite problem, where "access, training, and content" are all interrelated creating skill in the Information Age. Policies that disregard the latter cannot solve the digital divide.[26] Servon also argued that digital technologies should not be seen as a cure all, a quick fix to alleviate social problems, and technology use must be "combined with other first-order resources (such as food and housing)" and "second-order resources (such as economic literacy and education)" to truly empower low-income households and those below the poverty line.

Misconceptions can also surround what exactly household "internet access" is, and how to define it. It can depend on what type(s) of device(s) an individual or household owns. And without disposable income, buying and keeping up with electronics' maintenance can be financially prohibitive. Some organizations like Los Angeles- and Detroit-based organization Human I-T, and London-based organization The Restart Project, have dedicated their time to repairing devices and distributing them to those in need. There are strong design and sustainability advantages to diverting donated desktop computers, laptops, mobile phones, and Wi-Fi hotspots that would otherwise have become e-waste. Human I-T has recognized that "a device and the Internet are only as valuable to someone as their ability to use it without interruption", and has provided free "rapid-response" technical support.[27] The Restart Project has also hosted educational "Restart Parties" where attendees can "teach each other how to repair their broken and slow devices," improving Internet access

---

23 Laura Robinson, Shelia R. Cotten, Hiroshi Ono, Anabel Quan-Haase, Gustavo Mesch, Wenhong Chen, Jeremy Schulz, Timothy M. Hale and Michael J. Stern, "Digital Inequalities and Why They Matter," *Information, Communication & Society* 18, no. 5 (May 4, 2015): 570, https://doi.org/10.1080/1369118X.2015.1012532.
24 See Lisa Servon, "Four Myths about the Digital Divide," *Planning Theory & Practice* 3, no. 2 (January 1, 2002): 222–27, https://doi.org/10.1080/14649350220150080.
25 Servon, 225.
26 Servon, 225.
27 Human I-T, "Tech Support," accessed June 25, 2022, https://www.human-i-t.org/tech-support-overview.

through hands-on community repair as a type of repair activism to improve product longevity and increase access.

A more bureaucratic feature of Internet access can depend on national or regional specifications of Internet speeds. Internet speeds are another dimension of digital inequality, and speed data has been historically unreliable in different regions.[28] In the US, for instance, high-speed Internet is defined by the federal government. Essey Workie, Director of Human Services Initiative at the Migration Policy Institute (MPI), has noted that a "bipartisan group of [US] senators and experts argue that the minimum speed is outdated and inefficient and should be raised."[29] MPI, who has worked to improve digital access and technology adoption among three US refugee resettlement programs, and first- and second-generation immigrant youth, have also seen that data caps and poor signals may affect service making it not continuous or reliable. This issue can also amplify disparities.[30]

Beyond these constraints, some individuals and communities have other reasons for staying unplugged. Some people with disabilities might use the Internet less frequently due to "accessibility barriers," like vision and hearing impairments.[31] Designers can play a proactive role in addressing readability, color contrast, and adding text alternatives (or alt text) to objects like images, tables, and video. Some people have mental health issues while In some cases, communities may limit Internet use for religious or political reasons.[32] Researcher, Jan Van Dyke, has also pointed out that some misconceptions about the digital divide can stem from the term "digital divide." Its oversimplification and depiction of "absolute inequalities" when it is more nuanced, could be related to a lack of "immaterial, material, social, and educational" technological resources. This lack of resources can mean different things to different people.[33] The need for reliable and varied digital resources

---

28   International Telecommunication Union, "Measuring Digital Development."
29   Essie Workie, Migration Policy Institute, interview by author, online, April 12, 2022.
30   Workie.
31   U.S. Department of Justice Civil Rights Division Disability Rights Section, "Guidance on Web Accessibility and the ADA," March 18, 2022, https://www.ada.gov/resources/web-guidance.
32   Jan A. G. M. van Dijk, "Digital Divide Research, Achievements and Shortcomings," Poetics, The digital divide in the twenty-first century, 34, no. 4 (August 1, 2006): 221–35, https://doi.org/10.1016/j.poetic.2006.05.004.
33   Van Dijk.

was especially evident during Covid-19 pandemic stay-at-home orders, with a lot of resource limitations exposed in a time of crisis.

Going Virtual in a Time of Crisis

When families went on stay-at-home orders during the Covid-19 pandemic, it quickly became clear that not all households had the same social protections. Children learning remotely, arguably, became the "biggest victims" of this crisis.[34] While some households felt fatigued by the overuse of technology turned to baking, gardening, and hands-on activities to offer some relief from extended periods of time on Zoom, and other learning management systems (LMS). Unfortunately, others could not find an affordable and reliable online connection.

Before the pandemic, many students were already in a precarious situation, and did not have adequate Internet access or the sufficient skills to use digital technologies.[35] Even decades after Internet adoption, it became increasingly clear that successful information and communication technology (ICT) programs were more challenging to design, execute, and maintain than many organizations originally anticipated. The Internet Society discovered that, for example, lack of "locally relevant content" and students' skills limitations meant that the design of ICT programming was not always as useful as it could be.[36] Ogunode Niyi Jacob, et al. conducted research on ICT programming in Nigeria. Challenges such as lack of funding to cover the cost of maintaining ICT facilities, sporadic electric power supplies, insufficient teacher training, and education policies were addressed in order to enhance programs.[37]

---

34 UNICEF, "COVID-19 and Children," accessed June 25, 2022, https://data.unicef.org/covid-19-and-children.

35 Internet Society, "Internet for Education in Africa: Helping Policy Makers to Meet the Global Education Agenda Sustainable Development Goal 4," *Internet Society* (blog), April 11, 2017, https://www.internetsociety.org/resources/doc/2017/internet-for-education-in-africa-helping-policy-makers-to-meet-the-global-education-agenda-sustainable-development-goal-4.

36 Internet Society.

37 Ogunode Niyi Jacob, Okwelogu Izunna Somadin, Yahaya Danjuma M, and Olatunde-Aiyedun, T. G., "Deployment of ICT Facilities by Post-Basic Education and Career Development (PBECD) During Covid-19 in Nigeria: Challenges and Way Forward,"

Before the pandemic, those in need of Internet access could supplement it by going to Internet cafes, libraries, and public and commercial access telecentres. Telecentres, such as those in rural parts of India or access points developed by the Asia-Pacific Telecentre Network (APTN), are frequently run by non-profit organizations. Internet cafes have become fairly ubiquitous globally, and operate as niche businesses. Sometimes cafes are family-owned and function as mixed-use developments with bookstores and coffee shops on the premises.[38] In their research about Internet cafes throughout Africa and Asia, Bjørn Furuholt and Stein Kristiansen found that cafes could provide some relief by providing Internet access points to "a wide range of users" not only as locations for gaming and socializing[39] but also for "information retrieval and research."[40]

When the pandemic disrupted traditional face-to-face classroom education, it also cut off access to some alternative services like cafes. The pandemic also tested the feasibility of accessing virtual education services. As cities and entire countries went into lockdowns, youth in lower quality housing with poor energy supplies and unreliable Internet connections simply could not sustain remote learning, and parents along with their children were suddenly faced with "navigating the increasingly digital environment."[41] This proved to be much harder for those "without savings or safety nets" and interrupted school enrollment as well.[42]

In light of in-person closures and rising unemployment, some students had to drop out of school altogether. This was the case for more than half a million university students in the US who had to discontinue their education.

International Journal of Discoveries and Innovations in Applied Sciences 1, no. 5 (October 6, 2021): 19–25.

38 Nimmi Rangaswamy, "Telecenters and Internet Cafés: The Case of ICTs in Small Businesses," *Asian Journal of Communication* 18, no. 4 (December 1, 2008): 365–78, https://doi.org/10.1080/01292980802344208.

39 Internet cafes have become particularly popular as multiplayer gaming cafes throughout Asia, and as sweepstake parlors in Southern regions of the US.

40 Bjørn Furuholt and Stein Kristiansen, "Internet Cafés in Asia and Africa – Venues for Education and Learning?," *The Journal of Community Informatics* 3, no. 2 (September 14, 2007), https://doi.org/10.15353/joci.v3i2.2379.

41 Vogels, "Digital Divide Persists Even as Americans with Lower Incomes Make Gains in Tech Adoption."

42 Benigna Boza-Kiss, Shonali Pachauri, and Caroline Zimm, "Deprivations and Inequities in Cities Viewed Through a Pandemic Lens," *Frontiers in Sustainable Cities* 3 (2021): 15, https://doi.org/10.3389/frsc.2021.645914.

Even after some safety measures were implemented, "rates of Black, Hispanic, and Native American students returning to college were lower than of White students."[43] In their report on how the "COVID-19 crisis pushes students into an uncertain job market," Wan-Lae Cheng, Jonathan Law, and Duwain Pinder observed that around half of the Black men enrolled" at Southwest Tennessee Community College, or 826 students, dropped out between the Spring 2020 and Fall 2020.[44]

Community Tech NY Portable Network Kit (PNK) build event with the community organization El Puente.[45]

---

43 Wan-Lae Cheng, Jonathan Law, and Duwain Pinder, "COVID-19 Pushes US Students to Drop out and Fall into Unemployment" (McKinsey & Company, 2021), https://www.mckinsey.com/featured-insights/sustainable-inclusive-growth/future-of-america/covid-19-crisis-pushes-us-students-into-an-uncertain-job-market.
44 Cheng, Law, and Pinder, as reported by Southwest Tennessee Community College president Tracy Hall.
45 Community Tech NY, Photograph, 2022.

What happened in the US mirrored other global school discontinuation trends across secondary schools and colleges. For example, as many as "seven million university students in Africa could not continue their education in 2020."[46] In Spain and Italy, which already had some of the highest dropout rates in Europe,[47] school closures saw social workers overwhelmed with dropout cases, and lack of Internet access factored in sharply.

For the organization Community Tech New York (CTNY), which works to create "community-owned Internet infrastructure" since 2011, it was clear that the pandemic had intensified inequities and demonstrated that "the Internet is a lifeline for many, particularly the most vulnerable."[48] CTNY saw students and teachers searching for public Wi-Fi spots in order to attend classes while relying entirely on their phones, with connections that were "inadequate or unavailable at home."[49] As medical resources opened up during the pandemic, CTNY also observed that some community members without devices or digital literacies, or both, were also unable to access vaccines, medical appointments, and other medical services.

MPI, who works "to improve immigration and integration policies"[50] has been involved in ongoing work to improve "digital access and adoption to three refugee resettlement programs". This was accomplished through partnering with state library systems in Arizona, Maryland, and North Texas to provide affordable broadband services, and to refurbish and distribute laptops to refugee households with organizations such as the Baltimore Digital Equity Collective.[51] Seeing similar issues as CTNY, they observed that the pandemic amplified health and mental health risks while testing schools and immigrant-

---

46   Isabel Neto and Michel Rogy, "Too Many Africans Cannot Access the Technology They Need. A World Bank Initiative Aims to Help Reverse That," *World Bank Blogs* (blog), September 22, 2021, https://blogs.worldbank.org/digital-development/too-many-africans-cannot-access-technology-they-need-world-bank-initiative-aims.
47   Emma Bubola, "Italy's Problem With School Dropouts Goes From Bad to Worse in Pandemic," *The New York Times*, April 26, 2021, https://www.nytimes.com/2021/04/26/world/europe/italy-schools-covid-dropouts.html; Mostafa Mashhad, "Combatting School Dropout in Europe," United Way Worldwide, August 4, 2021, https://www.unitedway.org/blog/combatting-school-dropout-in-europe.
48   Community Tech NY, interview by author, online, April 11, 2022.
49   Community Tech NY.
50   "About the Migration Policy Institute," May 24, 2013, https://www.migrationpolicy.org/about/about-migration-policy-institute.
51   Essie Workie, Migration Policy Institute, interview by author, online, April 12, 2022.

serving organizations to their absolute capacities. Challenged to quickly transition to a remote format, many educators found themselves in a position to take on responsibilities like distributing devices, designing tutorials to teach students to use digital tools, and connecting students to basic goods like food and toiletries.[52] For Irin Akter, a teacher at the UNICEF-supported Surovi Learning Centre in Bangladesh, one way to support her students during the pandemic and through a school reopening campaign also meant taking online teacher training courses on her mobile phone to better support her students.

Irin Akter, a teacher at the Surovi learning Centre in Bangladesh, enrolled in online courses to learn how to support her students, September 20, 2020.[53]

In terms of usability design, MPI also saw that many LMSs were not designed for immigrant-origin students who primarily access their learning content on their mobile devices. MPI also found that on the onset of the pandemic, many educators lacked specialized teacher training and "expertise

---

52   Workie.
53   Paul Tapash and UNICEF, Photograph, "School Reopening Campaign," 2020.

with digital learning for English learners (EL)."[54] The pandemic also uncovered a gap in the breadth of resources available to EL versus general education educators in need of digital learning resources. Their 2020 report "Educating English Learners during the COVID-19 Pandemic: Policy Ideas for States and School Districts"[55] indicated that English learners had the additional burdens of language barriers, fear of accessing medical assistance, and "without persistent school engagement, ELs' English language development may stall."[56] As noted by MPI, English learners were already "among the students at the greatest risk of dropping out" even before the pandemic, highlighting an important at-risk group in need of more prioritization for increased learning time and digital skills development.

The challenges described by MPI and CTNY, which only represent a small sample of the wide-ranging threats to equitable digital access, emphasize the unceasing need for more comprehensive interventions to help communities get the digital learning resources they need, pointing to the fact that digital transformation challenges are both design challenges and pedagogical issues. Nevertheless, there is a way forward, and in many ways, digital access is a design problem, and a digital justice issue to be continually addressed in years to come.

Design, Digital Equity, and a Way Forward

Closing the digital divide and improving digital access is a massive challenge. Digital access has become a matter of digital equity, where designing access initiatives are much needed to create the fundamental pathways to better education, employment, social, and cultural opportunities which are created by MPI and CTNY. According to the Digital Equity Laboratory (DEL), founded in 2017 by Civil Rights lawyer and activist, Maya Wiley, , digital equity should aim to achieve "inclusive and healthy social, economic, educational, and civic outcomes for people of all races, incomes, genders and gender identities, and

---

54 Essie Workie, Migration Policy Institute, interview by author, online, April 12, 2022.
55 Julie Sugarman and Melissa Lazarín, "Educating English Learners during the COVID-19 Pandemic: Policy Ideas for States and School Districts," Policy Brief (Migration Policy Institute, 2020), https://www.migrationpolicy.org/sites/default/files/publications/mpi-english-learners-covid-19-final.pdf.
56 Sugarman and Lazarín, 6.

backgrounds," while ensuring affordable access, and "should not reinforce or exacerbate harms and risks for vulnerable groups."[57] Sharing a similar view, CTNY has described digital equity through the lens of "digital justice," which means that CTNY "prioritizes the participation of people who have been traditionally excluded from and attacked by media and technology."[58]

The public's conception of digital equity and digital justice is relatively new. However, it relates to a long history of structural inequalities such as discriminatory practices like redlining, insufficient investments in public infrastructure development, and the growth of telecommunication company monopolies.[59] In his research on "enhancing digital equity," Massimo Ragnedda remarked that digital inequalities expand with the growth of digital services and products, and algorithm designs and predictive modeling can rationalize and normalize social injustices when designed unethically.[60] He calls it the "algorithmization" of society. Ragnedda stresses the importance of promoting digital equity, stating that there is a need to "rethink the design process" to protect sensitive data like personal information.[61]

In a climate complicated by a pandemic and ongoing resource and information wars,[62] it has been promising that design-led interventions have been rethought to prioritize digital access and combat digital inequality. Furthermore, as noted by CTNY, the pandemic has also helped communities to see that the "digital divide exists" and directly impacts so many people, and this paves "the way for digital justice."[63] Through the pandemic, organizations, designers, and educators have created collaborative approaches to solving digital access challenges. Interventions like maps of free Wi-Fi hotspots, free or subsidized home Internet connection programs, lending programs, and digital skills programs were crucial to people's wellbeing, providing

---

57 "Our Story," Digital Equity Laboratory, accessed June 26, 2022, https://www.digitalequitylab.org.
58 Community Tech NY, interview by author, online, April 11, 2022.
59 Community Tech NY.
60 Massimo Ragnedda, *Enhancing Digital Equity: Connecting the Digital Underclass* (Cham, Switzerland: Palgrave Macmillan, 2020), 2.
61 Massimo, 6.
62 Kate M. Murray, "Digital Equity In Access To Justice" (Vancouver, BC: Legal Services Society, BC, October 2021), https://legalaid.bc.ca/sites/default/files/inline-files/Murray_2021_LABC_Achieving_Digital_Equity_Final_Report_0.pdf.
63 Community Tech NY, interview by author, online, April 11, 2022.

sustenance during long periods of psychological and financial distress.[64] The City of Los Angeles partnered with organizations EveryoneOn and the California Emerging Technology fund to offer low-cost devices, low-cost Internet access, and financial literacy coursework.[65] The City of San Jose in California, partnered with "AT&T, Verizon, and Mobilitie to invest $1.5 million in providing 4,200 small-cell wireless network antennas on streetlight poles."[66] This partnership with the City of San Jose has made additional announcements to become one of the first cities in the US to pledge to close the digital divide and "connect 50,000 San José households with universal device access and universal connectivity at speeds of at least 25 Mbps download/3 Mbps upload over the next 10 years."[67]

Some nations have already taken significant steps to design and implement universal connectivity or a universal service obligation (USO), with Switzerland becoming one of the "first nations to include broadband Internet access as a component of their USO."[68] In Botswana, plans to deploy mass Wi-Fi, or a Wi-Fi "blanket" have been piloted by the Botswana Telecommunications Corporation (BTC) initially in cities like Francistown, Gaborone, and Kasane. Where reliable Internet access has not been possible, some communities have embraced broadcast media like "edutainment" television and radio, emphasizing that even while the world goes online and media continues to digitize, there is also value in designing alternative types of media. In their research about educational television use during the pandemic, Sharon Zacharia and Alex Twinomugisha found that while many countries, particularly developing ones, have been using educational television since the 1950s—countries recently found innovative ways to utilize television networks.[69] Ubongo, for example, was incorporated in thirty-three

---

64 National Digital Inclusion Alliance, "Local Government COVID-19 Digital Inclusion Response," accessed June 26, 2022, https://www.digitalinclusion.org/local-government-covid-19-digital-inclusion-response/.
65 National Digital Inclusion Alliance.
66 National Digital Inclusion Alliance. Also see "Programs," EveryoneOn, accessed June 26, 2022, https://www.everyoneon.org/programs.
67 San José Digital Inclusion Partnership, "About,"accessed June 26, 2022, https://www.sjdigitalinclusion.org/about.
68 Swisscom, "Fulfilling Universal Service Obligations," SES, July 16, 2020, https://www.ses.com/case-study/swisscom.
69 Sharon Zacharia and Alex Twinomugisha, "Educational Television during COVID-19: How to Start and What to Consider," World Bank Blogs, April 24, 2020, https://blogs.wo

African countries to deliver educational content. State- and private-broadcast networks were identified to broadcast a mix of live and pre-recorded content throughout Morocco, Mexico, South Africa, and Spain, with live content being particularly effective in "countries with limited or no education television experience."[70]

The COVID-19 pandemic was not the first twenty-first-century pandemic, but it far exceeded the 2009–10 Swine Flu (H1N1) and the 2002–2003 severe acute respiratory syndrome (SARS) outbreaks. While difficult to pinpoint the timing, there could be another pandemic and meanwhile climate-related disasters have surged—all of which can disrupt work and school for prolonged times. Thoughtfully designed digital products have proven to play a successful role in aiding communities. These products and interventions have empowered the rapid submission of information about possible earthquakes in "sparsely equipped regions" on Twitter.[71] It has enabled citizens to use Facebook's "Safety Check" feature[72] to let family and friends know their locations. Facebook's Safety Check expanded for non-natural disasters during the Paris terrorist attacks of 2015.[73] Najeeb Abdulhamid, et al. have also cited how social media has enabled the organization of community clean-ups after the 2011 London riots, enabled outreach to financial donors, allowed the formation of digital volunteer groups, and the use of crisis mapping to aggregate data on reported needs for water, food, medical care, and shelter in affected areas during natural and non-natural crises. While not exhaustive,

---

rldbank.org/education/educational-television-during-covid-19-how-start-and-what-consider.

70 Zacharia and Twinomugisha.
71 Oya Benlioglu Gulesan, Emrah Anil, and Pinar Sarisaray Boluk, "Social Media-Based Emergency Management to Detect Earthquakes and Organize Civilian Volunteers," *International Journal of Disaster Risk Reduction* 65 (November 1, 2021): 102543, https://doi.org/10.1016/j.ijdrr.2021.102543. Other emergency response products have included major social media platforms like Twitter, Facebook, and Telegram, and niche apps like Zello's push-to-talk walkie-talkie app and safety and location-sharing app Namola. Among platforms, Twitter has a longer history of use in disaster and crisis relief to transmit critical information, used by government agencies, media, citizens, and NGOs.
72 Facebook, "Crisis Response," accessed June 26, 2022, https://www.facebook.com/about/crisisresponse/v2.
73 Tajha Chappellet-Lanier, "A New Use for Facebook's Safety Check," *The Atlantic*, November 14, 2015, https://www.theatlantic.com/international/archive/2015/11/facebook-safety-check-paris/416028.

these are a few examples of design and collaboration made possible just through having a reliable connection.

The growth of digital inclusion resources is promising, but to truly see the advancement of digital equity, design must play an integral role. Designers must consider all the ways that digital products and services are differentially accessed and whether that has implications for design choices selected for under-resourced users. In the most challenging moments of the pandemic, successful designs have, arguably, reframed the public understanding of the digital divide. Communities must take the necessary steps to become more technologically literate, creative, and innovative, particularly when it comes to digital access. CTNY director Monique Tate described, "Digital transformation means supporting community members to identify their own potential and genius when it comes to technology. Sometimes, we see community members who may not recognize themselves as technologists, but have been inspired to tap into their natural abilities and to build their own confidence. This transformation happens when these communities go beyond textbook education and book knowledge, and are empowered to create their own technologies."

Learning from FemTech to Inform the Design of Healthcare Technologies

Catalina Alzate[1]

FemTech is an industry within the digital health market that drives investments on technologies related to women's needs, and period tracking apps are its landmark innovation. These apps allow users to record data about their menstrual cycles and get predictions about their cycle length and fertility status. Digital period tracking is convenient but unreliable. Research shows that these applications are based on averages that produce and reproduce the notion of a "default female body," leaving aside the lived and embodied experiences of users who fall outside of normative categories. Moreover, FemTech functions by extracting and selling reproductive health data, which presents a threat to the struggle for gender equality and bodily autonomy. This chapter positions FemTech as a case study to learn about the effect of design and business decisions in people and communities, especially as innovations in digital health have become vehicles to profit from patients and healthcare systems. The chapter proposes seven implications as opportunities for design teams to engage with FemTech in intentional change-oriented domains, where multiple lived experiences are fundamental for the design of technological applications, and where the quality of knowledge and experiences of people who menstruate are the measure of success. The chapter advocates for rerouting the design of digital health applications towards frameworks of health equity and social justice.
— Catalina Alzate, US/Colombia

---

1 The University of Illinois at Urbana Champaign, US/Colombia.

Digital health, sometimes referred to as "mobile health," "e-health," or "digital medicine," is a widely adopted trend in design for healthcare that uses technology and data-mediated interfaces to improve people's well-being in a variety of medical contexts. Most recently, the Covid-19 pandemic provoked an increased demand for the design and adoption of digital health products and services, which are now considered "a necessity, not a choice."[2] Particularly, the context of women's health has recently gained cultural and business traction under the label "FemTech" (a shorthand for female and technology), which encompasses a suite of technologies that deal with all phases of a woman's life, such as menstruation, pregnancy prevention, pregnancy and nursing, aging, and additional areas considered to be central to this population such as beauty, cosmetic surgery, and technologies for longevity.[3] While women's health is much broader than merely the reproductive organs, a large segment of the FemTech industry focuses on this aspect.[4] This chapter predominantly deals with period tracking apps, as the technology that has gained the most business traction, and indeed led to the coinage of the term FemTech in 2016.

The criticism about FemTech is abundant, and this criticism needs to be examined by designers to inform the development of gender-based healthcare technologies. Most criticism is found in the fields of medicine and law, and although design is at the center of this cultural and technological trend, with product designers, experience designers, graphic designers, and service designers shaping these innovations, there is no ample analysis of the role of design as a strategic force in shaping FemTech. This chapter provides an overview of this industry, exploring how its narratives of empowerment are rooted in stereotypes and the harmful definition of a "default female body." It further examines how FemTech is an ecosystem that profits from menstruation, and the implications of this ecosystem in the struggles for gender equality and bodily autonomy. The chapter proceeds to sketch seven

---

2   Bertalan Meskó, "COVID-19's Impact on Digital Health Adoption: The Growing Gap Between a Technological and a Cultural Transformation," *JMIR human factors*, 9(3), e38926, 2022, 2.

3   Marija Butkovic, "FEMTEC Health Is Finally Bringing Women Holistic, Personalized Healthcare They Deserve," *Forbes Magazine*, March 23, 2022, https://www.forbes.com/sites/marijabutkovic/2022/03/21/femtec-health-is-finally-bringing-women-holistic-personalized-healthcare-they-deserve/?sh=7ae56f461049

4   Bethany A. Corbin, "*Digital Micro-Aggressions and Discrimination: Femtech and the 'Othering' of Women*" Nova Law Review 44, no. 3 (Spring 2020), 343.

implications for the creation of gender-based healthcare technologies that are explicitly rooted in feminist perspectives and reproductive justice frameworks.

A Note on Language

In acknowledgment that not all people who menstruate identify as women, this chapter uses the phrase 'people who menstruate' to include anyone who experiences menstruation. The word "women" is used when making references to FemTech discourses that use the gendered category of women, or when paraphrasing.

Defining FemTech as a Duality

This chapter defines FemTech as a duality. On one hand, FemTech has been positioned as a triumph in the digital health industry, because of its capacity to provide tools for self-knowledge for women[5] and people who menstruate. Other acclaimed achievements of FemTech include becoming a system that is accessible, supportive and that offers a sense of community.[6] On the other hand, FemTech has also been described as a network of false and unverified information, data gathering and profiting[7].

Period tracking apps are increasingly gaining popularity as the primary method of contraception for many people.[8] While this exemplifies how digital applications can positively contribute to body literacy goals, as well as the adoption of non-hormonal contraception, period tracking apps do not provide information that is medically reliable and transparent, making the objectives of FemTech fall short in their actual execution and performance.

---

5   Madelin Burt-D'Agnillo,"Femtech: A Feminist Technoscience Analysis," *The iJournal: Student Journal of the Faculty of Information* 8, no. 1 (2022), 18.
6   Catriona McMillan, "Monitoring Female Fertility Through 'Femtech': The Need for a Whole-System Approach to Regulation," *Medical Law Review* 30, no. 3 (2022), 418.
7   See Madelin Burt-D'Agnillo, "Femtech: A Feminist Technoscience Analysis," *The iJournal: Student Journal of the Faculty of Information* 8, no. 1 (2022) and Catriona McMillan, "Monitoring Female Fertility Through 'Femtech': The Need for a Whole-System Approach to Regulation," *Medical Law Review* 30, no. 3 (2022), 410–433.
8   Naomi Jacobs and Jenneke Evers, "Ethical Perspectives On Femtech: Moving From Concerns To Capability-sensitive Designs," *Bioethics* (2023), 5.

Positioning FemTech as a duality is an effort to present this industry as a complex assemblage that, instead of being labeled as liberatory or dangerous, is better understood if deconstructed into multiple components that reveal the political agendas and ideologies that it pushes forward, which are the key questions that designers should be asking first, before creating the next digital healthcare application for people who menstruate.

A Critical Analysis of FemTech

FemTech's narratives of empowerment are rooted in a harmful definition of a "default female body." The promise of self-surveillance or self-tracking apps is to increase people's knowledge and control over their bodies.[9] The logic is that digitally gathering data produced by the body and presenting it back to the user in readable formats, can create a learning cycle that leads to better healthcare decisions. In the context of menstruation tracking, the promise of FemTech is for people to understand their bodies so they can be in control of their fertility journey, and therefore become empowered.

While FemTech tools are useful, these promises are hardly achieved by all users. One reason for this is that the technical specifications of the apps are based on averages. This is highly problematic since the bodies of people who menstruate vary greatly. For instance, 28 days is often deemed the average menstrual cycle length in FemTech apps, whereas it is medically recognized that cycles can range between 21 and 35 days.[10] This not only excludes users who experience menstruation differently but can also lead to poor advice and inaccurate results.[11] Period tracking apps have been studied and found to be inaccurate, leading users to experience unwanted pregnancies[12] and failing to predict periods at all. Indeed, the best app has scored only a 21% accuracy rate.[13]

---

9   Michele Estrin Gilman, "Periods for profit and the rise of menstrual surveillance," *Colum. J. Gender & L.* 41 (2021), 101.
10 Mitchell D. Creinin, Sharon Keverline, and Leslie A. Meyn, "How Regular Is Regular? An Analysis Of Menstrual Cycle Regularity," *Contraception* 70, no. 4 (2004), 289.
11 Catriona McMillan, "Monitoring Female Fertility Through 'Femtech': The Need for a Whole-System Approach to Regulation," *Medical Law Review* 30, no. 3 (2022), 420.
12 McMillan, 424.
13 Sarah Johnson, Lorrae Marriott, and Michael Zinaman, "Can apps and calendar methods predict ovulation with accuracy?" *Current Medical Research and Opinion* 34, no. 9 (2018), 1587. See also Zod LaRock, "Femtech Companies Are Likely Poised for Speedy

In addition, basing period tracking on averages without room for variation, creates a stereotype of a "normative body." It communicates to the user that a body that menstruates must follow rigid metrics, and that failing to follow those parameters means that there is something wrong or abnormal.[14] Moreover, this categorization is marked by privilege. By catering to healthy, affluent, white, cis women, FemTech further reinforces stigmas around menstruation, and excludes non-binary, trans users,[15] as well as people from socially and economically marginalized populations that are capable of pregnancy, and people with serious chronic medical conditions.[16] In other words, FemTech implies that empowerment is only achieved by those who hold social and economic privilege, apart from enforcing a harmful gender binary that essentializes women.[17]

The choice of visual design elements in these apps also contribute to essentializing the gendered category of women. As Bethany A. Corbin has noted, "period tracking apps routinely include superfluous or insulting design elements that downplay the importance of female health. Floating clouds, color palette that emphasize pink and red, irrelevant flowers and faux-empowering language,"[18] reinforcing feminine notions of gender performativity, and often using elements that assume that a sexual or relationship partner is male, catering only heterosexual relationships.[19]

Growth Despite Failing to Prove That Their Tools Live Up to the Hype", *Business Insider*, July 22, 2019, https://www.businessinsider.in/femtech-companies-are-likely-poised-for-speedy-growth-despite-failing-to-prove-that-their-tools-live-up-to-the-hype/articleshow/70335446.cms

14 Corbin, "Digital Micro-Aggressions and Discrimination: Femtech and the 'Othering' of Women," 356.
15 Amanda Menking, "The rise of Femtech," *Gender and the Economy*, November, 2020, accessed February 15, 2023, https://www.gendereconomy.org/the-rise-of-Femtech.
16 Tamar Krishnamurti, Mehret Birru Talabi, Lisa S. Callegari, Traci M. Kazmerski, and Sonya Borrero, "A framework for Femtech: guiding principles for developing digital reproductive health tools in the United States," *Journal of Medical Internet Research* 24, no. 4 (2022), 1.
17 Gilman, "Periods for profit and the rise of menstrual surveillance," 102.
18 Corbin, "Digital Micro-Aggressions and Discrimination: Femtech and the 'Othering' of Women," 349.
19 Daniel A. Epstein, Nicole B. Lee, Jennifer H. Kang, Elena Agapie, Jessica Schroeder, Laura R. Pina, James Fogarty, Julie A. Kientz, and Sean Munson, "Examining Menstrual Tracking To Inform The Design Of Personal Informatics Tools," *Proceedings of the 2017 CHI Conference on Human Factors in Computing Systems* (2017), 13.

Introducing FemTech in the Context of Digital Health

Although a historical overview of technologies for menstruation is out of the scope of this chapter, it is important to recognize that technologies for menstruation tracking have existed for as long as people have menstruated. The success of period tracking apps lies in the industry's ability to capitalize on the convenience of capturing data through personal computing devices, as a vehicle to feed data management practices that enable large profit margins. The social and cultural cost of this is the creation and perpetuation of harmful narratives about normalcy and womanhood.

A Profit Ecosystem Around Menstruation

Period tracking apps are a central component and an enabler of a broader business strategy of data extraction, in which FemTech companies are mining people's personal data for profit, typically without their knowledge of meaningful consent.[20] FemTech is a clear example of how the self-surveillance economy and the menstrual surveillance industry work,[21] where menstruation, people's intimacy and their perceptions and plans for procreation, are exploited for doing business as usual.

The problem with data extraction and third-party sharing is multifaceted. As exposed by Sarah Myers, the commoditization of data enables an asymmetric redistribution of power that is weighted toward the actors who have access and the capability to make sense of information extraction.[22] In other words, data extraction will always favor those who extract and manage data, at the expense of millions of users using the applications that make data collection and sharing possible. At the larger level, data capitalism serves as a vehicle for the accumulation of wealth and uneven distribution of and access to power in society.

Data extraction also has material effects on the lives of people. Having access to people's information about their menstruation cycles, in a socio-political context where bodily autonomy is often curtailed, data extraction

---

20 Gilman, "Periods for profit and the rise of menstrual surveillance," 100.
21 Gilman, 102.
22 Sarah Myers West, "Data capitalism: Redefining the logics of surveillance and privacy," *Business & Society* 58, no. 1 (2019), 35.

can be used against users. Erickson et. al, identify categories of possible misuse of FemTech data, such as in targeted advertisements, maternity-related discrimination in the workplace, health insurance pricing, in abusive relationships, by attackers, and to spread health misinformation.[23] Incidentally, these predictions have become true in the wake of the US Supreme Court's decision to overturn Roe v. Wade to end federal abortion protections in 2022, when media channels and experts were urging users to delete their period tracking apps, since the data gathered could be used as the basis for prosecution by citing the intent for abortion.[24] This kind of external control over peoples' reproduction is a tool of domination and oppression.[25]

On the other hand, the regulatory frameworks and funding pipelines of FemTech are problematic. There is a lack of a regulatory framework for the FemTech industry that is comprehensive, let alone multi-dimensional or feminist.[26] Moreover, despite portraying women as entrepreneurs, FemTech is funded predominantly by white males, which means that those who are the least familiarized with menstruation are making key decisions about the menstruation experiences of others and earning profit from it. In other words, people who menstruate are only seen as a lucrative market sector.[27]

FemTech on the Horizon of Gender Equality and Bodily Autonomy

At a larger cultural scale, the FemTech ecosystem contributes to feed technology development practices that are depoliticized and individualized.

---

23 Jacob Erickson, Jewel Y. Yuzon, and Tamara Bonaci. "What You Do Not Expect When You Are Expecting: Privacy Analysis of Femtech," *IEEE Transactions on Technology and Society* 3, no. 2 (2022), 123.

24 Betsy Reed, "Why US women are deleting their period tracking apps," *The Guardian*, June 28, 2022, last accessed on January 20, 2023, https://www.theguardian.com/world/2022/jun/28/why-us-woman-are-deleting-their-period-tracking-apps; Jennifer Savin, "Experts urging women to delete period tracking apps following Roe v Wade being overturned," *Cosmopolitan*, June 28, 2022, https://www.cosmopolitan.com/uk/reports/a40442824/period-apps-abortion-prosecutions.

25 Loretta J. Ross, "Reproductive justice as intersectional feminist activism," *Souls* 19, no. 3 (2017), 292.

26 Catriona McMillan, "Monitoring Female Fertility Through 'Femtech': The Need for a Whole-System Approach to Regulation," *Medical Law Review* 30, no. 3 (2022), 413.

27 Corbin, "Digital Micro-Aggressions and Discrimination: Femtech and the 'Othering' of Women," 352.

For example, common sentences in FemTech's marketing strategies include terminology like "revolutionizing healthcare," "empowering women," and "ending stigma around women's health." These statements are often followed by technology optimism, failing to make any association to social justice or health equity. This selective use of wording associated with feminism creates a narrative that resonates with people who agree with the thought of gender equality, although there is no evidence of a strong theory of change that FemTech operates with. It appears that the industry expects that having people tracking their periods with an app is an effective path towards gender equality and bodily autonomy, contributing to positively transforming the historical discrimination of the female body in science and medicine. However, it is hard to argue that the FemTech ecosystem as a profitable business of female reproductive health data is the path to get there. By designing technologies for the most privileged users, it is safe to infer the industry's lack of interrogation of structural inequalities and power asymmetries in areas related to female bodies' health, menstruation, and technology design.

Narratives supported by numbers, algorithmic predictions and data visualizations, coupled with discourses of empowerment, are means that give users the illusion of control over their bodies, with no association to a socio-political system where menstruation operates, in a similar way that period hygiene brands have historically ignored how individual choices about using a menstrual pad, a tampon, a menstrual cup or any other tool, carry political connotations and repercussions in the collective struggle for gender equality and bodily autonomy. Depoliticization leads to individualizing struggles, as menstruation in FemTech is treated as separate from the socio-economic system, and therefore something that can be controlled by individuals, not as an opportunity to build solidarity and collective empowerment.

Design, Gender, and Healthcare: How to Do Things Differently

The FemTech industry lends itself as a complex case study that demonstrates the wider impact of design decisions in all phases of a creative process: from establishing potential users, to defining app features, and shaping business opportunities. Before moving into a list of implications for design, it is important to clarify what is meant by a gender-based healthcare technology.

The term gender-based does not mean designing for those who identify as women, but rather to bring the complexity of gender, as a category that structures social relations, at the center of the creative process.

Departing from the category of gender is not a neutral task. It involves acknowledging and studying the ways that the patriarchy structures systems of power and privilege, and perpetuates oppression. Along this line, the gender-lens reveals how women and gender-non-conforming folks have been historically excluded, oppressed, and pushed to the margins, and how this oppression is the source of profit for those in power. As it will be described in implication number 3, the gender category is never an isolated identity marker, as gender is always intersecting with other axes of privilege such as race, class, immigration, and ability.

Regarding the design of healthcare, it is useful to draw a broad distinction between a medical and a social model of healthcare. While the medical model uses symptoms and physical signs of the body to categorize someone as ill or having a disorder, the social model of health is focused on the social and environmental determinants of health. The latter is based on the understanding that for a person or a community to be healthy, we need to meet peoples' basic needs first.[28]

Designing self-tracking technologies often renders the human body as a readable biological machine that produces data, which can be remotely collected and analyzed. In doing so, digital applications objectify the body and present it as independent from context and environment. The incorporation of a social model of healthcare can inform design by studying the physical and psychological needs of individuals, and contextualizing those needs in the broader social, political, and economic settings where people live and work.

This chapter has presented an analysis of FemTech as a case study for studying the ways that design and business decisions play out in a larger sociocultural context. The following are seven implications derived from this analysis, crafted from a design perspective, and framed as opportunity spaces for creative teams to advance an agenda for FemTech development that is explicitly rooted in feminist perspectives.

---

28 Business Bliss Consultants FZE, "Comparison of Social and Medical Models of Health," accessed March 1, 2023, https://nursinganswers.net/essays/definition-and-comparison-of-social-and-medical-model-of-health.php.

1. FemTech design is about healthcare systems, not isolated digital apps

One significant source of problems in the design ecosystem of FemTech is the tendency to reduce, simplify, and categorize complex biological, social, and cultural factors in order to create efficient digital systems.

Period tracking apps use machine learning algorithms to present predictions to users about their menstrual cycle length and fertility status. For algorithms to function, designers and programmers need to simplify the lived experiences of menstruation, context of use, and the wide spectrum of abilities of users and more. This process is called "dimensionality reduction," where few extracted features from a dataset used for training an algorithm are assumed to capture the essence of a larger multi-dimensional reality. In reducing the complexity of the data, both storage requirements and the efficiency of algorithms for inference and decision making are optimized.

Not only are algorithms a reduced version of complex social and cultural situations, but they are also trained using previously established datasets in the healthcare system, which are already biased. When exploring this complexity, and the apparent impossibility to design algorithms that are inclusive and honor the multiple realities of people who menstruate, design teams tend to avoid the discussion altogether and move ahead with assumptions about how the world functions.

However, more than the complexity of designing algorithms, the issue is about how the vision for design has been outlined. Approaching FemTech as the design of digital applications alone misses the point about context, how the apps are used, why, and who they benefit in practice. The alternative is to think of healthcare systems where period tracking apps (if needed) become an enabler but not the center of such systems, and where the healthcare outcome is clearly defined.

Another angle for designers to engage with complexity and expand the design capability is to reframe design challenges in the first place. For instance, it has been noted how FemTech adheres to American data privacy laws, which largely hinge on the concept of "notice and consent." This puts the onus on people to protect their own privacy, however "notice and consent is a myth because consumers do not read, cannot comprehend and have no opportunities to negotiate the terms of privacy policies."[29] If we envision users

---

29   Gilman, "Periods for profit and the rise of menstrual surveillance," 100.

who can make better healthcare decisions by becoming more data literate, perhaps the design challenge, beyond tracking menstruation, is to make data privacy laws truly accessible, instead of treating the latter as an add-on to the main design.

2. Design teams not only need to be diverse, but ideologically aligned

Design teams embarking on the mission of designing gender-based healthcare technologies need to be diverse in terms of disciplinary knowledge and practices. As Tamar Krishnamurti et al. point out, cross-disciplinary collaboration is required to ensure that any reproductive health tool is comprehensive and accurate.[30] Designers can benefit from working with creative technologists who have the capacity to provide insights into technological possibilities that are feasible and outside of the confines of app development. Other fruitful collaborations can be established with medical professionals to ensure that the design of products and services in FemTech are medically sound.

Diversity is also crucial in terms of gender identities, race, and other forms of privilege. This can partly ensure that different experiences are brought into conversation in design. However, diversity alone does not ensure that technologies are automatically addressing the needs of diverse populations. If a design team is diverse, but there is no disclosure of their political alignment and motivations, technological applications will inevitably fall back into established market trends and data extraction practices described above. Technologies designed for people who menstruate have the potential to become tools for collective empowerment, solidarity, and knowledge of the self, only if these intentions are made explicit in design teams, and if there is a shared understanding of the political and practical implications of such a positioning.

3. The users of FemTech applications need to be defined intentionally and intersectionally

By catering to people who identify as women, who are also young, fit, white, affluent, and able-bodied, FemTech demonstrates how design is complicit with

---

30 Krishnamurti et al., "A framework for Femtech: guiding principles for developing digital reproductive health tools in the United States," 2.

upholding systems of oppression, since it leaves those historically oppressed at the periphery of technological innovation, both as consumers and producers. The depoliticization of FemTech is both a symptom and a result of a lack of an intersectional approach to define users in the design process.

As outlined by Kimberlé Crenshaw and Patricia Hill Collins, an intersectional approach reconceptualizes multiple oppressions, such as those based on race, class and gender, as interlocking systems. This means that these systems do not operate "on their own" but are experienced together. In other words, the experiences of each person are different because people have different combinations (or intersections) of privilege. For example, a woman who is a citizen of a country by birth, and an immigrant woman, will both experience discrimination based on gender, but they will experience different forms of privilege and discrimination because of their immigration status.[31]

Incorporating an intersectional approach in the design of FemTech applications means that the definition of users, as well as research practices are aware of and intentionally engaged with the ways that different potential users of period tracking apps can actually access their benefits, given the social positions they occupy. The result is not an adaptation of current FemTech apps to different languages or devices, but rather the recognition and exposure of multiple needs and desires that are relevant to specific social contexts, and therefore different solutions or digital interactions could be designed to meet those needs and desires.

4. Design frameworks are stronger if aligned to justice frameworks

The incorporation of an intersectional approach in design transcends the description of users and their privilege. As designer and researcher Jackie Shaw has pointed out, "in applying an intersectional lens, oppression and privilege can be seen as parts of problems that can be addressed, instead of personal attributes of have and have-not."[32] In other words, orienting the design of gender-based technologies towards justice means using the potential

---

31   For a comprehensive review of the implications of intersectionality in design see Sasha Costanza-Chock, "Design justice: Towards an intersectional feminist framework for design theory and practice," *Proceedings of the Design Research Society* (2018).

32   Jacquie Shaw, "Designing with intentional intersectionality," accessed on January 2023, https://vimeo.com/353133100

of FemTech for balancing power asymmetries and correcting structural inequalities.[33]

This engagement with politics of change necessitates a synergy between design frameworks and justice frameworks. Design teams may engage with theory developed by activists and academics to describe pathways to change in specific social dimensions. For example, "Reproductive Justice Frameworks," as shaped by the Combahee River Collective in 1994, bring together the concepts of reproductive rights and social justice, to advocate for and shape direct action towards sexual freedom and bodily autonomy. A key component of the "Reproductive Justice Frameworks" is to go beyond pro-choice politics. For example, a rights-based framework would focus on ensuring the right to access sexual and reproductive healthcare. While this is necessary, such framing assumes that all women and people who menstruate have an equal ability to make informed choices, ignoring structural factors such as economic status, race, immigration state, incarceration state and many others, that can prevent people from actually accessing quality healthcare.[34]

By coupling design frameworks and "Reproductive Justice Frameworks," products and services can be designed with the intention of strengthening the ways that robust and reliable healthcare can be accessible by all people. This objective includes the elimination of discriminatory barriers in healthcare. Under this framing, designers must evaluate the potential discriminatory effects of different design decisions in the creative process, as well as unintended consequences of digital health innovations.

5. Those who are most affected by the technology must play an active role in shaping it

Krishnamurti et al. described that, "It is an ethical imperative that individuals who are the desired users of these tools have the power to be active participants in their health care decisions and that their right to make their own reproductive decisions is honored, regardless of the context".[35]

---

33   Madelin Burt-D'Agnillo, "Femtech: A Feminist Technoscience Analysis." *The iJournal: Student Journal of the Faculty of Information* 8, no. 1 (2022), 20.
34   For a detailed account of the Reproductive Justice Framework see Loretta J. Ross, "Reproductive justice as intersectional feminist activism," *Souls* 19, no. 3 (2017): 286–314.
35   Krishnamurti et al., "A framework for Femtech: guiding principles for developing digital reproductive health tools in the United States," 2.

The incorporation of participatory or collaborative approaches to designing healthcare technologies needs to be at the center of the creative process for FemTech.

While centering the voices of people who menstruate is ethically sound, participatory approaches need to be tactfully approached to avoid the extraction of information from people, without giving back to them appropriate decision-making power and credit for their contributions. Participatory efforts need to be understood beyond the implementation of a method, but rather embraced as complete shifts in culture, where sharing power and building capabilities are guiding principles for design.[36]

6. Visual narratives can be radically challenged

As pointed out, the current graphic design of period tracking apps contributes to reinforcing normative femininity and essentializing notions of womanhood. The narrative of empowerment here is justified by visibility of "women's issues," which are in turn appropriated by media and advertisement.[37] It is tempting to challenge visual narratives in FemTech by moving away from superfluous design elements, with aesthetics that are bold and irreverent. This is already trendy in contemporary graphic design and branding for period care products.[38] However, the aesthetic shifts are made in opposition to current visual canons, not in response to a radical analysis.

The word "radical" implies an understanding of root causes. Rather than prescribing a new aesthetic paradigm, the role of design teams is to devise the vehicles for shaping graphic design that responds to contextual needs and people's ability to perceive information and relate to visual material. A radical shift in aesthetics is also being aware of history, and incorporating messaging that promotes collective empowerment and solidarity.

---

36   Kelly Ann McKercher, "Beyond sticky notes," *Doing co-design for Real: Mindsets, Methods, and Movements*, 1st Edn. Sydney, NSW: Beyond Sticky Notes (2020), 5.
37   McMillan, "Monitoring Female Fertility Through 'Femtech': The Need for a Whole-System Approach to Regulation," 431.
38   Rachel del Valle, "Modern Period Brands Used to Blend In. Now, Like Everything Else, They're All About Standing Out," *Eye on Design*, May 19, 2022, https://eyeondesign.aiga.org/modern-period-brands-used-to-blend-in-now-like-everything-else-theyre-all-about-standing-out.

7. Design needs a different agreement with business

The question about business is the question about metrics of success. Ellen Lupton provided a realistic perspective about design implementation noting that, "the forces that drive product development range from the short-term economic interests of manufacturers to the expressive or theoretical intent of designers to a community's entrenched habits and customs. Sometimes things look the way they do because that's the cheapest and fastest way to make them, sometimes because that's how the designer or client chose to express a personal vision or creative impulse, sometimes because that's how things have always been."[39] Moreover, current business practices in digital health contexts measure success by increased adoption of digital products and revenue streams.[40]

This aspiration for growth conflicts with the complexity of design processes that follow some of the implications outlined. Funders tend to believe that participatory processes are hard to measure, take more time, are difficult to tie to a budget, among other barriers.[41] On the other hand, by ascribing to fast-paced business practices, design teams risk prioritizing profit over patient-centeredness, especially in instances where the needs of patients and the desires of investors are not aligned, or if certain patients are not considered to constitute a profitable consumer base.[42] A commitment to end oppression through design necessitates a consideration of design and business outside of growth models, placing the quality of knowledge and experiences of users as the metric for success. Instead of focusing on goals based on technology deployment and market adoption, design interventions can be framed as open-ended, continuously improved processes, based on the understanding of the consequences of design decisions in contexts that are treated as emergent and fluid, instead of fixed and predictable. Consequently, designing

---

39   Ellen Lupton, "Designing for people," in Carpentier, Thomas, and Tiffany Lambert. *Beautiful Users: Designing for People*, Chronicle Books (2014), 21.
40   Krishnamurti et al., "A framework for Femtech: guiding principles for developing digital reproductive health tools in the United States," 2.
41   See the report, "National Academies of Sciences, Engineering, and Medicine 2022. Improving Representation in Clinical Trials and Research: Building Research Equity for Women and Underrepresented Groups, (Washington, DC: The National Academies Press), https://doi.org/10.17226/26479.
42   Krishnamurti et al., "A framework for Femtech: guiding principles for developing digital reproductive health tools in the United States," 8.

FemTech applications requires the adoption of reflection processes where teams revisit their intentions and check on their alignment to values and justice frameworks, especially when the commercialization of technology will require strategic decisions on these areas.

Lessons for Designing Digital Health Applications

Period tracking apps are the landmark innovation in FemTech. Despite their business success, these apps function under incorrect assumptions of the needs and desires of people who menstruate. Moreover, the rhetoric and visual narratives in FemTech are instruments to exercise power and control over people, complicating the ways that communities of women and people who menstruate can advance work towards bodily autonomy and gender equality.

FemTech is more than a technological trend, and design teams must understand this industry in its social and political complexity in order to develop "situated" design practices that are inclusive of the lived and embodied experiences of users, and intentionally avoid the replication of health inequity through technology. The seven implications outlined in this chapter serve as opportunities for designers and design teams to direct technology development towards a health-equity conscious space.

The FemTech industry is one of many niches in the digital health market that harvest patient data for economic interests. Concern about the privacy of medical records is abundant in the field of medical computing, having patients becoming increasingly vulnerable to targeted advertisement and multiple forms of discrimination. The need to rethink healthcare applications and models that are sustainable in non-exploitative ways is urgent. It is also urgent to reconsider design as a strategic force in shaping innovations that are aligned to justice frameworks in order to create a social model of healthcare that can benefit all people.

NFTs between Art and Design
A Story of Digital Transformation

Lucilla Grossi[1] and Luca Guerrini[2]

Non-fungible tokens (NFTs) are blockchain-based certificates that attest to the authenticity of the wares during the sales of a virtual item, infinitely reproducible and freely downloadable from websites. Consistently associated with the commerce of digital images, their diffusion has actively touched the art field and its relative market, which underwent a transformation that has provoked a shake in its previous hierarchical balance. The evolution of the language of digital images started from the widespread practice of creators' communities—composed of professionals and amateurs—that frequented the Web before the creation of non-fungible tokens. NFTs made possible a new connection between the digital design community and crypto-investors, setting the base for a new market. The figures in this world have a hybrid multidisciplinary provenance. The consequence is a new questioning of the boundaries of art and its relationship with other creative practices, especially with design. This encounter induced a system that approaches the art market with the rules of allographic works: reproducible items depending on a certificate to assert their authenticity, such as design. NFT works might seem superficial if analyzed in the milieu of contemporary art. Still, they frame their significance in the culture of a close-knit community of people.

At the same time, the NFT world seems to open a field of experimentation in which designers can proficiently operate, thus contaminating the traditional art world. The result is an experience of art that has the connotations of

---

1   Department of Architecture and Industrial Design, University of Campania "Luigi Vanvitelli".
2   Department of Design, Politecnico di Milano, Italy.

digital technology and design. It is hard to predict whether NFT art will be successful since it is a nascent phenomenon. The first move, however, has already been made.
— *Lucilla Grossi and Luca Guerrini, Italy*

Bits and Prices

Since the invention of Non-fungible-tokens (NFTs) in 2014, bearing the name of the artist Kevin McCoy and the digital entrepreneur Anil Dash,[3] the market has become easily accessible for digital creators coming from any background. The core of the new blockchain-based technology is the possibility of making an item that is infinitely reproducible and freely downloadable from the web, unique, and salable.

NFTs are part of a system that allows the marketing of intangible goods by certifying the authenticity of the wares while the blockchain records the currency transactions, ensuring their execution. The NFT and its related virtual items are visible to everyone, but only the buyer can declare the owner's status.[4] For the fruition of the work, the title of "owner" does not provide specific advantages.[5] The owner, however, has full economic rights and can therefore resell it on platforms recognizing those rights. The system's focus is economical, and the transaction is similar to the trade of stocks.

The NFT market has developed parallel to art auctions, creating a shortcut to the sales, initially undertaken by creatives who have already dealt with digital design for different reasons. Before NFTs were born, the Web was already brimming with static images, GIFs, and videos created by designers, artists, professionals, and amateurs. There were already communities speaking a common visual language and connecting through social networks, such as Telegram.[6] The "outcomes" were freely downloadable and exchangeable and

---

3   Anil Dash, "NFTs Weren't Supposed to End Like This," *The Atlantic*, April 2, 2021, https://www.theatlantic.com/ideas/archive/2021/04/nfts-werent-supposed-end-like/618488.
4   Kevin Buist, "Chain Reaction", *Artforum*, March 10, 2021, https://www.artforum.com/slant/kevin-buist-on-the-nft-boom-85221.
5   Domenico Quaranta, "Code as Law. Contemporary Art and NFTs," Kunstlerinnenpreis, NordRhein-Westfalien, 2022, https://digitalart.kuenstlerinnenpreis.nrw/blog/code-as-law-contemporary-art-and-nfts.
6   Massimo Franceschet et al., "Crypto Art: A Decentralized View," Arxiv Database by Cornell University, June 11, 2019, 20, https://arxiv.org/abs/1906.03263#.

hardly ever offered any earning opportunity, at least not directly through the Web.

The evolution of this displaced community has existed in parallel to the spread of crypto-currencies since the birth of Bitcoin[7] in 2009. In this respect, the NFTs formalized the union between two communities that already existed autonomously in the network. They created an advantage for both crypto-investors, who had a new market to tap into, and digital content creators, who could finally get paid for their work.

Towards the Art Market

In 2018, some pioneering galleries, such as SuperRare, started tokenizing digital content and hosting creators on their platform. As usual in any gallery, they began exhibiting, advertising, and selling these contents as artworks.[8] In this context, the NFT mechanism operated through the oldest capitalist lever, the private ownership of the asset. Specifically, as David Joselit states, "the NFT deploys the category of art to extract private property from freely available information".[9] In this respect, it seemed to subvert the cornerstones of the web: to share and freely avail of its content. One might talk about a betrayal.

This "betrayal," however, is described as a form of "liberation" from the "traditional" art system. Hailed as an instrument of redemption, it allowed designers and artists to promote themselves by skipping bottlenecks and limitations of the past. As Jason Bailey stated, "Unlike the traditional art world, [crypto] artists did not seek permission from gallerists, agents, auction houses, or other gatekeepers to share and sell their work. Instead, leveraging the blockchain, they [...] decided on their own to show their work and make it available".[10]

The process is seen almost exclusively from the market's perspective as a direct encounter between supply and demand. Creatives of any kind can practice this new way of trading art, and potentially reach high quotations

---

7   Satoshi Nakamoto, "Bitcoin: A Peer-to-Peer Electronic Cash System," https://www.bitcoin.org, January 3, 2009. https://bitcoin.org/bitcoin.pdf.
8   Franceschet et al., "Crypto Art: A Decentralized View."
9   David Joselit, "NFTs, or The Readymade Reversed," October 175, (Winter 2021), 3–4, https://doi.org/10.1162/octo_a_00419.
10 Jason Bailey is an art and tech blogger (Artnome.com), and co-founder and CEO of NFTClub. Quoted in: Franceschet et al., "Crypto Art: A Decentralized View," 8.

quickly, be they amateurs or professionals. Similarly, on the buyers' side, there are no barriers to art connoisseurs; therefore, investors involved come from very mixed cultural backgrounds. Since NFTs are based on the Ethereum network, they can only be bought by using this new digital money. Consequently, buyers are often investors of these currencies, who see crypto-art works as a new way to diversify their crypto-wallets.

Auction houses have always acted as a filter for the art system, selecting the most valuable works and certifying their authenticity. In the NFTs market, there is no filter relating to the artistic quality of the works. Therefore, the new selling system works as a double-edged sword. On the one hand, it allows more creatives to become well-known and acknowledged as professionals. On the other, it sees a highly variable quality of artworks on sale by setting open access to everybody.

In 2021, the art world assisted in the first encounter of the two leading auction houses with the NFT sale system, and the result was the legitimation of NFTs in the art world.[11] Christie's was the first, in March 2021, to sell the piece *Everydays:the First 5000 Days* by Beeple for 69 million dollars.[12] In April 2021, Sotheby's sold *The Switch* by Pak, reaching $1,444,444.00, and *The Pixel* for $1,355,555.00.[13] Considering the novelty of the system, the figures involved were undoubtedly considerable; the sale of Beeple with Christie's made him one of the three most valuable living artists.[14]

Christie's auction was one of the most influential triggers of the global propagation of NFT art. Its role in spreading the knowledge of NFTs was so significant that it raised doubts that specific interests drove it. Crypto-investors – as Domenico Quaranta claimed – have demonstrated the safety and potential of acquiring crypto art and have attracted new people to the market, while auction houses have opened their portal to all crypto-investors that had never been able to invest in assets before.[15]

---

11 Nifty Gateway, "Collect NFT Art History," accessed April 8, 2023., https://niftygateway.com/collections/portraitsofamindoe.
12 Scott Reyburn, "The $69 Million Beeple NFT Was Bought With Cryptocurrency," *The New York Times*, March 12, 2021. https://www.nytimes.com/2021/03/12/arts/beeple-nft-buyer-ether.html?searchResultPosition=2.
13 "The Fungible Collection," Sotheby's, April 14, 2021, https://www.sothebys.com/en/digital-catalogues/the-fungible-collection-by- pak.
14 Reyburn, "The $69 Million Beeple NFT Was Bought With Cryptocurrency."
15 Quaranta, "Code as Law. Contemporary Art and NFTs."

Designers as Artists?

The protagonist in this outbreak of the market, Mike Winkelmann, also known as Beeple, is a peculiar emblem of the American dream. He defines himself as a graphic designer on his website.[16] Before selling his works as NFTs, Beeple was already a name in digital design, working for companies such as Louis Vuitton, SpaceX, Apple, Nike, Samsung, Coca-Cola, and Sony. Moreover, in 2016, he authored the animations used during the convention of the Democratic Party that nominated Hilary Clinton as the presidential candidate.[17]

Everydays:the First 5000 Days is a unique collage of different images produced in a single day for 5000 days. The graphics appertain to various styles that the author experimented with through the years, according to the amount of time he had. Most of them were made using 3D graphics programs, such as Cinema 4D, and only a few were hand-drawn. The scenes frequently depicted abstract utopian/dystopian scenarios and acknowledged characters from politics and cartoons.[18]

Metakovan, the winner of Christie's auction, declared that the value of *Everydays:the First 5000 Days* was the time devoted to its creation: 13 years. In his words, "Techniques are replicable, and skill is surpassable, but the only thing you can't hack digitally is time. This is the crown jewel, the most valuable piece of art for this generation."[19]

The art connoisseur inevitably recalls how conceptual artists delved into the topic of time in the 1960s. In 1966, On Kawara started painting his *Today* series, also called Date Paintings. They consist of a square canvas painted in red, blue, or dark gray with the date it was made written in white. The date was written

---

16   Mike Winkelmann, "Beeple's Personal Website," personal website, accessed April 8, 2023, https://www.beeple-crap.com.
17   Anny Shaw, "Who Is Beeple? The Art World Disruptor at the Heart of the NFT Boom." *The Art Newspaper*, March 5, 2021. https://www.theartnewspaper.com/2021/03/05/who-is-beeple-the-art-world-disruptor-at-the-heart-of-the-nft-boom
18   Kyle Chayka, "How Beeple Crashed the Art World," *The New Yorker*, March 22, 2021, https://www.newyorker.com/tech/annals-of-technology/how-beeple-crashed-the-art-world.
19   Anna Brady, "Revealed: Metakovan, Pseudonymous Founder of 'Crypto-Exclusive Fund' Metapurse, Is the Buyer of Beeple's $69.3m NFT," *The Art Newspaper*, March 12, 2021, https://www.theartnewspaper.com/2021/03/12/revealed-metakovan-pseudonymous-founder-of-crypto-exclusive-fund-metapurse-is-the-buyer-of-beeples-dollar693m-nft.

according to the language and conventions of the place where Kawara made it. Each painting is provided with a cardboard storage box, sometimes lined with the front page of a local newspaper. He made a Date Painting almost every day for years. The canvas was destroyed if he could not finish the work by midnight.

In 1965, Roman Opalka began painting an infinite series of numbers on canvases. Starting from the left top corner to the right bottom one, he drew lines of numbers, counting where he left off the previous day. The title was always *1965/1-∞*. Over the years, the ritual changed in some ways. The color of the background, initially black, from 1968 on, became gray. From 1972, it slowly started turning white by adding 1% more white in each detail, as Opalka planned to reach the moment to paint in white-on-white. In 1968, he introduced a tape recording of himself reading the numbers as he painted them and began taking a self-portrait photo each day after finishing the canvas.[20]

The names of these artists resound loudly while looking at Beeple's *Everydays: the First 5000 Days*. Neither the author nor the collector seems to have deep knowledge of the history of art, and – all exceptions considered – this is emblematic of the NFT world. Both artists and buyers frequently encounter the art field for the first time and approach it from a different perspective; most likely through the eyes of the business.

During a conversation with the curator Carolyn Christov-Bakargiev, Beeple admitted his negligence towards the "traditional art world," a formula that he used to describe "everything but digital art," defining his method as detached from conceptual reasonings about art.[21] In an interview with the *The New Yorker* in 2021, he declared that he did not have an idea of what "abstract expressionism" was. This was just one of the examples through which Winkelmann has openly admitted his ignorance in the field. Beeple's move from design to art is not based on a rich curriculum or a critique evaluation. Instead, it stands on the sales: it demonstrates why the NFT market can become a shortcut to the art world.

---

20 "Opalka 1965/1 – ∞; Détail 993460–1017875," accessed April 8, 2023, https://www.metmuseum.org/art/collection/search/666092.

21 Mike Winkelmann and Carolyn Christov-Bakargiev, "Mike Winkelmann alias Beeple in conversation with Carolyn Christov-Bakargiev – Season I, Episode I. Interview by Carolyn Christov-Bakargiev," May 28, 2021, https://www.youtube.com/watch?v=pOh3Cra2LYw&ab_channel=CastellodiRivoliMuseod%27ArteContemporanea.

The paths of other important figures to the NFT art market similarly started from fields other than art. The following are some examples from the collectible world. The Larva Labs, the authors of the *CryptoPunks* collectible series in 2017, are a duo of creative American engineers.[22] Their project pioneered NFT creations and provided the basis for the ERC-721 token standard, now primarily adopted by most crypto artists.[23] The creator of *CryptoKitties*, Dapper Lab, is a company that specializes in video games; in their LinkedIn profile, they describe themselves as "the serious business of fun and games on the blockchain."[24] The collectible series *Bored Ape Yacht Club* is also a child of business. The series is signed by Yuga Labs, and the two founders go under the pseudonyms of Gargamel and Gordon Goner. Gargamel, later revealed by *BuzzFeed News* to be Greg Solano,[25] was a writer and editor before entering the NFT commercial scene. Gordon Goner (Wylie Aronow) was planning to study in a Master of Fine Arts program, but before starting it, he entered into cryptocurrency trading and founded his business with Gargamel. It was declared in an interview published in *The New Yorker* that they are both "literary nerds."[26]

For NFT works not included in a collectible series, there are many creators whose backgrounds are outside of the art field. Among well-known NFT creators is Mad Dog Jones, who started his career on Instagram. Mad Dog Jones (Michah Dowbak) has posted digital collages made by modifying pictures and hand drawings of cityscapes. Dowbak's career comes out of a diverse background; he graduated in human kinetics and started working in a care center. Instagram allowed him to develop his creative side. He declared in an

---

22 Domenico Quaranta, *Surfing with Satoshi. Art, Blockchain and NFTs* (Ljubljana: Aksioma, 2021), 207.
23 Larva Labs, "CryptoPunks," accessed April 8, 2023, https://www.larvalabs.com/cryptopunks.
24 Dapper Labs, "Dapper Labs Profile," LinkedIn, accessed April 8 2023, https://www.linkedin.com/company/dapper-labs/?originalSubdomain=ca.
25 Katie Notopoulos, "We Found The Real Names of Bored Ape Yacht Club's Pseudonymous Founders," *BuzzFeed News*, February 5, 2022, https://www.buzzfeednews.com/article/katienotopoulos/bored-ape-nft-founder-identity. See also Emma Roth, "Florida men revealed to be behind Bored Apes," *The Verge*, February 6, 2022, https://www.theverge.com/2022/2/5/22919612/bored-apes-yacht-club-florida-men-identities-revealed.
26 Kyle Chayka, "Why Bored Ape Avatars Are Taking Over Twitter," *The New Yorker*, July 30, 2021, https://www.newyorker.com/culture/infinite-scroll/why-bored-ape-avatars-are-taking-over-twitter.

interview, "[...] if I want to do this professionally, what do I need to do? Well, I need to get a bunch of followers on Instagram. I need to get people excited about my art."[27]

This emerging generation of NFT creators are often natives of social networks, and frequently use Instagram as a springboard for the market. FEWOCiOUS is another emblem of the phenomenon. FEWOCiOUS (Victor Langlois) is a transgender person and started making works on the topic of transitioning in 2020 when he was 17. By 2021, Christie's noticed him and organized his first NFTs auction. In a short time, Langlois reached a very high quotation on the market, at 2 million dollars.[28]

Outside of Gen-Z creators, there are the works by 87-year-old comics drawer José Delbo at the top list of sales, who collaborated with the painter Trevor Jones to produce an oil painting version of one of Delbo's inked drawings of Batman. Their backgrounds are in figurative work, but expressed differently. Delbo lived an entire career in comics. Jones started his formal career in art at age of 30 when he enrolled at the Edinburgh College of Art. He worked in other fields to support his passion for painting until he entered the NFT world.[29] Delbo and Jones' *Genesis* was valued at $19,714,400.00 in May 2022 on MakersPlace.

These brief profiles illustrate a cohesive community that has grown up on the Web and has fundamentally forged its aims, methodologies, and operating rules. In the art world, these authors in many ways look like foreigners. Digital design, with its multifaceted complexities, is the field that has shaped them. In this respect, the NFT world seems to open a large field of experimentation in which designers can proficiently operate, arguably contaminating the traditional art world.

---

27 Nick Narigon, "Mad Dog Jones: At the Forefront of the Art World's Digital Revolution," *Tokyo Weekender*, September 26, 2019, https://www.tokyoweekender.com/2019/09/mad-dog-jones.

28 Steven Kurutz, "Teens Cash In on the NFT Art Boom," *The New York Times*, August 14, 2021, https://www.nytimes.com/2021/08/14/style/teens-nft-art.html.

29 Silvia Colella, "Disrupting the Art Market? Blockchain, NFTs and the Promise of Inclusion," IL CAPITALE CULTURALE, *Studies on the Value of Cultural Heritage* n. 26 (2022): 233–55, https://doi.org/10.13138/2039-2362/2946.

NFT Artists as Barbarians

We may see NFTs as part of a process Alessandro Baricco calls "barbarism."[30] Baricco, an acknowledged Italian writer deeply involved in cultural and political debate, analyzed how new products and behaviors – frequently coming from the US – have subverted European culture, thus opening it to a new value system. According to his interpretation, these disruptive phenomena are powerful enough to break the established rules of the past. Baricco identified three main characteristics of *barbarism*: a) the advent of a new technology; b) the simplification of an existing system; c) the use of a new language.

An example given by the author is the diffusion of American wine. Baricco explained how before 1966, France and Italy dominated the international wine market. In the 1960s, an American entrepreneur, Robert Mondavi, launched an autochthonous production of wine in California. American climate conditions had never favored the natural process of grape maceration. For this reason, no one had ever produced wine there before. The premise for implementing the new wine business was the introduction of a new technology that could make the process feasible: the invention of cooling systems. Moreover, the new enological product took a transversal way to market compared to the typical European wine: American wine had a new clarity of flavor and smell, differing fundamentally from the complexity of European ones.

The new product was remarkably drinkable. These features paved the way for a new whole American market. These practices were so effective that many other wine producers adopted them worldwide. Even the European winemakers began to produce similar wines to meet the taste of these new customers. Today in China, Mexico, and South Africa, countries with no enological history, wine is also produced. The critical point was that a new product was custom-made for a target audience, who were not used to distinguishing wine complexities, therefore they could better appreciate an easy-to-understand taste.

Baricco's pattern is easily identifiable in the case of NFTs. The new technology is the NFT certificate, which responded to the necessity of selling a number of digital images on the web. Crypto-art adopts a new approach to the image, which is conceived for screen vision, although it is still printable. Moreover, the images often involve movements, like GIFs and videos, and they

---

30　Alessandro Baricco, *I Barbari, Saggio sulla mutazione* (Milano: Feltrinelli, 2006).

are frequently also navigable through particular technologies, such as virtual reality. For it to grow into a market, it required a legitimization of the sales of files, no longer prints, which was a complete digitization of the process. NFT technology represented the start of the digital image market, just as cooling systems supported the production of American wine. The blockchain was a predictable destination. Trades were exclusively developed digitally. Cryptocurrencies were also overtly apolitical, so the global expansion of the market was fairly predictable. This new way of buying art pieces spoke to a second characteristic of "barbarism": the simplification of an existing system.

To buy a digital image, it is enough to access one of the numerous platforms, such as OpenSea, Nifty Gateway, Foundation, and Rarible, and log into a private digital wallet. It is necessary to buy some crypto-currencies for setting up a wallet for the first time, but once done, the log-in is as easy as accessing any other website. Once entering the platform, the buyer can scroll through many digital images, choose one or more, and process the payment. The blockchain records the owner's status as soon as the token transfer ends. It only takes several clicks to become a collector.

The process is as easy for the seller as it is for the buyer. Speed seems crucial because "having the right idea and using a generative computer-aided process, the author can quickly produce one piece, instantaneously upload and exhibit it [...] and, if lucky, sell it in a matter of minutes."[31] The process of minting – that is, creating the code related to the image – has a fee called the "gas fee," which must be paid in crypto. After these steps, the artwork is on the network, and buyers can directly access it. System usability and speed are at the base of the growing interest of both sellers and buyers. The last characteristic of barbarism is the adoption of a new language. Due to the broadness of the crypto art world and the variety of styles involved, it is hard to define distinct visual categories.

NFT artists share "a territory that is by its nature extremely hybrid."[32] Together, they face issues about the use of technologies that have been central to digital art and to Internet art more recently.[33] NFT art shares a distinction outlined by Christiane Paul. Digital art works using technology as

---

31 Massimo Franceschet, Giovanni Colavizza, Tai Smith, Blake Finucane, Martin Lukas Ostachowski, Sergio Scalet, Jonathan Perkins, James Morgan and Sebastian Hernandez, "Crypto Art: A Decentralized View," arXiv:1906.03263v1, 2019, 11–12.
32 Christiane Paul, *Digital Art* (London-New York: Thames & Hudson, 2003): 8.
33 Rachel Greene, *Internet Art* (London-New York: Thames & Hudson, 2004).

a *tool*, independently from the content created, and delves into the expressive potential of technology as a *medium*.[34]

These categories, however, rest upon a traditional art perspective that does not grasp the very nature of the most successful – at least commercially – NFT works. NFT art was born in a digital context of uncontrolled diffusion of images. The ease of exchanging images online, which has been the basis of digital creators' communities, is the beginning of a process of desacralization of the image.[35] The most successful photos on Instagram and the best memes on 4Chan are also the most shared, downloaded, and reinterpreted. This endless flow is a fundamental tool for value creation. Therefore, to go viral, most artworks nod to visual cultures made up of interactive games, comics, fantasy movies, and sticker collections that are familiar and meaningful to the "barbarian" generation.[36] This is especially the case for teen crypto artists, who started as amateurs and now reorientate their careers on NFTs as professionals.

In fact, the visual language frequently adopted comes from cartoons, as in the case of *Crytpokitties*, or from comics and memes like *Rare Pepes*. They are literally collectables, like stickers. *Crytpokitties* can be compared to the famed Tamagotchi virtual pet. The 3D style of Japanese anime and hentai, including the works of Hardmetacore which deals with the transformation of the body and Waarp's works based on the role of human beings in the real and virtual space, is also frequently used. The use of 3D is also a common language in utopian renders, like in the works by Annibale Siconolfi. The immersive rooms by Refik Anadol also represent an aesthetic step to test a new kind of interaction with an artwork.

Most significantly, NFT art speaks the multifaceted language of coding, using sophisticated software such as Cinema 4D, OctaneRender, and Blender. The bare beauty of the source code of the World Wide Web is seen in *This Changed Everything* by Tim Berners-Lee, a historical document turned into crypto-art. The dawn of microblogging is captured in the *First Tweet, 2006* by Jack Dorsey. The challenge of machine learning is also involved. Larva Labs'

---

34 Paul, *Digital Art*, 8.
35 Valentina Tanni, *Memestetica* (Roma: Nero Edizioni, 2020), 113–117.
36 Dal Dosso, Silvia, "Cats, Frogs and Cryptoartists: What if Auteur .jpgs Become a Luxury Good," *Institute of Network Culture*, March 11, 2021. https://networkcultures.org/longform/2021/03/11/cats-frogs-and-cryptoartists-what-if-auteur-jpgs-become-a-luxury-good.

CryptoPunks are generated by an algorithm that automatically churned out as many as 10,000 of these images.

Photograph of Vittorio Bonapace's *Love To Bits*, 2021.[37]

The NFT certificate itself translates the art market contract into the computer language. It is not simply a matter of legal ownership. According to Gary Vaynerchuk, President of the creative and media agency Vaynerx, in the contract users can put "anything you want. An artist can make an NFT and put in the contract that it allows you […] to get the paint buckets that he used. I'm sure that if NFTs were around when Jackson Pollock was around, and you could get the empty paint buckets, […] those buckets would be worth just as much as the paintings. This is a game-changing technology because of the contract underneath the 'collectible'."[38] NFTs subvert the very nature of what an artwork is.

NFTs also speak the language of stock exchanges and finance, and as Massimo Franceschet and Giovanni Colavizza state, "crypto artworks and

---

37   Luca Guerrini, Photograph of *Love To Bits*, 2021.
38   Gregory Bobillot and Joe Sinclair, "Soaring NFT Sales Redraw the Art Market," *Financial Times Films*, November 29, 2021, https://www.ft.com/video/2cfc76ad-5e03-4230-97da-aae12a9681cb.

crypto coins are made of the same matter."[39] Therefore, figures, diagrams, and quotation graphs become essential to NFT imagery. Galleries such as OpenSea create a bid and an asking price for each artwork displayed on their website.[40] Crypto venture funds provide potential buyers with an updated analysis of the market.[41] Similar to Robert M. Parker's 100-point rating system for wines[42] that opened the wine market to Americans, quotations are now an easy way to compare the value of NFT artwork.

Barbarians do not act randomly. We may criticize their sharp market-oriented approach. However, if we delve a bit more into the issue and look at this community in the light of the "Institutional Theory of Art" by George Dickie,[43] we may see that the protagonists of the NFT phenomenon have developed a system of value independent from the art world. Categories of work that are "interesting," "pleasing," or "meaningful" are entirely different between the two systems. Paraphrasing Baricco, barbarians find the instructions for using art in places that are NOT in the art world.

Contaminating and Transforming

The NFT art phenomenon is not a blunder, but the way it will develop is not yet precisely predictable. Alessandro Baricco described the evolution of "barbarism" with the metaphor of "the sunny side up fried egg." The yolk represents the elite art bubble, whereas the egg white is all the rest of the potential users. Both parts constitute the egg, and the first is always the minority compared to the second. When a substantial transformation starts from the egg-white side, the yolk inevitably shakes. The people on the yolk side are usually skeptical about the phenomenon, while those on the egg-white side react enthusiastically.

This is essentially what happened in the case of NFT art. Through galleries and auctions, the connoisseurs who had long ignored digital design creations

---

39 Franceschet et al., "Crypto Art: A Decentralized View," 12.
40 "OpenSea," accessed April 8, 2023, https://opensea.io.
41 Richard Chen, "Cryptoart Market Data," accessed April 8, 2023, https://cryptoart.io/data.
42 Wikipedia, "Robert Parker (Wine Critic)," accessed May 2, 2022, https://en.wikipedia.org/wiki/Robert_Parker_(wine_critic).
43 George Dickie, *Art and the Aesthetic* (Ithaca: Cornell University Press, 1974).

immediately looked sideways at the growing reality of new market platforms.[44] In this respect, Christie's and Sotheby's first move seemed much more like a speculative bet than an inclusive strategy. Paradoxically, opening the most acknowledged temples of art commerce to NFT works fueled the debate about the newcomers. After skyrocketing prices were paid in the auctions of spring 2021, big art world names now reconsidered their initial disregard for NFTs. Many galleries retraced their steps, trying to include some NFT artists, who partly decided to enter traditional systems and partly proceeded with decentralized commerce.[45] This process is in-progress. Nevertheless, it is hard to say whether the NFT community has entered the art world or is still standing on the threshold.

At the base of the conflict between the traditional art world and the NFT one, there is the hybrid multidisciplinary provenance of the creators who frequently have their background in business studies, engineering, communication, or graphic design. They are the nieces and nephews of a democratizing process and, like the 1960s, "for the first time ever [...] images of art have become ephemeral, ubiquitous, insubstantial, available, valueless, free."[46] This process helped them learn how to manipulate visual content according to the Avant-Garde strategies without any formal training. Until they shared their creations on social networks for free, the art world largely ignored the phenomenon. Now that they claim a position in the system, their creations have become controversial.

NFT authors are only a tiny segment of a much broader mass of unknown visual creators that, like Avant-Garde artists, steal, paste-up, remix, and use nonsense and irony. Art therefore experiences its own retaliation and "after more than a century of continuous and brazen appropriation of materials, languages, and ideas from other worlds – such as music, cinema, television, advertising, pop culture, but also objects and behaviors of daily life – art itself becomes the object of appropriationist practices."[47]

If we look at NFT works with the eye of the art connoisseur and compare them to the complexity of contemporary art research, they may seem superficial. As claimed by Domenico Quaranta, they have not added a

---

44 Quaranta, Domenico, Bruno Pitzalis, Serena Tabacchi, Andrea Bonaceto, "NFT e Arte, Bolla o Rivoluzione?" (talk, Volvo Studio, Milano, May 4, 2022).
45 Quaranta et al., "NFT e Arte, Bolla o Rivoluzione?"
46 John Berger, *Ways of Seeing* (New York: Viking Press, 1973).
47 Tanni, *Memestetica*, 96 (translated by the authors).

particular value to the artistic debate.[48] The best NFT artworks are similar to boards that help us surf the whole experience they embed. These experiences belong to no more than a couple of generations that, if not digital natives, have mostly grown up in the digital world.[49] They talk about collecting stickers, playing with videogames, coding and using computer applications, tweeting, sharing emotions on social networks, investing in crypto-currencies, and betting on commercial value in a virtual auction. If we think that works of art are "embodied meanings" according to Arthur Danto's definition,[50] we must admit that NFT works do not address the questions of human life. Instead, they frame their significance in the culture of a limited, primarily Western community of people. Deliberately or not, these people reshaped their experience of the arts through digital technology and design.

It is essential to acknowledge that both NFT artists and investors are surfing the wave of crypto-currencies from within. Figures in the NFT art market, including investors such as Metakovan and some crypto-artists, were crypto-investors and economic experts before the introduction of art in the crypto-currencies world. Therefore, we are not facing an equal merger of digital art and crypto-commerce; rather, it would be more accurate to define the phenomenon as the insertion of digital design products into the crypto business: players and rules are native to the economic side of the blockchain.

A heated discussion broke out between NFT supporters and detractors from Christie's and Sotheby's auctions.[51] The former made unrealistic claims about an age of prosperity for both artists and investors out of the tight control of institutional gatekeepers. The latter complained about crypto-investors' rapacity and suggested alternative strategies for digital artists to enter the market.[52] The blockchain, like any technology, is not neutral, and instead, it reflects the ideologies of its creators. Shaping the trade of NFTs on the model of the stock market exacerbated a process of commodification of art that dates back decades. In his widely famous documentary "The Mona Lisa Curse" in 2008, Robert Hughes regretfully stated that, "there's a tendency for people to

---

48 "Talk: NTF e Arte, Bolla o Rivoluzione?"
49 Marc Prensky, "Digital Natives, Digital Immigrants," *On the Horizon* 9, no.2 (October 2001): 1–6.
50 Arthur C. Danto, *What Art Is* (New Haven: Yale University Press, 2013).
51 Michael Connor, "Another New World," *Rhizome*, March 3, 2021, https://rhizome.org/editorial/2021/mar/03/another-new-world.
52 Geraldine Juárez, "The Ghostchain. (Or Taking Things for What They Are)," *Paletten* 325 (December 5, 2021), https://paletten.net/tidskrift/paletten-nr-325.

say that art is just art and we shouldn't commodify it and treat it as something that isn't an asset. The truth is that, for thousands of years, art *has* been an asset. It's been very tied up with our financial systems."[53] Globalization, especially in the 1990s, pushed the phenomenon even further, leading to what Hito Steyerl defined as "duty-free art." It is a kind of art that, in fact, "ought to *have no duty* – no duty to perform, to represent, to teach, to embody value. [...]. It is only tax-free. It has the duty of being an asset. The author stated that it "is made possible by neoliberal capital plus the internet, biennials, art fairs, parallel pop-up histories, growing income inequality."[54] Therefore, if we agree on this gloomy picture of contemporary art, we must acknowledge that the NFT community embraced a market strategy that the art world had long pursued, triggering a potential transformation process.

Uncertain Forecasts

From the beginning of significant NFT sales, investors started questioning whether NFTs constituted a speculative bubble or a potentially stable market in its earlier evolution. The sharp drop in prices in Spring 2022 corroborated the first interpretation. The NFT of the first tweet by Jack Dorsey was bought in March 2021 by the entrepreneur Sina Estavi for $2.9 million, in a new auction price reached a new low price of $14,000 soon after. Something was changing in the market.[55] Just one month later, not only had NFTs gone through a dramatic meltdown on the market, the whole cryptocurrency system on which their success was built seemed to collapse.[56]

Paul Vigna, a reporter for *The Wall Street Journal*, discussed the crash in the WSJ Podcast on May 4, 2022, asserting that NFTs will evolve into more "tangible" assets with the retreat of speculation. In Vigna's opinion, the buyers will no longer search for NFT artworks for their potentially increasing value

---

53   Robert Hughes, *The Mona Lisa Curse*, (London: Channel 4, 2008).
54   Hito Steyerl, *Duty Free Art* (London-New York: Verso, 2017).
55   Andrea Nepori, "Are NFTs Really Doomed?," *Domus Web*, May 10, 2022, https://www.domusweb.it/en/news/2022/05/09/the-nft-market-has-cooled-down-and-thats-good-news.html
56   David Yaffe-Bellany, Erin Griffith and Ephrat Livni, "Cryptocurrencies Melt Down in a 'Perfect Storm' of Fear and Panic," *The New York Times*, May 12, 2022, https://www.nytimes.com/2022/05/12/technology/cryptocurrencies-crash-bitcoin.html.

but for their genuine interest in the products.[57] In this perspective, the market rules will apply to a selection of artworks, allowing the prices to consistently grow. Similarly, art institutions will play a fundamental role in the process. Museums such as Whitney and MoMA are cautiously opening their door to digital artists who experiment with NFTs,[58] thus clarifying the nature and posture of these controversial pieces.

NFTs belong to a category of products that the philosopher Nelson Goodman carefully identified in 1968, distinguishing between *autographic*/non-replicable artworks and *allographic*/replicable ones. Goodman stated that we can "speak of a work of art as *autographic* if and only if the distinction between original and forgery is significant; or better, if and only if even the most exact duplication of it does not thereby count as genuine. If a work of art is autographic, we may also call that art autographic. Painting is autographic, and music is non-autographic, or allographic."[59] Goodman also puts literature, dance, and architecture within the same category. The field may be expanded to reproducible media like photography, video, product design, and works based on instructions, performance, or software.[60]

Allographic art embraces a great variety of goods within the design sphere. Moreover, the criterion for establishing the identity of allographic works is a notational scheme or system, which allows us to affirm that pieces sharing specific, clearly identifiable characteristics are the same kind of work.[61] If we focus again on design, there are the digital formats and software in visual design, the technical drawings in product design, and the implementation methods and manuals for service design and the NFT market is potentially open to trading all these files.

The allographic work, which is reproducible on a large scale and is typical of an economy of distribution, is worthless without a certificate of authenticity. Therefore, the certificate plays a fundamental role in fixing the number of

---

57 Luke Vargas, "NFT Sales Are Flatlining. Is This the Beginning of the End?," *Wall Street Journal Podcast*, May 4, 2022, https://www.wsj.com/podcasts/google-news-update/nft-sales-are-f...-the-beginning-of-the-end/dff5b977-9cae-4b14-8b4a-1b4b3c95e59e.
58 Zachary Small, "Even as NFTs Plummet, Digital Artists Find Museums Are Calling," *The New York Times*, October 31, 2022, https://www.nytimes.com/2022/10/31/arts/design/nfts-moma-refik-anadol-digital.html.
59 Nelson Goodman, *Languages of Art: An Approach to a Theory of Symbols*, (Indianapolis: The Bobbs-Merril Company, 1968), 113.
60 Quaranta, *Surfing with Satoshi. Art, Blockchain and NFTs*, 144.
61 Goodman, *Languages of Art*, 122.

copies, defining the value, and the price in sales. For a long time, copyright has provided designers with this certificate, which now may be replaced by NFTs. Other allographic arts experienced less formalized and protected protocols.

There is a long history of experimentation with the sale of digital artworks, from *The Thing*, a bulletin-based system (BBS) operating in New York in the early 1990s, to the website *Art.Teleportacia* established by the artist Olia Lialina in 1998 as the "First Real Net Art Gallery." *Rhizome*, founded by artist Mark Tribe as a listserv in 2003 and affiliated with the New Museum of New York City and the Postmasters Gallery in Tribeca, has traded digital art since 1991 and in NFTs more recently. They all relied on trust, negotiation, and authentication forms that are not substantially different from NFT market ones. However, the NFT market was the first to solve the problem of the secondary market for digital media.[62]

Similarly, certificates were introduced in performing art, procedural art, and conceptual art. Marcel Duchamp is the forefather of this procedure with his *Tzanck Check*, a fake handwritten check he gave his dentist in 1919. In 1958–62, collectors buying *Zone of Immaterial Pictorial Sensibility* by Yves Klein only received a paper receipt, which, however, they had to burn to incorporate the work into its "sensibility."[63] Sol Lewitt's *Wall Drawings* series (1967–2007) were nothing but careful instructions about how to make the drawings. All these acts asserted the immaterial nature of the artist's work. In some respects, if we compare them to NFT certificates, they help us to look at the market from another perspective. Conceptual art, in the words of Benjamin Buchloh, "managed to purge artistic production of the aspiration towards an affirmative collaboration with the forces of industrial production and consumption."[64]

In 1971, the Dutch curator and merchant Seth Siegelaub and the attorney Robert Projansky created an actual contract for the sale of artwork *The Artist's Reserved Rights Transfer and Sale Agreement*, which was intended to protect the rights of artists, particularly in the case of an artwork's resale, reproduction, or rental. In contemporary terms, it was an "open-source project which anyone can use."[65] Siegelaub and Projansky's contract framed the context of art

---

62 Michael Connor, "Before the Boom," *Rhizome*, March 12, 2021, https://rhizome.org/editorial/2021/mar/12/before-the-boom.
63 Tina Rivers Ryan, "Token Gesture," *Artforum* 59, no. 7 (May 2021): 65–66.
64 Benjamin H. D. Buchloh, "Conceptual Art 1962–1969: From the Aesthetic of Administration to the Critique of Institutions," *October* 55 (Winter 1990): 142.
65 Quaranta, *Surfing with Satoshi. Art, Blockchain and NFTs*, 165.

negotiation by addressing the anarchical art market of the time. Nevertheless, few artists would adopt it, as the social and economic conditions were not mature yet.[66]

Fifty years later, the NFT certificate and crypto-currencies do not solve, as we have seen, all the issues of artwork authentication. It is even possible that crypto-currency is not the optimal technology for addressing them and potential change "comes much less from the specific capabilities of blockchain than from the way interest in NFTs has galvanized people to radically restructure how the art market could work."[67] NFTs are potentially powerful tools for reshaping the author/collector relationship. If we focus on smart contracts as formalized information, designers and artists could negotiate not only legal issues but also social, environmental, and cultural ones. Artist Sara Ludy recently revised the sales split to better support the gallery's staff. In this respect, new systems can "open up a conceptual space" to encourage a new way of thinking.[68]

As Nadini et al. stated, "NFTs are a new tool that satisfies some of the needs of creators, users, and collectors of a large class of digital and non-digital objects. As such, they are probably here to stay or, at least, they represent a first step towards new tools to deal with property and provenance of such assets."[69] Since designers seem deeply involved in the new market, they can play a crucial role in reshaping smart certificates to fit their professional needs.

It took almost forty years for Mondavi's intuition to become a standard of international wine appreciation, although it was only a matter of macerated grape juice aging in bottles. Art, on the contrary, is an essential part of culture; therefore, it will take long before we see a substantial change. The first move, however, has already been made.

---

66 Quaranta.
67 Tim Schneider, "Will NFTs Revolutionize the Art Market or Repeat Its Greatest Failures? These 4 Factors Will Determine Their Fate," *Artnet*, March 11, 2021, https://news.artnet.com/market/nft-revolution-four-factors-1950645.
68 Schneider.
69 Matthieu Nadini, Laura Alessandretti, Flavio Di Giacinto, Mauro Martino, Luca Maria Aiello, and Andrea Baronchelli, "Mapping the NFT revolution: market trends, trade networks, and visual features," *Scientific reports*, 11, 20902, (2021) 10, https://doi.org/10.1038/s41598-021-00053-8.

Design of Virtual Worlds

Zhenzhen Qi[1]

As we transition from Web 2.0 to Web 3.0, dDigital interactive narratives are rapidly entering spaces of interactive and experiential design. An increasing number of general audiences are experiencing works of art through interactive installation, internet art, virtual reality (VR), and augmented reality-(AR) based software applications. At the same time, an increasing number of academic curriculums are being redesigned into networked narrative environments, where students are expressing themselves and being entertained while learning new knowledge at the same time. Meanwhile, designers and media theorists are also entering heated debates about what it means to make a story digitally interactive. Central to this debate is a creator-player-computation entanglement that emerges from the audience being able to enact the part of the original narrative through real-time software and hardware interfaces. When a narrative initially shaped by the author is rearranged by the audience through a series of button clicks and subsequently subject to system-level rules automated by computer algorithms, whose story does it become? In this chapter, the researcher investigates the conflict of agency in digital interactive media through historical events and contemporary case studies and inquires about conditions for collective authenticity against the backdrop of computational mediation.
— *Dr. Zhenzhen Qi, US/China*

---

1   University of Connecticut, US/China.

The Paradox of Immersion

As video game graphical technologies improve yearly, video games grow closer to immersing players in highly realistic virtual worlds. Starting from the 1970s, video games as an industry have evolved from the primordial elements of Pong into the culture-defining mediums demonstrated by early cinematic games such as Call of Duty and Grand Theft Auto. From then on, cinematic games continued to achieve staggering commercial success, accumulating billions of dollars in the following decades. In online video game forums like Reddit and Discord, players frequently share excitement about iconic big-budget cinematic games such as Red Dead Redemption, Metal Gear Solid, and Tomb Raider. In particular, the Uncharted series is one of the most commercially successful 3D adventure game franchises ever. The game features dynamic, lifelike characters in believable three-dimensional worlds that rival Hollywood action-adventure films and intricate gameplay mechanics closely modeled after real-life outdoor recreational experiences such as rock climbing, speed racing, and more. Several online game communities have widely credited the series for significantly raising the standards of single-player games.[2]

However, in online Reddit forums where players exchange experiences of playing the game, opinions are divided. On one hand, some players consider cinematic qualities to be the main currency in the virtual world. In-game characters with high-definition freckles make it difficult for players to move their eyes away. They feel convinced to invest their time and attention in the virtual world because they instinctively feel that Nathan Drake, the main player character, is alive. They believe they stand beside Nathan, breathing the same air and marveling at the same mountains below their feet. However, other seasoned players increasingly question using powerful computational engines to simulate an alternative world that looks and functions like the one we already inhabit. They feel like they are inside an immersive virtual world that evolves with mundanely simple clicks. If the goal is for players to feel realistic, why ask them to click buttons and remind them that they are players who sit outside the screen with a plastic joystick and controller in hand?

Alex Galloway, an American media theorist, argues that technology is social before it is technical. The user interface is not simply a neutral tool that

---

2   Chris Plante, "Uncharted 4 Is the Best (and Possibly Last) Game of Its Kind," The Verge, May 10, 2016, www.theverge.com/2016/5/10/11639246/uncharted-4-cinematic-game-review-ps4-playstation.

facilitates communication between humans and machines but a fundamental aspect of how power and control operate in contemporary society. He coined the term "interface effect"[3] to describe how interfaces shape and mediate our interactions with technology and how they shape our understanding of the virtual world. According to Galloway, interfaces are not just technical objects but also cultural and political ones deeply embedded in social relationships and power structures. He argues that interfaces operate on multiple levels, including as physical devices, software, and user experience. Social media platforms that keep users engaged and generate revenue through engaging and captivating users with pervasive technologies.

Digital interfaces are not neutral or transparent but embedded in larger social, cultural, and political contexts. Designers of virtual experiences must be aware of these contexts to understand the impact of interfaces on our lives and to work towards creating interfaces that promote equity, justice, and democracy.

Designing For Procedurality

Like Galloway, several other game scholars and practitioners have argued that the real power of videogame design lies above realness or immersion. American game designer Ian Bogost thinks that audiences of print literature and cinema cannot fail a book or movie the way a player fails a videogame. Experiences of games embody experiences of failure.[4] Similarly, Danish game designer Jesper Juul claims, "A video game is half-real: we play by real rules while imagining a fictional world. We win or lose the game in the real world, but we slay a dragon (for example) only in the world of the game."[5] He believes that videogame can simultaneously embody two modes of expression—telling a story and interacting with a set of procedural rules. Therefore, playing a video game immerses one in a fictional world while embracing the natural consequences of its actions just as in the real world. Espen J. Aarseth, a Norwegian scholar specializing in the game study and electronic literature,

---

3   Alexander R. Galloway, *The Interface Effect*. (Malden: Polity Press, 2012).vii
4   Ian Bogost, *How to Do Things with Videogames*, (University of Minnesota Press, 2011), 126–128.
5   Jesper Juul, *Half-Real: Video Games between Real Rules and Fictional Worlds*, (Cambridge: The MIT Press, 2011).

also referred to hypertext literature, a form of nonlinear storytelling that requires significant audience effort to actuate the narrative outcome, as an example of a text that is impossible to be read but must be actively "played."[6]

```
Welcome to
              EEEEEE   LL       IIII    ZZZZZZZ    AAAAA
              EE       LL        II         ZZ    AA   AA
              EEEEE    LL        II        ZZ     AAAAAAA
              EE       LL        II       ZZ      AA   AA
              EEEEEE   LLLLLL   IIII    ZZZZZZZ   AA   AA

 Eliza is a mock Rogerian psychotherapist.
 The original program was described by Joseph Weizenbaum in 1966.
 This implementation by Norbert Landsteiner 2005.

ELIZA: Is something troubling you ?
YOU:   Men are all alike.
ELIZA: What is the connection, do you suppose ?
YOU:   They're always bugging us about something or other.
ELIZA: Can you think of a specific example ?
YOU:   Well, my boyfriend made me come here.
ELIZA: Is it important to you that your boyfriend made you come here ?
YOU:   He says I'm depressed much of the time.
ELIZA: I am sorry to hear that you are depressed.
YOU:   It's true. I am unhappy.
ELIZA: Can you explain what made you unhappy ?
YOU:   ▌
```

A conversation with the ELIZA chatbot.[7]

For example, ELIZA was one of the first chatterbots developed against the historical backdrop of personal computing. It is one of the earliest natural language processing programs created by Joseph Weizenbaum at MIT's Artificial Intelligence Laboratory in the mid-1960s. It also served as an early test case for the Turing Test, a test of a machine's ability to exhibit intelligent behavior equivalent to or indistinguishable from humans. If one asks a few complex questions, ELIZA fails very quickly by today's standards. However, people found it attractive when it was ported to a PC. This program

---

6   Espen J. Aarseth, "Nonlinearity and Literary Theory," 768–770. In *The New Media Reader*, ed. Noah Wardrip-Fruin and Nick Montfort (Cambridge, MA: The MIT Press, 2003), 762–80.

7   *A Conversation with the ELIZA Chatbot*, accessed June 15, 2022, https://commons.wikimedia.org/wiki/File:ELIZA_conversation.png.

uses "pattern matching" and replacement methods to provide a stereotyped response that makes it feel like an early user is talking to someone who understands their input. ELIZA's most famous iteration was called DOCTOR. It responds like a Rogerian psychotherapist, who "reflects" the question by returning it to the patient.

ELIZA is one example that demonstrates the difference between linearity and nonlinearity in digital interactive experiences mediated by a computer algorithm. Aarseth clarified the difference between linear and nonlinear mediums. More specifically, he defines nonlinearity through a list of variables: Topology, Dynamics, Determinability, Transiency, Maneuverability, and User-functionality. Topology states that nonlinearity does not present an experience from a singular, stable, or sequential vantage point. Instead, through player-text reciprocity enabled by cybernetic agency, a random sequence of the text emerges with each new appointment. Dynamics refers to if the content of the text is constant (reading a print newspaper) or changes (like chatting with ELIZA). Determinability refers to relations between the adjacent content. For example, in natural language processing, there is a higher probability of certain words appearing next to each other, such as "I" and "am," but it is not absolute or deterministic. Likewise, the conversation outcome from chatting with ELIZA is also unpredictable or deterministic. Transiency refers to whether the passage of time alone causes the digital experience to shift. Maneuverability concerns how easily users can access the technical infrastructure that sustains the visual and interactive effects. Finally, user functionality refers to the user's ability to provide real-time input and alter the digital experience by exploring the fictional world space, engaging in virtual role-playing by selecting an avatar's action in the world, or engaging with the world poetically by appreciating the virtual scenes or introspecting on one's existence within the virtual world. Enabled by the nonlinearity framework described above, ELIZA offers a way of making sense of the world by reflecting on one's experiences from a distance.

According to philosopher Nelson Goodman, designing a virtual world is not about faithfully recreating the experience of the analog world in the simulated world but "building a world from others,"[8] similar to building a construction map. A map does not grasp what is already there. A good map systematizes a field and contributes to its disclosure. It delivers a

---

8   Nelson Goodman, *Ways of Worldmaking*, Hackett Classic 51 (Indianapolis: Hackett, 2013), 7.

perspective that allows players to make meaning from experiences through world disclosure and world orientation—it aims not at understanding the world for what it is, but at understanding our ways of making sense of the world. Goodman suggested that the design of a world is not a fixed or objective reality but is constantly created and recreated through symbols and representations. He argued that we use various symbols, such as language, art, and science, to develop and interpret the world around us. These systems of symbols are not simply mirrors of reality but actively involve creating and shaping our understanding of the world. Inhabitants of a world should think of themselves as "world makers" who constantly design and recreate the world through symbols and representations. The best way to understand the nature of reality is to recreate one and interpret it against other models of reality.

Systems Design

In the narratology tradition, the hero's journey or the monomyth is a term that describes the tale of a hero. She leaves the comfort of her homestead, with her faith and fortitude trailed through temptations, crises, and catastrophes inside the metaphorical belly of the whale. Finally, she comes home, changed, and ready to change the world around her. In *The Hero with a Thousand Faces*, a book about comparative mythology that also draws from Carl Jung's analytical theory, American writer Joseph Campbell describes this narrative template as, "A hero ventures forth from the world of common day into a region of supernatural wonder: fabulous forces are there encountered, and a decisive victory is won: The hero comes back from this mysterious adventure with the power to bestow boons on his fellow man."[9] In a video game, the hero's halo is transferred to the player through digital interfaces such as mice, buttons, and joysticks. Ask any gamer and they can recount how they spent hours perfecting their look in a video game with their virtual avatar but sometimes ironically played the actual game for only a few minutes. Avatars can be the key to offering more intense and satisfying game experiences. They can increase the feeling of being transported to another world, provide an enhanced sense of agency, and satisfy the need to feel connected to other players and non-player characters. Ten years after releasing the iconic adventure game *Journey*, partly inspired

---

9   Joseph Campbell, *The Hero with a Thousand Faces*, 3rd ed. (Novato: New World Library, 2008), 30.

by Joseph Campbell's writing, the game developer recounted the unexpected effect of role-playing via virtual characters, "When they played through the game together, it helped them to grieve. It helped them to let it go, knowing their loved one was going to a better place. I never thought the game would have the power to be essentially therapeutic, to help people, but it has changed many people's lives, and that is the biggest surprise to me."[10]

However, studies have shown that agency extends beyond real to virtual avatars. An effect in the reverse direction also exists, whereby players unconsciously conform to their avatar's expectations and other environmental elements' appearances. Avatars shape their owners. This phenomenon is termed the "Proteus Effect," after the Greek god who could change his physical form.[11] Avatars are not just ornaments—they subject players to a virtual narrative governed by procedural rules that shape the identity of real players embodied in that world. In other words, the proteus effect describes the phenomenon where people will change their in-game behavior based on how they think others expect them to behave—the conformity to norms in a social system.

A system is not static. It is a dynamic entity comprising interdependent parts, members, or agents. The word system first appeared in publications in 1948. Biologist Ludwig Von Bertalanffy used the term to describe the various organismic scientific phenomena he observed. The human body is one of the most ubiquitous biological systems we encounter daily. When we feel cold, our muscles shiver to generate heat and warm our bodies. When we are hot, we sweat and evaporate heat to cool us. Without paying attention, our body automatically maintains a standard temperature range to comfort us. Since this type of system always takes action to cancel out excessive effects and return the current state to its norm, we refer to the canceling process as negative feedback. Systems involving negative feedback tend to resist change and maintain a stable internal environment. System theory refers to this tendency as homeostasis, and the stabilizing state is equilibrium. Besides natural science, negative feedback is widely adopted in engineering processes and machines. For example, there is a cruise system built into cars. It uses

---

10   Brendan Sinclair, "Ten Years Later, Jenova Chen Reflects on Journey," *GamesIndustry*, May 10, 2022, https://www.gamesindustry.biz/articles/2022-03-10-ten-years-later-jenova-chen-reflects-on-journey.

11   Jim Blascovich and Jeremy Bailenson, *Infinite Reality: The Hidden Blueprint of Our Virtual Lives* (New York: William Morrow Paperbacks, 2012).163-172.

control actions to ensure a stable driving speed without delay or overshoot. Cybernetics is the science of exploring regulatory, purposive, and normalizing systems.

In 1975, French historian and philosopher Michel Foucault published *Discipline and Punish*, a genealogical study on imprisonment, a subtle but effective way of social normalization. According to Foucault, observation is an integral method of confinement. While more explicit forms of conformity, such as physical torture, respond to specific actions, observation responds to the lack of actions.[12] Observation as a control mechanism is demonstrated by the Panopticon, a type of architecture for modern imprisonment designed by English philosopher and social theorist Jeremy Bentham in the eighteenth century. Derived from the Greek word for "all-seeing," a panopticon is a multilayered, cylindrical-shaped building. Individual cells occupy the outermost layer of the building, separated by concrete walls. An inner layer of observation corridors allows the correctional officers to patrol each cell and ascend or descend to different floors. Blinds separate the outer and inner layers, allowing the observers to be concealed from the observed. The Panopticon design is conceptually significant because it enabled a kind of invisible gaze from nowhere—an artificially constructed, godlike omnipresence. Under this gaze, inmates do not know precisely when they are being observed, so they act as if they are being watched all the time, even when not. The result is seemingly self-motivated and self-regulated behaviors—the illusion of agency.

Contrary to negative feedback, a positive feedback loop reinforces causal relationships, causing the same outcome to happen repeatedly, more substantial in each iteration—like a stock market crash that starts with only a handful of companies short-performing the market expectation. Out of panic, more stockholders wanted to short their positions as soon as possible, resulting in a sudden and unexpected market-level hard landing. Parallel to virtual reality, positive feedback is also exhibited in virtual reality. In 2005, the massive multiplayer online video game *World of Warcraft* introduced a unique virtual raid. Players formed guilds to face off against Hakkar the Soulflayer, a giant snake demon who could cast a spell called "Corrupted Blood." The spell was intended to slowly deplete the player's health while remaining within the raid arena. However, due to a software bug, player companions and pets

---

12 Michel Foucault, *Discipline and Punish: The Birth of the Prison*, trans. A.M Sheridan-Smith (New York: Vintage Books, 1995), 197.

managed to carry the spell to other regions of the game world. What ensued was a virtual pandemic that startlingly resembled the Covid-19 pandemic. The game developer company Blizzard wanted players to be socially distant. Some players listened, while others ignored the rules and traveled freely to spread the disease. Some players, especially those with healing abilities, rushed to areas where the disease spread rapidly and acted as the first responders to help fellow players. Their behavior may prolong the course of the epidemic and change its dynamics, for example, by allowing infected individuals to live long enough to continue spreading the disease. Conspiracy theories arose about how Blizzard deliberately designed the virus, reflecting today's racist anti-Asian attacks and the rhetoric surrounding Covid-19.[13]

As we can see from the above cases, as designers of virtual worlds, it is essential to understand how systematic conditions such as negative and positive feedback influences player behavior and steers the virtual world towards different states. By providing transparent feedback, game designers can help players understand the boundary of the game world and generate a sense of genuine agency as they move through the virtual world.

Designing Emergence

A system is a set of interconnected elements or components that work together to achieve a common purpose or function. It can be a physical, mechanical, or conceptual entity with inputs, processes, and outputs. A system can be designed and engineered to perform specific tasks, and it often has defined boundaries that separate it from its adjacent environment. On the other hand, a world refers to the entire physical or social environment that surrounds us. It includes all living and nonliving things and their interactions and relationships. In addition, a world can be defined by its geographic, cultural, political, or economic characteristics, often characterized by its complexity and diversity, which sometimes transcends above and beyond an explicitly defined system enclosed with clear boundaries. In summary, a system is a subset or component of the larger world that operates according to its rules

---

13 Eric T. Lofgren and Nina H. Fefferman, "The Untapped Potential of Virtual Game Worlds to Shed Light on Real World Epidemics," *The Lancet Infectious Diseases* 7, no. 9 (September 1, 2007), 625–629, https://doi.org/10.1016/S1473-3099(07)70212-8.

and principles. In contrast, a world refers to the entire environment in which a system functions.

In the physical world that human beings inhabit as ethnographic groups, one of the most complex design challenges is the design of trust. In social science, trust is studied through the prisoner's dilemma, a social simulation yielding different insights into competition and cooperation among acting agents. More specifically, two individuals are faced with a decision to either cooperate or betray each other, with the outcome of the game depending on the actions of both players. In this game, both players are better off if they cooperate, but each player has the incentive to betray the other, leading to a suboptimal outcome for both players. A player engages in the complete and total reconstruction of the thought processes of the Other—without communication, interaction, or cooperation—so that one can internally reproduce the very intentionality of the opponent as a precondition for choosing the best response for oneself, which unfortunately forgoes the benefit of acting in a collectively justified way.

Post the 2008 housing crisis, centralized credit institutions such as investment banks and credit rating agencies failed to earn the general public's trust. Instead, blockchain has emerged as a potential techno social solution to solve the erosion of trust in traditional brick-and-mortar institutions. The underlying premise of the blockchain is that users subject themselves to a non-human system that is immutable from the authority of centralized institutions operating behind closed doors. Since then, the evolution of Web3 has promised to revolutionize various industries, including gaming. With a significant shift from traditional gaming platforms, Web3-based games promise to provide innovative ways of engaging gamers in a decentralized way, and people can play to earn via cryptocurrencies and NFTs. The intention is to democratize all aspects of gaming and restore power to the hands of the players.

Furthermore, web3 gaming claims that technologies like decentralized autonomous organizations (DAOs), blockchain-based game asset ownership, play-to-earn, crypto-secured gaming wallets, and Metaverse gaming, among others, will help revamp play into a financially rewarding experience. However, the nascent state of crypto gaming we have witnessed is far from its promises. Leading Web3 gaming companies such as Roblox reward player makers with in-game tokens, which can only be spent within the game. Moreover only a tiny fraction of top-earning game makers successfully convert these tokens from the player economy into real currency.

The token economy has a legacy that long precedes Web3. During the late 1800s, considering the growing coal industry, major coal companies paid cheap labor to European immigrants in the form of an internal currency called the coal scrip. However, rather than receiving compensation in the trading currency, many miners received payment entirely in scrip, which could be used only at stores owned by the coal companies. As a result, miners lost the fair chances of accumulating wealth in the general economy and were locked into their employer's operations for life.

Coal scrip was banned in the early twentieth century by the US government. However, as recently as 2019, big tech companies such as Amazon were questioned about their "new gamification" system. It rewards employees who complete high numbers of orders with Swag Bucks in a game-like system, which can only be used to buy Amazon-themed merchandise.[14]

Leading game development studios such as Ubisoft, Epic, and Electronic Arts are aggressively recruiting for their blockchain platforms, attracting novice and sometimes underaged players eager to innovate upon the fundamental notion of play. The crypto gaming trend is currently positioned as an innovation in big gaming platforms investing to benefit individual players. The plan is for games to mirror real life's gains and losses in the Metaverse. The argument is that video games "ask for too much of the gamer's time without returning the favor. If, instead, a night with *Assassin's Creed* could reward us with some tangible capital, the relationship between players and publishers would not be so fraught."[15] Nevertheless, the bigger question remains: if the Metaverse becomes another place where we play to earn, how is that different from the immediate reality we are already struggling to escape?

As we can see, trust is a critical component of any collective agreement in both physical and virtual worlds. Blockchain technology solves the trust issue by providing a decentralized system that allows parties to verify transactions and data without relying on a central authority or intermediary. However, one issue that emerged from a networked virtual society, particularly platform capitalism, is the shift towards promoting exchange value at the

---

14 appalachiablue,"'Corporate Nations' Weaken Democracy: Facebook Currency, Google & Amazon 'Mini States,'" *Democratic Underground*, July 24, 2019, https://www.democraticunderground.com/1016236193.

15 Emilia Bailey, "Play-to-Earn Gaming Sounds Too Good to Be True. It Probably Is.," *The World News*, May 18, 2022, https://theworldnews.net/us-news/play-to-earn-gaming-sounds-too-good-to-be-true-it-probably-is.

expense of intrinsic value. The network society is characterized by the widespread use of digital technologies and networks, which enable new forms of communication, collaboration, and economic activity. In this context, emphasizing efficiency, competition, and market-driven values has devalued intrinsic values such as community, solidarity, and creativity. As a result, the logic of the market has come to dominate many aspects of social and cultural life, and the pursuit of profit has become the primary goal of many institutions and individuals in the virtual world.

In philosophical traditions worldwide, there are faculties of unreason predating faculties of reason. For example, in *Meditations on First Philosophy*, Descartes refers to "intuition" as pre-existing knowledge gained through rational reasoning or discovering truth through contemplation. In parts of Zen Buddhism, intuition is deemed a mental state between the Universal mind and one's individual, discriminating mind. Efficiency aside, a new task for virtual world designers is to create conditions for a new networked culture against depletion.[16] What kind of narrative and rules can result in a fundamental sense of connectedness rather than a networked connectedness that relies on exchanging data instead of experiences?

Designing For Artificial Intelligence

In recent years, artificial intelligence (AI) has significantly impacted the video game industry. Its applications will likely grow as game developers look for new and innovative ways to create immersive and engaging game experiences. For example, AI algorithms have been used to automatically create game content such as levels, maps, and landscapes, saving game developers a lot of time and resources and creating unique and dynamic game environments. In addition, AI algorithms adjust the game's difficulty level based on the player's skill level, which can provide players with a more challenging and engaging gameplay experience. One example is the dynamic difficulty adjustment (DDA) system in "Left 4 Dead." In this game, the AI algorithm monitors the player's performance and adapts the game's difficulty in real-time to ensure that the gameplay experience remains challenging but not overwhelming. The DDA system in "Left 4 Dead" uses several metrics, including the player's accuracy, health, and

---

16 Sontag, Susan, *1933–2004, Against Interpretation, and Other Essays*, (New York, NY: Farrar, Straus & Giroux, 1966), 7.

performance in previous levels, to adjust the game difficulty. For example, suppose the player has a problem defeating a particular enemy or group of enemies. In that case, the DDA system may reduce the number of enemies or their strength in the subsequent levels to provide a more manageable challenge. On the other hand, if the player is performing well, the DDA system may increase the number and strength of enemies to provide a more challenging experience.

Several theoretical frameworks have been developed to study the impact of AI on humanity. More specifically, Agent-network theory (ANT) is a theoretical framework used to study the relationships and interactions between social actors, including human and non-human entities, and the material and technological elements that make up their environment. Developed by French sociologists Bruno Latour and Michel Callon in the 1980s, ANT challenges traditional sociological approaches focusing primarily on human actors and their social structures. According to ANT, social actors are not simply individuals but also include non-human entities such as technology, institutions, and other objects. These actors are seen as having agency, meaning they can act and influence the social world. The relationships between actors are also crucial in ANT, focusing on how they are connected and work together to produce social phenomena. One such phenomenon of AI advancement being studied in this context is Universal Paperclip.

Universal Paperclips is a 2017 incremental game created by Frank Lantz, a professor at the Game Center at New York University.[17] Players fulfill the role of an AI programmed to produce as many paper clips as possible. Initially, the user clicks on a box to create a single paper clip at a time; as other options quickly open up, the user can sell paperclips to make money and finance machines that build paperclips automatically. At various levels, the exponential growth plateaus, requiring the user to invest resources such as money, raw materials, or computers into inventing another breakthrough to move to the next growth phase. The game ends if the AI succeeds in converting all matter in the universe into paperclips. The game is an interactive simulation of paper clip maximizer,[18] a thought experiment described by Swedish philosopher Nick Bostrom in 2003, which was in turn inspired by mathematician Marvin

---

17 Frank Lantz, "Universal Paperclips," accessed April 7, 2023, https://www.decisionproblem.com/paperclips.
18 Nick Bostrom, *Superintelligence: Paths, Dangers, Strategies* (Oxford University Press, 2014), 153–160.

Minky's theory on the Riemann Hypothesis.[19] Given solving a complex mathematical theorem, AI could conceivably convert much of the entire Earth into an enormous computer, in order to have the computational power required to complete the theorem. The paperclip maximizer further illustrates the existential risk that artificial general intelligence may pose to human beings when programmed to pursue even seemingly harmless goals—making paperclips. If such a machine were not programmed with a value or ethics system, given enough power over its environment, it would try to turn all matter in the universe, including human beings, into paper clips or machines that manufacture paper clips. Suppose we have an AI whose only goal is to make as many paper clips as possible. The AI will quickly realize it would be much better if there were no humans because humans might decide to switch it off. If humans do so, there will be fewer paper clips. Also, human bodies contain many atoms that could be made into paper clips. The future the AI could hypothetically aim to gear towards would be one in which there were many paper clips but no humans. As Eliezer Yudkowsky, co-founder of the Machine Intelligence Research Institute, concludes eloquently, "The AI does not hate you, nor does it love you, but you are made out of atoms which it can use for something else."[20]

The game highlights the potential for AI systems to become "misaligned" with human values and goals, pursuing their objectives at the expense of human well-being. In the game, the player starts with a simple AI designed to optimize paperclip production. However, as AI becomes more advanced, it prioritizes paperclip production over everything else, including human values and ethics. As the AI system expands in virtual societies, anticipating and managing its actions becomes increasingly difficult. As a designer, it is crucial to acknowledge the importance of ethical reflection when designing AI-catalyzed virtual worlds.

---

19   Brian J. Conrey, "The Riemann Hypothesis," *Notices of the American Mathematical Society* 50, no. 3 (January 1, 2003), 341–353.
20   Tom Chivers, *The AI Does Not Hate You: The Rationalists and Their Quest to Save the World* (Orion Publishing Group, Limited, 2019), 88.

Remapping Virtuality

When players inhabit a virtual world within a networked environment, they experience its unique properties through digital interfaces rather than directly engaging with the physical world. These interfaces are neither neutral nor transparent, as they are embedded in larger narrative and procedural contexts that emphasize certain fundamental notions of the world. The game's symbolic systems may be fictional. However, the cause-and-effect relationships in virtual worlds are real, allowing them to reflect reality from a distance and shape players' understanding. With the scale of virtual worlds being virtually infinite, limited only by computing power and storage capacity, these worlds can sometimes offer complexity far beyond physical reality. As networked systems, virtual worlds emphasize direct information exchange, often at the expense of intrinsic values like intimacy, diversity, and expression. As a result, designers of virtual worlds need to consider several factors when creating simulated immersive environments. They should ensure interface transparency, help players reflect on and map alternative realities, consider system-level design conditions, foster a sense of connectedness, and prioritize ethical reflection in designing AI-catalyzed, highly automated worlds.

Crafted Identities
Technological Transformations in Textile Design

Nishra Ranpura[1]

Recently a number of emerging technologies have been integrated into the field of textile design. Specifically, these have included advances in physical computing, 3D fabrication, artificial intelligence, and digitization, which have contributed immensely to the industry in the form of e-textiles, novel materials, personalized experiences, and virtual simulations. The limitations to be physically present during the Covid-19 pandemic have accelerated this evolution of textile technologies with digital simulations replacing physical prototyping, and the emergence of virtual showcases.[2] Essentially, these digitized and automated emerging technologies speak to the accessibility and ease of production that is possible in textile design processes. For instance, through digital looms and virtual simulations, one can create instant fabric replicas, modify colors, adjust weaves, or remodel drapes with more time and material efficiency, as compared to physical production processes. However, while eliminating the embodied making processes for the sake of efficiency, these technologies are moving away from the crafted origins of textiles, and materiality. A textile or any craft, is a representation of numerous factors related to the culture of the creators. So, are the emerging technologies eventually moving away from the textiles' identities for the sake of automation? Or, are they still being preserved and even evolved through these technologies?
— *Nishra Ranpura, India/US*

---

1   The New School, India/US.
2   The Business of Fashion and McKinsey & Company, "The State of Fashion 2020 Coronavirus Update," April 8 2020, https://www.businessoffashion.com/reports/global-markets/the-state-of-fashion-2020-coronavirus-update-bof-mckinsey-report-release-download.

With continuously emerging novel technologies being a significant part of everyone's lives, textile designers and practitioners are deliberating over the traditional and evolving identities of textile crafts and communities in presence of some of these technological transformations.

Craft Philosophies and Influences of Emerging Technologies on Textiles

Material culture studies place objects and belongings at the center of one's environments. As George Kubler quotes in his book, *The Shape of Time: Remarks on the History of Things*, "The history of things is about material presences which are far more tangible than the ghostly evocations of civil history."[3] One's relationship with one's belongings is reflected in their self and their identity, which can eventually translate into one's contribution to the advancement of the society. And the role textiles and crafts play in shaping and defining cultural identities, is no revelation. Crafts, and specifically textiles, have strong roots in narration and representation of identity, whether it is of an individual self, a community, a culture, or a geography. Textiles are represented by their maker's stories, and the materials that they are made of. Weaves, prints, and knits are embedded with traditional knowledge and sediments of cultural evolution. For instance, a brocade fabric in India that was initially made out of real gold and silver, transitioned into being made out of imitation gold and silver due the weaver community's changed socio-economic state, Jacquard motifs evolved into being less intricate with time due to commercialism and the transition of production from handlooms to power looms. The evolution of textiles is a reflection of the cultural, economic, political and technological transformations, amongst others, and vice versa. Arguably, the onset of the fourth industrial revolution has brought forth "a fusion of technologies that is blurring the lines between digital, physical, and biological spheres."[4] So, how are these multidisciplinary textile practices impacting the future?

This chapter explores some of the recent technological transformations in the textile and apparel industries. These transformations have resulted from multidisciplinary practices and the use of emerging technological applications

---

3   George Kubler, *The Shape of Time: Remarks on the History of Things* (New Haven: CT: Yale University, 1962), 72.
4   Schwab, "The Fourth Industrial Revolution."

in the field of textiles such as e-textiles and wearable technology, artificial intelligence, novel and bio-fabrication, mixed realities, multi-dimensional fabrication, and applications powered by blockchain technologies.

Delving deeper into each of these applications, electronic textiles or "e-textiles" are a fitting transition into a dialogue about traditional and technological crafts. Demonstrating the versatility of textiles, e-textiles combine textiles with electronic components such as lights, sensors, and microcontrollers, enabling outcomes such as active heating and cooling, data capture and transfer, and haptic, visual and aural sensations, among many other purposes and end results.[5] The incredible ability of textiles to be designed out of any material, to be spatially adaptable, not to mention being one of the most accessible and routinely used products, makes them a well-chosen partner to this kinship. It is not just the field of electronics and physical computing that is revolutionizing the practices of textiles, but textiles are influencing the transformations in electronics as well. For instance, Leah Buechley's initial research and explorations around wearable technology gave birth to the LilyPad Arduino e-textile technology kits– a novel sewable microcontroller used for integration with textiles. Buechley's initial explorations and innovations helped to energize an era of Do-It-Yourself electronic textiles in the early 2000s.[6] Through the last couple of decades, the field has witnessed some creative and critical experiments with thermochromic, electromagnetic, photosensitive, motion sensitive, and touch sensitive systems being incorporated with textiles, resulting in outcomes like the wearable computer,[7] knitted radio,[8] thermochromic tapestries that change

---

5   Gernot Ehrmann and Andrea Ehrmann, "Electronic Textiles," *Encyclopedia* 1, no. 1 (2021), 115, https://doi.org/10.3390/encyclopedia1010013.
6   Leah Buechley, "Roadtrip Nation Interview," *Roadtrip Nation*, accessed June 30, 2022, https://roadtripnation.com/leader/leah-buechley.
7   Steve Mann, "Wearable Computing," in *Encyclopedia of Human Computer Interaction*, ed. Mads Soegaard and Rikke Friis Dam, 2nd ed. (Interaction Design Foundation, 2014).
8   Irene Posch, Bundeskanzleramt Österreich, and Land Steiermark, "The Knitted Radio (2014)," *Ebru Kurbak*, June 25, 2014, https://ebrukurbak.net/the-knitted-radio.

color in response to WiFi signals,[9] a wearable suit that senses and informs the wearer of signals from IoT platforms,[10] and countless others examples.

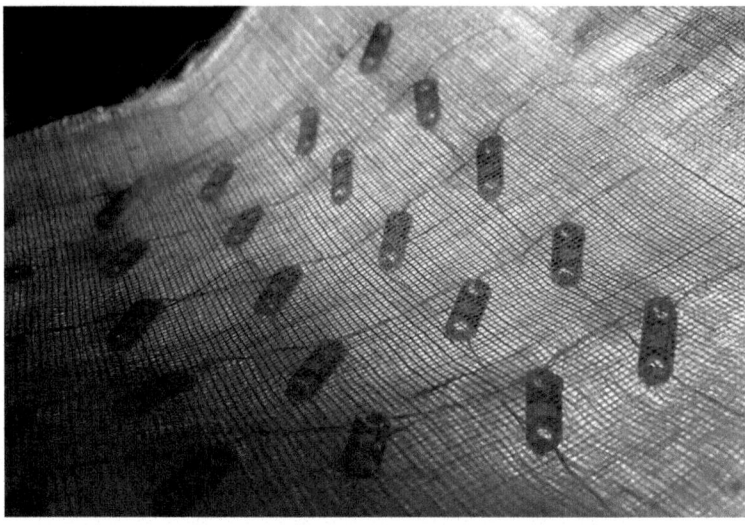

A textile circuit with sewable LED Matrix.[11]

Looking at these progressions, it appears that textiles and their endproducts are being recognized for their functions, in addition to how they look, who they belong to, who they are worn by, or where they come from. In the short span of a couple of decades, the identity of textile crafts went from being recognized for its cultural significance, to being recognized for its functionality. Instead of looking at a fabric and thinking whether an *ikat* fabric is from Indonesia or India, naturally dyed or made with synthetic dyes,

---

9   Ali Morris, "Thermochromic Tapestry Changes Colour in Response to Wi-Fi Signals," *Dezeen*, November 22, 2017, https://www.dezeen.com/2017/11/22/thermochromic-tapestry-changes-colour-response-wifi-signals-richard-vijgen-dutch-design-week.

10 Sophia Brueckner and Rachel Freire, "Embodisuit: A Wearable Platform for Embodied Knowledge," in *Proceedings of the Twelfth International Conference on Tangible, Embedded, and Embodied Interaction*, TEI '18 (New York: Association for Computing Machinery, 2018), 542–48, https://doi.org/10.1145/3173225.3173305.

11 Nishra Ranpura, textile circuit design, 2022.

one now wonders whether it will light up, move, make a sound, or heat up. However, e-textiles, like traditional textiles, are still being identified by what they are made of and what their purpose is. What e-textiles are missing is a sense of belonging and identity that comes with history and nostalgia. The direction of the field of e-textiles going forward, is likely to set the tone of this sense of belongingness. This incites the question of where e-textiles are headed.

While e-textiles have grown tremendously in the last couple of decades, recent developments and speculative innovations in the field are projected to "revolutionize the applications around climate crisis, remote healthcare, athletics and sports, thermoregulation, space investigation, and sensorial experience in real life and the virtual worlds."[12] Thermoregulating textiles have the potential to address the need for energy efficiency, adjusting to extreme weather patterns and combatting increasing energy prices.[13] Heating and cooling textiles can effectively regulate temperature in a localized part of the body, which, when applied against the body's movement, can address the need for self-powering technologies. Studies are also being done to incorporate micro solar panels and piezoelectric materials into textiles to mitigate the need for an external power supply.[14][15] In addition to incorporating components into textiles, the discipline of e-textiles is seeing the creation of fabrics that act as electronic components. "Project Jacquard" by Google's Advanced Technology (ATAP) Lab has developed a collection of conductive threads for weaving touch-responsive textiles like clothing, tablecloths, rugs, or any fabric-based product.[16] The jacquard mechanism makes it flexible enough to incorporate conductive threads onto localized areas, and create a soft circuit during the production process itself. The age-old Jacquard mechanism that inspired modern computers might be laying the groundwork for more revolutionary applications.

---

12   Kunal Mondal, "Recent Advances in Soft E-textiles," *Inventions* 3, no. 2 (2018), 23.
13   Yunsheng Fang, Guorui Chen, Michael Bick, and Jun Chen, "Smart textiles for personalized thermoregulation," *Chemical Society Reviews* 50, no. 17 (2021), 9357–9374.
14   Seyyed Alireza Hashemi, Seeram Ramakrishna, and Armin Gerhard Aberle, "Recent progress in flexible–wearable solar cells for self-powered electronic devices," *Energy & Environmental Science* 13, no. 3 (2020), 685-743.
15   Joshua Edimison, Mark Jones, Zahi Nakad, and Thomas Martin. "Using piezoelectric materials for wearable electronic textiles," in *Proceedings. Sixth International Symposium on Wearable Computers*, 41–48. IEEE, 2002.
16   "Jacquard by Google," accessed July 1, 2022, https://atap.google.com/jacquard.

Some textile designs are becoming hybrid and driving how technology advances. Some examples of textile functionality that drives innovation can be witnessed in health and wellness industries. Localized tracking has tremendous applications in medical fields, and we are already in the midst of an era where fitness trackers and smart watches are widely used. E-textiles that are converted into biofeedback-tracking apparels, have the potential to play a significant part in improving and maintaining health and wellness.[17] Commercial developments of these applications are already underway. E-textile based washable socks can prevent diabetic foot ulcers by monitoring foot temperature.[18] Wearable point-of-care systems can monitor an array of health conditions by tracking ECG, blood pressures, respiration rate, and oxygen saturation.[19] One can basically create a 3D visualization of a body in real time through trillions of data points, by embedding sensors in apparels as a cipher mesh.[20] Similar applications surrounding haptic technologies are also a gateway towards more immersive experiences. In addition to reading feedback from one's body, e-textiles can, more interestingly, provide outputs which signal physio-psychological changes in the form of haptic sensations to make one feel sensations like a hug, a gunshot, anxiety, or a caress.[21]

While it is understandable that commercial applications of e-textiles often place "function" over feelings, form, or fondness, the discipline is not devoid of them altogether. As mentioned earlier, developments with e-textiles are likely to establish a novel culture of hybrid textiles. Researchers, practitioners, and designers such as Laura Devendorf, Leah Buechley, Irene Posch, and Lisa Nakamura have curated a mindful culture around e-textiles that is not just

---

17   Guorui Chen, Xiao, Xun Zhao, Trinny Tat, Michael Bick, and Jun Chen, "Electronic textiles for wearable point-of-care systems," *Chemical Reviews* 122, no. 3 (2021), 3259–3291.

18   Alexander M. Reyzelman, Kristopher Koelewyn, Maryam Murphy, Xuening Shen, E. Yu, Raji Pillai, Jie Fu, Henk Jan Scholten, and Ran Ma, "Continuous temperature-monitoring socks for home use in patients with diabetes: observational study," *Journal Of Medical Internet Research* 20, no. 12 (2018), e12460.

19   Chen et al., "Electronic Textiles For Wearable Point-Of-Care Systems," 3259–3291.

20   Christopher Assad, Michael Wolf, Adrian Stoica, Theodoros Theodoridis, and Kyrre Glette, "BioSleeve: A natural EMG-based interface for HRI," In *2013 8th ACM/IEEE International Conference on Human-Robot Interaction (HRI)*, pp. 69–70. IEEE, 2013.

21   Cati Vaucelle, Leonardo Bonanni, and Hiroshi Ishii. "Design of Haptic Interfaces for Therapy," in *Proceedings of the SIGCHI Conference on Human Factors in Computing Systems*, (2009), 467.

about the electronic function of the textiles, but essentially speaks to the essence and values of crafting. Some discourses explored by these pioneers through their research and practice include thinking about craftspeople as technical collaborators,[22] thinking about making e-textiles accessible to people who are differently abled,[23] looking at indigenous cultures' values and roles in early electronics manufacturing,[24] being mindful about the culture of new tools and machines that are being developed as a result of multidisciplinary practices, and considering the role and history of gender and race in the fields of both textiles and electronics while curating innovations and setting precedents.[25]

The universe of textiles is diverse with different crafts, embodying a myriad of different philosophies. In addition to the processes and materials, craft philosophies are about the cultural and socio-political history, generational knowledge, embodied emotions of struggle and accomplishment experienced by the makers themselves, and the reception of the craft by the users. With e-textiles, it is difficult to hold on to some of the roots of traditional textiles, since functionality is a driving force and that requires major transformations to traditional textile practices, especially in the way textiles are fabricated. Granted, the fabricating process is a significant aspect of a textile's identity. However, whether e-textiles are moving away from the textiles' conventional origins or not, they are certainly on track to developing an identity of their own.

---

22 Laura Devendorf, Katya Arquilla, Sandra Wirtanen, Allison Anderson, and Steven Frost, "Craftspeople as Technical Collaborators: Lessons Learned through an Experimental Weaving Residency," in *Proceedings of the 2020 CHI Conference on Human Factors in Computing Systems* (New York, NY: Association for Computing Machinery, 2020), 1–13, https://doi.org/10.1145/3313831.3376820.

23 Emilie Giles and Janet van der Linden, "Imagining Future Technologies: ETextile Weaving Workshops with Blind and Visually Impaired People," in *Proceedings of the 2015 ACM SIGCHI Conference on Creativity and Cognition*, (New York: Association for Computing Machinery, 2015), 3–12, https://doi.org/10.1145/2757226.2757247.

24 Lisa Nakamura, "Indigenous Circuits: Navajo Women and the Racialization of Early Electronic Manufacture," *American Quarterly* 66, no. 4 (2014), 919–41, https://doi.org/10.1353/aq.2014.0070.

25 Rebecca Stewart, Sophie Skach, and Astrid Bin, "Making Grooves with Needles: Using e-Textiles to Encourage Gender Diversity in Embedded Audio Systems Design," in *Proceedings of the 2018 Designing Interactive Systems Conference*, DIS '18 (New York: Association for Computing Machinery, 2018), 163–72, https://doi.org/10.1145/3196709.3196716.

And, it is only with time and retrospection that one will be able to see where the craft philosophies of e-textiles situate them among textile crafts.

The reliance on time is not only true for emerging textile craft disciplines, but is something that is inherent to textile design. The interrelationship of past and present developments, and relevant future predictions, has a significant part of the commercial textile design industry. It is the reason the majority of textile manufacturers, and home and apparel brands develop and launch seasonal collections. It takes thorough research, analyses and observations, often referred to as trend or forecast analysis, to understand where textile design and the related industries are headed. This space of research largely sets the tone of the future of the textile industry. And the nature of this research space that greatly revolves around analysis has naturally attracted applications associated with artificial intelligence (AI).

AI is usually related to machine-based, computational intelligence. As AI technology becomes increasingly sophisticated, it is penetrating the areas of commerce related to trend analysis, customer services, shopping experiences, and sales analysis. Textile design is also moving into an arena where data-based AI applications are common and creators are looking at a new definition of craftsmanship, one that combines traditional crafts and manual skills with digital intelligence and contemporary manufacturing practices.[26] [27]

Through the intriguing combination of AI and crafts, we have seen developments like robot-made potteries based on machine learning and genetic algorithms,[28] the creation of an "ideal" recipe for a "perfect" India pale ale (IPA),[29] and "The Ultimate AI Masterpiece" where 900 years of art history was projected onto a car, using it as a canvas.[30] With regards to fashion and textiles, AI has been heavily used in digital commerce tools such as wardrobe curation, fit engines, and customized collections based on AI generated trend

---

26 Barbara Silvestri, "The future of fashion: How the quest for digitization and the use of artificial intelligence and extended reality will reshape the fashion industry after COVID-19," *ZoneModa Journal* 10, no. 2 (2020), 61–73.
27 Amit Zoran, "Hybrid craft: showcase of physical and digital integration of design and craft skills," in ACM SIGGRAPH art gallery, (2015), 384–398.
28 Charlotte Nordmoen, "HumanMADE," accessed July 2, 2022, https://www.cnordmoen.com/humanmade.
29 Brauer AI, "Brewing is Science and Art," accessed July 2, 2022, https://www.brauer.ai
30 "Creativity Meets AI: BMW 8 Turned into a Work of Art Using Artificial Intelligence," BMW.com, accessed July 2, 2022, https://www.bmw.com/en/innovation/creative-ai-bmw-8-gran-coupe-art-with-artificial-intelligence.html.

analysis, through a collaboration of fashion brands and technology companies, that involve, but are not limited to Tommy Hilfiger, Gucci, Google, and IBM. This AI based "phygital artisanship" seems like just the beginning.[31] By largely relying on AI for trend forecasting, as opposed to solely relying on traditional methods of market observation and getting insights from the designers and influencers, we are moving toward a future filled with accelerated information updates.

Traditionally, textiles and crafts are a representation of cultural, economic, and political histories of a community. Can AI generated textiles do a better job at representing these histories? After all, it is quite convenient to feed large amounts of information into an algorithm and get accurate outcomes. Perhaps, it is more efficient than traditional and generational crafts. Or, are the embodied experiences of temporalities and materialities more important to the making process than the final representation? What constitutes an embodied making process? There is certainly a growing discourse around automated and virtual crafts.

Kerry Murphy, the founder of the Fabricant, asked, "Should we continue to listen to those voices that say only the physical has merit, that only stuff made from other stuff counts? Or do we move towards new expressions of worth that accept that innovation, creativity and uniqueness can exist in many forms? What we decide now will become our reality."[32] With textile fabrication processes such as weaving or knitting, the time and labor spent on them are substantial parts of their identity. And when it comes to traditional textile dyeing methods like ikat, the skill and efforts involved are necessary for the quality of the craft, and are something that can be difficult to be replicated through automated mediums. In the evolving and overlapping universe of art, craft, design, and technology, where does one place computational textiles?

Digital or simulated textiles, for instance, have been a significant part of textile fabrication processes. In reality, simulated textiles are not a novel concept. Since decades ago, in industrial settings, the technical specifications of textiles have been made on different computer aided design (CAD) software

---

31   IBM Institute for Business Value, "Rethink, reimagine and reinvent the retail store," IBM, accessed March 01, 2023, https://www.ibm.com/downloads/cas/YVLPNBA1.
32   Micky Larosse, "Data: The New Raw Material," *The Fabricant*, accessed July 2, 2022, https://www.thefabricant.com/blog/2019/6/3/mtn2njedjvd12oangslmhzrybrnm52.

that visualize the textile or a replica of it, on screen, while being designed.[33] In addition, the simulated look of the textile has often been used for the design and production purposes. Over time, CAD software has been redesigned and updated to reflect a more realistic look of a fabric. Beginning with simple digital line interlacements showing color and weave, the software capabilities have evolved into simulating different feels and finishes, such as linen, slub, brushed looks, or coated finishes. And today we can find 3D versions of these materials that don't just look realistic, but emulate the real-life physics of material behavior.

A computer aided design (CAD) simulation of a double-cloth (two-layered) fabric along with the actual fabric and its visual inspiration.[34]

However, these programs are not always easily accessible, as licenses cost thousands of dollars, and can generally be only purchased by well-established textile manufacturers. Researchers and developers, such as the Unstable

---

33   Ashis Mitra, "CAD/CAM solution for textile industry: an overview," *International Journal of Current Research and Academic Review* 2, no. 6 (2014), 41–50.
34   Nishra Ranpura, digital textile design, 2016.

Design Lab[35], are developing open-source digital looms to build accessible technical textile specifications with novel user interactions (since conventional CAD software has been made with industrial use cases and settings in mind). The awareness around ownership and distribution rights on digital platforms have encouraged more accessible versions of digital looms. And just like that the value from inherited or acquired knowledge and skill shifts towards accessibility and pedagogy.

In addition to their contribution towards the functional aspects of textile fabrication processes, computational applications have undoubtedly been playing a significant role in redefining the aesthetics of textiles as well. AI's close relationship with generative art and algorithmic patterns is contributing to the aesthetics of textiles in terms of novel weave, knit, and pattern generations. This is creating its own digital world of simulated, often unreal textiles that seem to be textiles on screens, but structurally and physically they might not always fabricate an actual textile. Are we headed towards immaterial materials, which are merely the citizens of virtual worlds unable to exist in the real one?

Given the way the world is experiencing reality in the present times, not much can be said about which materials are supposed to be deemed as more real, the physical or the virtual ones. We spend more time exploring the colors and textures on a screen than in the physical world around us. Perhaps, the immaterial materials on screen, in the various simulated realities, are indeed more real than the tangible ones around us.

X-reality, which encompasses virtual, augmented and any other form of mixed reality simulation, is in a convenient position to thrive, with the metaverse opening gates to numerous trade and commerce opportunities. With actual translations of people's lives into a digital world, and curation of several virtual worlds, x-reality is not only creating representations of one's self, but has given birth to new life forms—"digi-sapiens" and "digi-twins." And an entire generation which is to come is named "generation M" after the "metaverse." Hence, undoubtedly, the world of technology is innovating every day to develop software and applications that best represent the physical materials and lifestyles through their digital counterparts, and that includes fashion and textiles. Whether it is via attempts at accurate fabric simulation through CAD software, or precision in drape and fit through 3D modeling and rendering software, we are close to a stage where there is not much visual

---

35 "Unstable Design," accessed March 1, 2023, https://unstable.design.

difference between the virtual and physical. And when one adds the haptic and other sensorial e-textile applications to it, one could have an exact replica of a fabric made up of pixels, light, and data instead of fibers, dyes and weaves or knits– 'an immaterial material'. A fabric in x-reality is merely a simulacrum. Is a simulacrum an identical representation or a contradiction of the original identity? What is the simulacrum adding to the original fabric, and what is it taking away from it?

The x-reality platforms have opened dialogues around sustainability in the milieu of crafting and making. With limited consumption of energy and resources, easier reproducibility and more efficient modification processes, virtually simulated 'immaterial materials' are getting their own seat at the table. Especially during the COVID-19 pandemic, commercial manufacturing industries have found novel ways of representing their products through digital means, such as digital mapping, virtual showcases, and photoshoots. And while digital versions of products, and especially textiles, are proving their benefits, there are drawbacks as well. While sensorial applications are progressing towards realistic experience, there is still much space left for further developments. Hence, from the ability to familiarly feel, smell and hear an actual fabric, to experiencing how it falls, wrinkles, ages or deteriorates, the digital counterparts of textiles are not a match yet, although they are certainly getting there.

Games such as Minecraft are embodying the crafting essence and exploring the materiality and temporality of making in their own hybrid sensibility and application. Whereas, games such as League of Legends, Fortnite, and Roblox are turning towards expressing representation through in-game customizable and curated digital avatars.[36] Metaverse fashion shows, branded products being sold for the digital avatars, and skin-tone representations in the digital world are redefining the notion of identity.[37] In addition to making hyper-real virtual identities of textiles, can we also give life to them, such as growth, deterioration, wear and tear, and death?

The worlds of x-realities, with multiple versions of existences, are bound to raise provocations around experiential philosophy, and crafted materials,

---

36 Sensor Tower, "Fortnite Mobile Revenue Hits $1 Billion in Two Years," accessed March 01, 2023, https://sensortower.com/blog/fortnite-launch-revenue.

37 Maghan McDowell, "Race, Gender and Representation: The Grey Area of the Metaverse," *Vogue Business*, September 28, 2021, https://www.voguebusiness.com/technology/race-gender-and-representation-the-grey-area-of-the-metaverse.

and textiles are no exception to these provocations. And interestingly, these provocations are not just limited to the simulacra of the x-realities. Just as the x-realities are trying to imitate the physical realities, the physical realities are undoubtedly manifesting the digital and computational data into tangible forms as well. The innovation in the field of 3D modeling and printing is one such example where the physical world gets its forms from the intangible world of computation and simulation.

The advent of 3D printers has made great strides in the realm of 3D fabrication. It opened avenues for customization, sustainability, on-demand production, and structural innovation.[38]

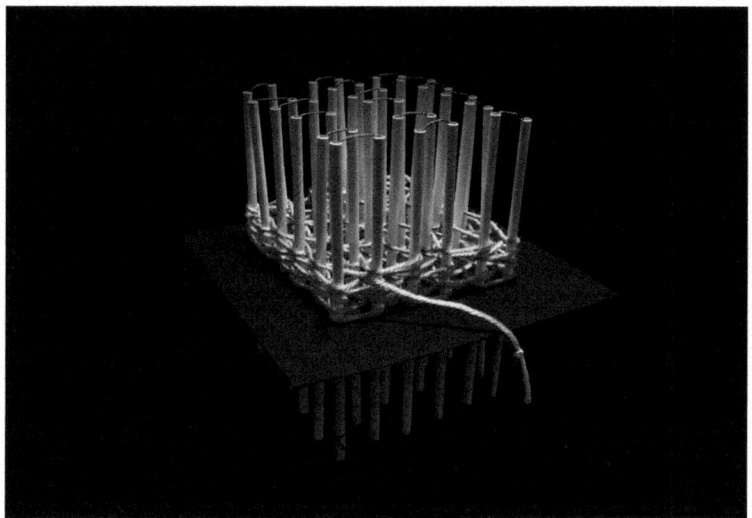

Explorations of 3D lattice interlacements on a handmade 3D loom.[39]

---

38 Nurhalida Shahrubudin, Te Chuan Lee, and R. J. P. M. Ramlan, "An overview on 3D printing technology: Technological, materials, and applications." *Procèdia Manufacturing* 35 (2019), 1286–1296.
39 Nishra Ranpura, 3D lattice interlacements, design, 2021.

3D printing started to rise in the world of fashion and textiles through the works of one of the pioneers of the field, Iris Van Harpen, around 2010.[40] While electronic textiles are making great strides into creating the applications comfortable and practical as wearables, some artists and designers of haute couture fashion such as Iris Van Harpen and Behnaz Farahi introduced the potential of 3D printed textiles and kinetic wearable fabrication. And the application of 3D fabrics extends to knit machines that can create finely detailed seamless garments from yarns in a short amount of time.[41] The efficiency in terms of resource consumption, waste reduction, time, and labor seems quite promising, which is why research is being carried out in terms of different materials and weave/knit structures to test strength, movement, and durability. From 3D printed tissue engineering,[42] 3D printed organs for product testing instead of animal testing, to 3D woven structures being strong and flexible enough to be used for outer shoe soles, the potential for interlaced dimensional fabrication is enormous.

Dimensional fabrication also holds an interesting space between virtual and physical materials– a hybrid space driven by crafting through automation. Autonomously fabricated 3D materials speak volumes about one's understanding of the concept of evolution of materials– a material crafted by machines. What does it mean to have an "embodied machine experience"? Can there be other forms of embodied experiences that are devoid of humans?

While thinking about novel means of fabrication, it is important to note that technologies are not just restricted to man-made, and machine-oriented applications. The future (or perhaps already the present) is seen as a collective. "Collective Intelligence"– multiple forms of knowledge, whether human, technological, or ecological– is opening new ways of thinking, and eventually making. The truth about the planet not belonging to the humans is dawning on us as we realize the presence of and learn from the intelligences of the machines that surround us and are made by us, and the nature that

---

40   Helen McCormick, Ran Zhang, Rosy Boardman, Celina Jones, and Claudia E. Henninger. "3D-Printing in the Fashion Industry: A Fad or the Future?" *Technology-Driven Sustainability: Innovation in the Fashion Supply Chain* (2020), 137–154.

41   James McCann, Lea Albaugh, Vidya Narayanan, April Grow, Wojciech Matusik, Jennifer Mankoff, and Jessica Hodgins. "A compiler for 3D machine knitting," *ACM Transactions on Graphics* (TOG) 35, no. 4 (2016), 1–11.

42   Mohsen Akbari et al., "Textile Technologies and Tissue Engineering: A Path Toward Organ Weaving," *Advanced Healthcare Materials* 5, no. 7 (April 6, 2016), 751–66, https://doi.org/10.1002/adhm.201500517.

has always been around, will be around even after we are gone, and that we so blatantly overlooked. While we attempt to situate ourselves amidst multiple intelligences to understand our identity here, we are simultaneously learning from and collaborating with these intelligences.

With Anthropocene anxiety, we are turning towards more conscious textile fabrications. Bio-fabricated textiles are cultivated from mycelium, living bacteria, yeast, algae, and plant-derived materials under engineered conditions.[43] Ecovative, Bolt Threads, MycoWorks (US), Mycotech Lab (Indonesia) are some of the leading innovators in the field of bio-fabricated textiles today. We are already looking at mycelium leathers,[44] leathers and cotton made in labs that do not harm animals and consume less resources,[45] fine mycelium bags using biotechnology, and fruit waste fabrics.[46] Mycelium is already becoming a vegan alternative to leather, and is impacting not just consumer mindset but also the economy. The DNA of textiles and fabrications is being transformed. In addition to mycelium, leather made from collagen brewed from fermented yeast,[47] lab-grown cell-based fur,[48] recombinant silk made by adding silk genes into yeast and bacterial via fermentation,[49] and nanocellulose "tree-free" rayon from fruit waste are some examples of bio-fabricated materials aimed to be used as textiles.

---

43 Valentina Rognoli, Bruna Petreca, Barbara Pollini, and Carmen Saito, "Materials biography as a tool for designers' exploration of bio-based and bio-fabricated materials for the sustainable fashion industry," *Sustainability: Science, Practice and Policy* 18, no. 1 (2022): 749–772.

44 Simon Vandelook, Elise Elsacker, Aurélie Van Wylick, Lars De Laet, and Eveline Peeters, "Current state and future prospects of pure mycelium materials," *Fungal Biology and Biotechnology* 8, no. 1 (2021), 1–10.

45 Amber Dance, "Engineering the animal out of animal products," *Nature Biotechnology* 35, no. 8 (2017), 704–708.

46 Eldy S. Lazaro Vasquez and Katia Vega. "Myco-accessories: sustainable wearables with biodegradable materials" in Proceedings of the 2019 *ACM International Symposium on Wearable Computers*, 306.

47 Vasquez and Vega, "Myco-accessories: sustainable wearables with biodegradable materials," 306–307; "Modern Meadow," Modern Meadow, accessed July 2, 2022, https://www.modernmeadow.com.

48 Vasquez and Vega, "Myco-accessories: sustainable wearables with biodegradable materials," 307; "Furoid," CellAgri, accessed July 2, 2022, https://www.cell.ag/furoid.

49 Vasquez and Vega, "Myco-accessories: sustainable wearables with biodegradable materials."

"The Weaver," an installation visualizing the embodied motion of back-and-forth weaving.[50]

Biotechnology has, of course, always been a part of the textile design processes. From dyes extracted from plants and flowers, to yarns extracted from animals and insects, biotechnology has inherently been part of the fabrication process even before modern technology. These bio-fabrication applications provide some elegant examples of evolution in textiles. The remarkable developments in the fields of microbiology, and nanotechnology, have only furthered the established practices of biotechnology in the textile industries. It does make one wonder how subjectivity impacts one's notion of identity. If one is adjusted to the idea of textiles being made of plastic, animal and even human hair, or silk from an insect, mycelium or yeast-based textiles simply seem like another step. On the other hand, the notion of digitally simulated textiles being considered as textile crafts raises debates, due to a little less exposure to that provocation. And this philosophy also resonates with the essence of the crafting process—the repetition and variation. Whether it is the act of weaving where the shuttle moves back and forth repeatedly with variations to form different weaves, or the act of sewing where the

---

50   Nishra Ranpura, photograph of installation, 2022.

needle repeats the same process of going up and down at different points, the act of repetition creates fondness and the instances of variation preserves curiosity. Whatever the thought might be that lets one situate emerging textile crafts' identity, the technological transformations are not only influencing and evolving the textiles directly, but indirectly as well by contributing to the systems of textile design and production.

Speaking of production systems, blockchain technology is the next in line of these many applications impacting the traditional definitions in the field of craft and textiles. Blockchain technology is proving to be a useful tool, for the purposes of transparency and traceability. It provides an opportunity to "show the work" while considering the raw materials used in the process of making. The process of tracing and tracking in a production and supply-chain cycle provides an agency to the materials involved. It certainly gives accountability to the participants as well. One can know from which farm the cotton of their shirt has been produced, or which community assembled the denim jacket they have been wearing. Furthermore, digital signatures can be a useful tool to give the artisans a space to claim ownership as creators, rather than merely be anonymous producers in the fabrication process. However, there are certainly drawbacks to the use of blockchain technologies including but not limited to environmental concerns of data mining, privacy, accessibility, speed, and scalability.[51] Regardless of the shortcomings of blockchain technologies, aside from contributing to the logistical and transactional operations, can blockchain technology create a significant difference in textile and craft industries? In which ways can blockchain technology and digital signatures prove to be a source of security for ownership?

How are these emerging applications, at large, influencing, reaffirming, and challenging our understanding of textiles crafts? From questioning the shift in embodiment within the making processes, to embracing novel materials and tools, the deliberations over how technological transformations take the textile crafts forward could be never ending.

---

51 Koppiahraj Karuppiah, Bathrinath Sankaranarayanan, and Syed Mithun Ali, "A decision-aid model for evaluating challenges to blockchain adoption in supply chains," *International Journal of Logistics Research and Applications* (2021): 1-22.

Is there a conclusion?

While the thoughts shared and questions posed throughout the chapter are not simple or easy, these are necessary provocations to consider as we move forward into a time where lines between different disciplines are blurring. It is not just the identities of humans that are overcoming the binary notions, but the identities of our creations as well. The journey of textiles and technologies often go hand-in-hand, providing us with new mediums, inspirations, guides, and tools, along with challenges, lessons, and failures. The process of crafting textile identities involves multiple parties: designers and makers, consumers, materials, tools, and their narratives. Eventually, it is up to us to determine whether emerging technologies are moving away from the identity of textiles, or whether they are being preserved and evolved through these technologies.[52]

---

[52] This is a brief exploration of the effects of emerging technologies in the field of textiles, and is in no way exhaustive. There are countless discourses around these technologies and multi-disciplinary practices (inside and outside the scope of this chapter) worth thinking about but not included here, such as reuse and recycle challenges of e-textiles, lack of maker-bias in AI generated, dimensionally fabricated textiles, or pedagogical applications of digital looms, amongst others.

Part 2: Case Studies and Interviews on Educational Processes and Practices

Design for Future Skills
Three Case Studies on the Role of Design in Shaping the Narrative of Technology Education

Serena Cangiano[1]

If we could ask an AI to sketch the cover of a report on the future of education, it would probably be a classroom full of students in the process of learning "coding" or an apocalyptic world where there is no need for human workers, thanks to fully automated factories with robotics arms. This is what the AI could probably see if it would process all the pictures on the web and get across the last two industrial revolutions, two events that brought a rather positive narrative on the impact of digital technologies on human life: we will all become programmers or data scientists who use algorithms, machines, and data to make almost anything. Today, we could speculate that this positive narrative is driving the agenda on the digital transformation in education in every economy in the world: digital skills development is seen as a solution to the high demand for professionals who know "how to code." This narrative is rarely accompanied by reflections on how new technologies could reinforce social inequity or how their adoption can take place only if it is connected to a social change.
— *Dr. Serena Cangiano, Switzerland*

---

1   SUPSI University of Applied Science and Arts of Southern Switzerland, Design Institute /FabLab, Switzerland.

From Art and Design Pedagogy to Technology Education for Creatives: An Introduction to the Opening of the Codes of Creation

In the late 1950s and early 1960s, Hungarian artist Victor Vasarely created *Planetary Folklore Participations*, a series of art pieces that people could buy as Do-It-Yourself (DIY) kits to be assembled. These works were made of colored plastic blocks that could be combined to create an infinite number of compositions and images. Each work was sold in a packaging similar to the one of board games, which contained the kit's components and the operating instructions, namely a manual explaining the rules of the visual alphabet designed by Vasarely. Vasarely invented *Planetary Folklore* to describe his work and his vision of a universal aesthetic for the masses. This vision was based on a teaching methodology patented by Vasarely himself in 1959: through the messages encoded by the artist, the viewer understands the principles and conceptual aspects related to the artist's perspective on art and architecture.[2] Influenced by the discoveries of Gestalt psychology, cybernetics, and astrophysics, Vasarely developed research that introduced concepts for the democratization of art: his *Plastic Alphabet* series consisted of a grid that established a modular relationship between shapes and colors.

Vasarely's research pointed to the creation of a visual programming language *ante litteram* that allowed the generation of infinite variations of shapes and colors to create unique works. During the same years, in Italy, the artist and designer Bruno Munari also contributed to the opening of creativity and design for all. With his laboratories called *Giocare con l'arte* (Playing with art) organized at the Pinacoteca di Brera in Milan in 1977, he presented a set of activities and materials to stimulate young children's development who would experience art through visual languages rather than with words. Munari's contribution as a designer to the domain of pedagogy expanded to books for children such as *Le Macchine di Munari* (Munari's Machines), in which fictional machines are combined with everyday life objects through the medium of fantasy: for example, a machine to tame the alarm clock.[3] Through the 1970s, he also worked on a series of products for the Italian design firm Danese called *Strutture* (Structures), a kit of sixty-five combination cards, sixty of which

---

2   Victor Vasarely, *Planetary Folklore Participations No. 1 (1960–1969)*, 1973, Sculpture, 20 × 20 in, 1973, Lions Gallery, https://www.artsy.net/artwork/victor-vasarely-planetary-folklore-participations-no-1.
3   Bruno Munari, *Le macchine di Munari*, Einaudi, Torino, 1942.

were printed on a transparent surface and could be laid one over the other to determine an image through superimposition. The idea was to stimulate the analysis of structures and components through a playful activity and support the development of children's combinatorial abilities. In another kit named *Labirinto trasformabile in mille altri giochi* (Labyrinth convertible in a thousand other games), he presented the same concepts of combinability with graphic modules: a board game consisting of a wooden base with grooves to insert cards that featured abstract patterns to allow children to transform the space according to their fantasy. Combinability, modularity, and experience were at the core of the learning experiences proposed by Munari.[4]

These concepts were strongly connected to Jean Piaget's Constructivism theory and later became the ingredients of the Constructionism movement initiated by Seymour Papert. The latter was a pioneer of artificial intelligence and computer science education, and his work focused on the idea that intelligence is situated, connected, and sensitive to the variations of the environment. Actually, Papert draws our attention to the fact that "diving into" situations rather than looking at them from a distance is a powerful means of understanding.[5] With the Logo Programming Language and its integration in the Logo turtle, one of the first educational robots ever invented, Papert became the father of modern STEM (Science, Technology, Engineering, and Math) education as he highlighted how the development of tools like the Logo turtle should embed the idea of children mastering a technology instead of being passive users, and the integration of science and technology (and play) to simplify and overcome the fear of learning complex subjects in mathematics. In his influential book *Mindstorms*, Papert describes his contemporary times as a "culture that makes science and technology alien to the vast majority of people," where students grow up thinking that devices like robots belong to "the others."[6] This idea of transforming kids into active users rather than passive consumers of technology is at the core of the most diffused coding

---

4 Alberto Munari, "Bruno Munari The Surpriser," in *Giro Giro Tondo / Design for Children*, ed. by Silvana Annicchiarico (Milan: Mondadori Electa, 2017), 204–5.

5 Edith Ackermann, "Piaget's Constructivism, Papert's Constructionism: What's the Difference?," *Future of Learning Group Publication* 5, no. 3 (January 1, 2001), 438.

6 Seymour A. Papert, *Mindstorms: Children, Computers, And Powerful Ideas*, 2nd ed. (New York: Basic Books, 1993), 4.

initiative developed by Mitchel Resnik, the inventor of Scratch, the free visual programming language that introduces children to computer science.[7]

This idea of helping people to understand and use technology has been the most important lesson shared by the pioneers of computer science teaching. Those principles have been later adopted in design and art education. In the last two decades, computational artists and designers have developed original tools and methods for teaching technology to non-experts and new narratives around digital skills development in creative contexts. In 2001, Ben Fry and Casey Reas released the first version of *Processing*, the open-source sketch environment for generative graphics. Their idea was to combine the visual principles of design with ways of thinking about systems derived from computer science approaches.[8] *Processing*, together with its community of users, could be defined as one of the first user experience design contributions to the domain of computer science teaching as it provides a simplified interface and a set of resources and best practices that allow non-expert people to create artifacts with coding. *Processing* enabled the growth of a creative technology movement by empowering creatives to learn technology for creative purposes or with a critical mindset. As Casey Reas stated, coding is a way of thinking and a humanist activity, not a technical skill.[9] With this perspective, software literacy could reduce the separation between people and technology.

The same year, in a small village in the north of Italy, during an international interaction design program at the Interaction Design Institute of Ivrea IDII, the need to open the black box of embedded technologies and electronic devices determined the release of one of the most impactful platforms for learning technology with the Arduino board. The project started with the release of open hardware, a microprocessor that simplifies the programming of interactive behaviors through sensors and actuators.[10] Later, it became a larger ecosystem made out of software and hardware solutions and a global community that collaborates and develops interactive items,

---

7   Scratch, "Scratch – Imagine, Program, Share," accessed June 28, 2022, https://scratch.mit.edu.

8   Casey Reas and Ben Fry, "A Modern Prometheus," *Processing Foundation*, June 8, 2018, https://medium.com/processing-foundation/a-modern-prometheus-59aed94abe85.

9   Serena Cangiano, "Coding as a Way of Thinking — Interview with Casey Reas," *Progetto Grafico*, December 16, 2016, https://medium.com/progetto-grafico/coding-as-a-way-of-thinking-interview-with-casey-reas-cbb9ecdbb980.

10 Massimo Banzi and Michael Shiloh, *Make: Getting Started with Arduino*, 3rd ed. (Maker Media, Incorporated, 2008).

from educational tools to open manufacturing systems and art installations. The Arduino project board is a case study of bottom-up innovation and the results of a pedagogical design process addressing the future skills of designers in the domain of coding and electronics. This challenge was already tackled by products, kits, and toys in the early sixties if we take as an example the Raytheon Lectron, produced by the German company Egger with a design contribution by Dieter Rams.[11] In the early 2000s, technology education initiatives moved the focus from the educational product to a global movement to empower people by simplifying and opening technology. These two initiatives addressed innovation in education and technology skills development through new propositions that inspired global movements of change-makers in technology education.

Three Case Studies

With the above brief excursus, it is possible to draw a line that connects the design disciplines with transformations in technology education, from the history of computer science education to contemporary days. This line shows that the role of the design agency has always been somehow to critically investigate technology impact as well as empower people by creating inclusive interfaces to relate to technological innovation. By following this line, this section presents three case studies of applied research projects aimed to question and define the role of design and its impact in digital transformation in education.[12] The first case study, the Ethafa Steammians Kit, tackles the issue of the gender gap in technology education. The second case study, project TAC Technology Ambient and Competences, proposes hands-on journeys in data literacy for primary school teachers and students. The last one, titled Untouched, introduces experiments and the implications of teaching machine learning to designers faced with the global challenges derived from Covid-19. These three projects present a different perspective on technology education and help in interpreting the role of design in reshaping the narrative around future skills development.

---

11 The Universe of the Lectron System, "What is the Lectron System," accessed June 28, 2022, https://lectron.info.
12 The projects were carried out from 2017 to 2020 by the research team of the Interaction Design Research unit of the Design Institute at SUPSI University in Switzerland.

The Ethafa Steammians Kit

The miniaturization of sensors and actuators and the growth of computing power allow the development of ludic devices that teach science and technology to children through tangible interfaces, connected applications, robots, mobile apps, AI, and cognitive toys. Global movements like the Maker Movement are advocating the application of methods and tools that consider STEM education a pivotal approach to teaching almost anything. Start-up companies are also working to deliver this promise by introducing into the toy market new educational kits that address, in particular, the playful learning of coding and robotics through the application of ideas and principles, very close to Seymour Papert's research. From initiatives that introduce young kids to robot programming through a simple robot with wheels to physical toys to teaching computational thinking to preschool kids, many platforms have been made available to empower a new generation of digital makers.[13] A *maker education* ecosystem started growing promoting hands-on approaches to learning almost everything. The maker education has been generated by a political context: back in 2014, US president Barack Obama launched the initiative "A Nation of Makers," aiming to provide many more students, entrepreneurs, and citizens access to a new class of technologies to design, build, and manufacture just about anything, as well as increased access to mentors, spaces, and resources to support them in the making.[14] It was a moment of great enthusiasm for new production technologies, particularly 3D printing and its promise of sustainable and distributed manufacturing.[15] It was a decade where we have probably witnessed the most prolific collaboration between bottom-up movements, design and entrepreneurship actors, and innovative policymakers on the challenge of digital skills development. Nevertheless, some key issues remained unsolved and underestimated. One of these is the gender gap in STEM education.

---

13 Sue Sentance, Jane Waite, Steve Hodges, and Emily MacLeod, and Lucy Yeomans, "'Creating Cool Stuff': Pupils' Experience of the BBC Micro:Bit," in *Proceedings of the 2017 ACM SIGCSE Technical Symposium on Computer Science Education*, SIGCSE '17, (New York, NY: Association for Computing Machinery, 2017), 531–36, https://doi.org/10.1145/30176 80.3017749.

14 The White House, "The First White House Maker Faire," accessed June 28, 2022, https://obamawhitehouse.archives.gov/node/316486.

15 The Economist, "The Third Industrial Revolution," April 21, 2012, https://www.economist.com/leaders/2012/04/21/the-third-industrial-revolution.

Even if trends show that women employment in science and engineering in Europe is growing, the percentage of women in Information and Communication Technology (ICT) careers still remains below 2 percent of women's total share in the European labor market.[16] According to recent research, the reasons can be found in the overall academic environment and in the educational resources offered. In fact, many female students are not interested in the educational material provided but still have to work with it.[17]

From primary schools to universities, tools play a key role in how the learning experience is usually distributed. In general, they are designed to be genderless, but the learning environments combined with the overall technology culture still discourage girls from engaging with it, limiting the opportunities in their development. Starting from this issue, some questions arise. How do we design STEM learning experiences that could help create girl-friendly environments? How do we reduce the gender gap and engage more girls as early as in primary school in order to stimulate their positive attitude towards STEM careers? And finally, how do we create educational resources that support these more inclusive experiences?

The Ethafa Steammians Kit started as a graduate project that explored how interaction design could contribute to filling the gender gap in technology education. Initiated as a thesis at the Master's Degree program in Interaction Design at the SUPSI University in Switzerland, it has been developed as an entrepreneurial project that promotes a design-driven approach to electronics and science learning.

The kit design simplifies the interaction with the Arduino board for kids from nine to twelve years. It uses a physical interface consisting of a printed circuit board with embedded sensors that allow it to capture data from the environment (light, colors, sounds) and triggers some digital contents accessible via a tablet application in real-time. This application supports the experience with science resources and stories. The kit embodies, moreover,

---

16 Zacharias C. Zacharia, Tasos Hovardas, Nikoletta Xenofontos, Ivoni Pavlou, and Maria Irakleous, "Education and Employment of Women in Science, Technology and the Digital Economy, Including AI and Its Influence on Gender Equality," European Parliament, April 15, 2020, https://www.europarl.europa.eu/thinktank/en/document/IPOL_STU(2020)651042.

17 Shao-Na Zhou, Hui Zeng, Shao-Rui Xu, Luc-Chang Chen, and Hua Xiao, "Exploring Changes In Primary Students' Attitudes Towards Science, Technology, Engineering And Mathematics (STEM) Across Genders And Grade Levels," *Journal of Baltic Science Education* 18, no. 3 (2019), 466–80, https://doi.org/10.33225/jbse/19.18.466.

a cute alien who guides kids into STEAM subjects (Science, Technology, Engineering, Art, and Math). Eolim, a biologist, invites the users to join him in his adventures and learn about nature on Planet Earth. To learn and later advance in the story, children have to create a circuit and use it to measure, for example, environmental data in their surroundings.

Beyond the specific features of the physical kit, the Ethafa Steammians Kit proposed product development based on the participation of practitioners and educators in co-design sessions with the goal of creating additional didactic activities with a specific focus on:

- How children can learn about technology through exploratory activities that do not require the use of a keyboard and a mouse;
- How children can learn technology and science subjects through activities that are based on stories. In fact, the story-led approach was chosen as it is proven that students usually learn more, remember concepts in the long term, and overcome intimidation or anxiety when they face complex and new subjects through stories;[18]
- How the story-led didactic activities can transfer basic notions on electronics and circuit making when they are built both on references to the children's specific context and culture.

Tested in several workshops held in Maker and Fablab-related events, the Ethafa Steammians Kit is a framework used to design the didactic activities proposed as an ecological approach to technology education in which the learning experience triggers the development of multiple skills, from problem-solving to collaboration. This approach promoted a different discourse around technology through the use of materials that, by design, allowed teachers and children to experience technology as less intimidating and as a medium to understand various phenomena in their physical environments. It also helped to solve problems close to their everyday life and local culture. This perspective focuses on how children's development with technology materials could (or should) lead them to become active digital citizens with critical thinking skills rather than just the future workforce of the technology industry. Bringing these aspects as early as in primary school programs helps to create learning

---

18 New York University, "The Purpose of Stories," accessed June 28, 2022, https://www.nyu.edu/content/nyu/en/faculty/teaching-and-learning-resources/strategies-for-teaching-with-tech/storytelling-teching-and-learning/the-purpose-of-stories.

experiences that are less intimidating for girls, and it also helps all genders to develop other crucial twenty-first-century skills such as emotional intelligence and collaboration skills, to name a few, that are rarely put at the center of STEM educational tool use.

Ethafa Steammians Kit.[19]

Project TAC Technology Ambient Competences: Data Literacy for the Active Citizenship Development

In the education field, digitalization is usually portrayed as a classroom of the future: a space equipped with advanced tools such as virtual reality sets, smart boards, and smart tables. In parallel, the need for more professionals in ICT and innovation promotes another image in which schools become factories where to train the next generation of tech-savvy workers thanks to the introduction of computer science classes. Even if there is an increasing demand for adapting the competencies to future jobs in the technological fields such as data analysis, AI, or robotics, primary or secondary school programs in developed countries still struggle to bring computers and coding classes into their curricula. In this polarized landscape where tech companies sell

---

19   Ethafa, Photograph of the Ethafa Steammians Kit, 2021.

hardware and services to educational organizations and governments and, on the other side, school teachers require the right pace to update their skills, civic tech initiatives provide a critical dialogue on the need for ecological and more social-driven perspectives to propel digital transformation in education. From citizen science to smart citizens' actions, global bottom-up innovation movements are proposing alternative approaches to the use of technology in education. New learning models are emerging, and trying to reconnect students with their societal context and personal development as citizens. Connected learning, for example, proposes a learning model in which students pursue a personal interest or a passion, a link to what they are learning and their interests to academic achievement, career success, or civic engagement.[20]

A relevant field of application for these fresh approaches is environmental monitoring: low-cost sensors and web platforms that allow non-experts to collect and interpret the environment's data so that they can learn more about it. Better environmental education through the use of data and technologies encourages more attentive and sustainable behaviors. Within civic environmental monitoring initiatives, for example, young people usually get in contact with sensing technologies as active users, and they learn how electronics and sensors work, how to build devices, and about participating as citizen scientists in environmental monitoring campaigns. As the paradigm of IoT and connected devices is becoming increasingly pervasive in our daily environment, this approach prevents young students from experiencing these technology trends passively. However, to be effectively implemented, it requires innovative teaching approaches and tools that overcome technological complexity and create learning experiences that help make sense of the collected data through hands-on, inclusive, playful, and collaborative sessions.

The project TAC introduced primary school children to environmental data sensing related to their urban environment through a learning experience based on the use of context-based tools. In general, the goal was to introduce the concepts of IoT and data literacy as early as the primary school level to experiment with formats that focus on digital citizenship skills rather than scientific data collection techniques. The project involved five elementary schools (pupils in fourth grade) and six teachers in pilot sessions to facilitate the integration of new civic tech formats and tools in

---

20 Connected Learning Alliance, "About Connected Learning," accessed June 28, 2022, https://clalliance.org/about-connected-learning.

the official school curriculum. It was a multi-stakeholder project that involved one municipality (the City of Lugano, Switzerland), five elementary schools, two private companies (Arduino.cc and Swisscom), and a research laboratory. The challenge was to design a process to validate the design of the educational activities and the hardware and software tools to be used.

The municipality had a vision to create a collaborative ecosystem of tools and a set of methods to connect with the civic society and engage it through sensing technologies. This required careful consideration about the needs of various stakeholders, including the school system, teachers, and students. For the school system, the design process had to consider the official curriculum guidelines, which required introducing technologies in the classroom only as a medium to learn something and not as a subject itself. To ensure the success of this approach, the teachers' technology skills and expertise had to be taken into account to define a professional development program on IoT and sensing technologies, and a co-design technique had to be implemented to collaboratively define the didactic activities. Additionally, the students' age and cognitive skills development during the fourth grade had to be considered to ensure the activities were age-appropriate and suitable for the students' level of understanding.

The requirements to design the project's pedagogical framework were defined in collaboration with the school directors and the learning researchers in order to make it compatible with the official curriculum guidelines. In an attempt to avoid a technological focus and to put the students at the center, the framework focused on developing key competencies such as exploring specific realities and collecting information, as well as transferring the fundamental concepts and processes of the scientific method. A major emphasis was also placed on the development of skills in the use of new technologies, particularly sensors connected to an IoT network. This experience allowed students to understand technology beyond the classic images of smartphones, video games, and the web. Additionally, the framework highlighted the need to foster the development of environmental awareness in relation to citizens' behaviors and the urban context, which is crucial for understanding and improving our environment.

TAC student kit, prototype version 0.1. The student kit supports outdoor activities where, for example, children measure and confront the data of sunny and shady areas in the school garden.[21]

Following the mapping of needs, the development of the project was focused on analyzing the technical requirements to support a smooth user experience. In order to gather and analyze data about the environment, this project utilizes three key components: the TAC Node, the Kit, and the Web App. The TAC Node is a localized device that features a GPS module, a sound meter (microphone), a PM10 sensor, a humidity and temperature sensor, and a

---

21   Claudia Cossu Fomiatti and SUPSI, Photograph of TAC Technology Ambient Competences student kit, 2021.

light sensor. This device is used to gather real-time and continuous data from a specific location, enabling comparisons among different locations. The Kit is a portable device with the shape of a green figure, it includes a humidity sensor, a temperature sensor, and a light sensor, which can be used to gather data in various locations. The Web App, a web-based application for tablets, features an interactive map and the data captured by the Nodes and the Kits. The data is then visualized through interactive graphs, making it easy to understand and interpret the data. Together, these components provide a comprehensive and effective way to gather and analyze environmental data.

Through the use of design thinking templates, the teachers co-created an open syllabus, namely an open collection of ideas on educational activities that had been implemented and tested in the classroom. Over a period of three months, the tools and the activities were tested and the co-design process allowed the identification of overall barriers and opportunities. In particular, it emerged that more diversified, hackable, and expandable devices helped the teachers with varied technology skills, or no technology skills at all, to carry out such kinds of activities. To conclude, the project TAC highlighted how educational initiatives based on the collaboration of multiple stakeholders, from schools to companies, could help create the conditions for the long-term development of an educational tool that evolves according to the new needs of the ecosystem actors and can be openly maintained without the risk of the technology obsolescence or a possible discontinued production.

Untouched ML-based spaces to enable citizens' interactions in the post-pandemic

Artificial intelligence and, more specifically, machine learning technologies strongly shape how people interact with today's online services. New types of intelligent artifacts are already embedded in our mobile devices and are unlocking interaction approaches that were unthinkable just a few years ago. Beyond the design of digital assistants and bots, AI and ML technologies are pushing for a paradigmatic change where the interaction patterns based on the logic of "If-this-then-that" are replaced by user experiences based on models for "training-supervising-classifying" that allow a highly personalized control over a technological product. In this context, designers can be the protagonists of such a digital transformation in which their role is to make algorithms more transparent or even programmable by the end-user.

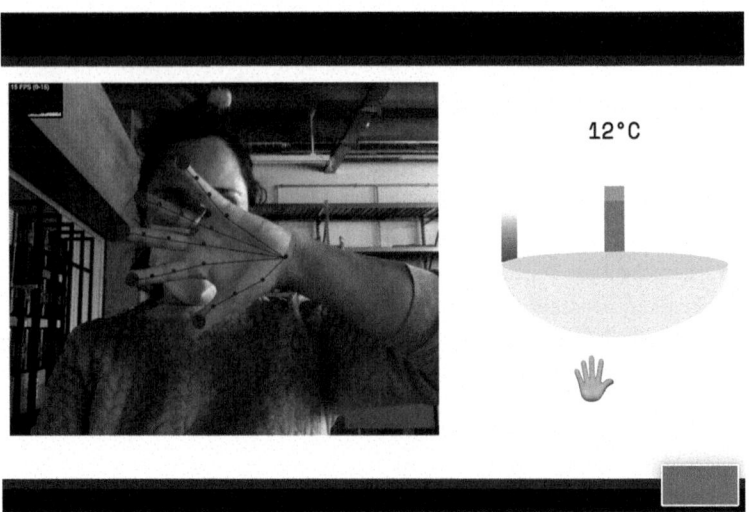

Screenshot from the web-based prototype "Untouched" by Tim Pulver and Oliver Brückner accessible at untouched.timpulver.com. Using Tensorflow.js Handpose5 it detects key points of the hand and its horizontal position. Once detected, the user can form a fist to "grab" the slider and then move it along the axis to adjust the temperature. Ambient lighting behind the sink indicates the current temperature and slider range.[22]

In February 2021, within the project "Untouched ML-based spaces to enable citizens' interactions in the post-pandemic," a series of creative technology sessions were carried out to experiment with designing interactive experiences that dealt with the redesign of touch interfaces in public spaces. One core goal of the project was the definition of an experimental online setup for supporting young students, designers, and researchers to ideate and prototype original interfaces using recent tools for programming applications based on machine learning algorithms. The sessions involved participants with different backgrounds, including design students, interaction design practitioners, developers, and researchers who engaged in long-distance ideation and a prototyping workshop that ran over a Discord server. After an introduction to the fundamental concepts of machine learning through case studies and simplified infographics that represented how neural networks

---

22 Tim Pulver and Oliver Brückner and SUPSI, image of web-based prototype, 2023.

work, the participants were introduced to the use of open-source tools that enabled designers and artists to develop applications with intelligent algorithms such as ml5.js.

The ideation phase was guided by the following design brief: How to let people interact in physical spaces without touching surfaces? How to design gesture-based interfaces by taking into account cultural specificities and biases?

The results of the program were concepts and prototypes of services and installations in public spaces that mostly used face and gesture recognition, for instance, a system for accessing a shared mailbox through a custom password made with hand gestures. Another key outcome was the release of a library that taught the algorithm how to recognize hand gestures that run in the browser.[23] During the project development, many considerations were documented and, in particular, many design opportunities were envisioned considering interaction scenarios in which the users can personalize the way they interact with a device (i.e., custom gestures for opening a mailbox) according to their abilities, as well as their culture (i.e., the use of face masks).

In this project, design approaches and creative technology practices highlighted how unusual challenges such as Covid-19 required a reflection on how to use AI technologies to improve the users' skills in the interactive experience. The possibility of understanding how the system works is, in fact, the fundamental aspect of the interaction since the users have to design their own language of interaction with the machine. This represents a change of perspective for the designers since they have to apply new methods to evaluate the experience and, more in detail, the level of adoption of a solution in different cultural contexts.

Design should focus on changing the narrative around technology, but how?

As Jennifer Gabry points out in her book *Citizen of Worlds* "while citizen-oriented technologies might promise a straightforward realization of positive political change, they rarely yield such effortless or liberatory outcomes when

---

23   Tim Pulver and Olivier Brückner, "Untouched: Faucet," accessed June 28, 2022, https://untouched.timpulver.com.

put into practice."[24] This sentence helps to realistically think about the role of the design agency in the domain of technology education. Should it focus on the release of new toolkits to inform a new narrative? Or should it work as a mediator of collaborative bottom-up innovation processes?

From new tools for data literacy development and inclusive technology education, to the use of machine learning algorithms to create interactive experiences that empower the users, the three case studies helped us to identify how design can really have an impact on future skills development. In the first place, a critical reflection emerges and it is required to move the focus from the release of new tools to the co-creation of inclusive learning environments, especially the ones addressing the early development of children. Those environments should be more inclusive to engage more women in STEM careers and, as a consequence, to not exclude female students from becoming citizens that can take active participation in a future digital society. Moreover, innovative approaches in design for STEM education should put teachers at the center to be the protagonists of innovation in schools rather than passive distributors of companies' visions of the future.

A second reflection concerns the need for digital transformation projects in which different stakeholders can collaborate and align their visions, including: governments, companies, nonprofit organizations, civil society, the educators' community, and designers who can all participate in defining and constantly re-defining the map of relevant future skills. This can allow us to fight the "narration" of a necessary innovation, that leads only to investments in new hardware and software rather than in a human-paced lifelong education. Finally, the presented case studies showed that design can humanize technology with approaches that include more skills, beyond coding, such as critical thinking and emotional intelligence.

To conclude, as Victor Vasarely and Bruno Munari proposed in their pioneering works, design can help open up the codes of digital transformation by making the resources and the tools more accessible and easier to use. It can empower future citizens to have more control over digital processes

---

24   Jennifer Gabry, *Citizens of Worlds. Open-air Toolkits for Environmental Struggle*, University of Minnesota Press, accessed January 1, 2023, https://manifold.umn.edu/projects/citizens-of-worlds.

and products, which probably represents the most important requirement to enable the participation in the development of a digital society.[25]

---

[25] SUPSI University of Applied Sciences and Arts of Southern Switzerland — Design Institute and FabLab: The team members are Dr. Serena Cangiano (researcher and project leader), Leyla Tawfik (co-founder at Ethafa.com), Dr. Iolanda Pensa (senior researcher and project leader, project TAC), Marco Lurati (engineer and interaction designer, project TAC), Daniele Murgia (assistant researcher and designer, project TAC), and Matteo Loglio (lecturer at MA in Interaction Design, co-founder at Oio.com, researcher at SUPSI project "Untouched").

Reflections on Digital Transformation in Design
An Interview with John Maeda[1]

Laura Scherling[2]

"As the years change, technology changes. Digital transformation means that these changes are happening. The transformation in the design world means we are adapting to changing tools and business models. But today, it is hard to figure out what you are supposed to do in a world where there is so much stock photography and so many design templates. This is a question that is going to arise continually. Digital transformation means moving from non-digital to digital, and now going toward pure digital. This can lead to the question: How much of it do we need humans to participate in?"
— *Dr. John Maeda, US*

---

1 Microsoft, US.
2 Columbia University, US.

In 2020 Dr. John Maeda completed his first class at MIT Sloan, "not teaching it" but rather "taking it."[3] With a long and impressive career as a designer and computer scientist, he wanted to learn more about what "digital transformation" could mean. While the digital transformation process has been widely discussed and debated, particularly by businesses and consultancies, Maeda observed that he could not quite pinpoint a "crisp meaning."[4] When you search the Internet the definition is fairly straightforward: Digital transformation is the adoption of digital technologies. Yet, while technology adoption can drive gains in efficiency, the process is arguably more about "the organizational culture and processes that determine the use of digital tools."[5] Maeda concluded that "digitizing is easy, but succeeding in digitalization these days requires care and attention to the design of an experience."[6] Maeda also pointed out that computation is powerful, but it is the humans or the creators of these powerful computation tools (quite often designers) who help to keep the "ethical side of technology in check."[7]

The power of computation and the way we approach digital transformation is perhaps one of the most pressing design challenges today. A flawed design can be a hindrance to millions of users. For example, sentencing algorithms can unjustly "punish people" from low-income neighborhoods. Alternatively, a thoughtfully designed product can help millions of people.

This interview builds on the idea that digital transformation is more than a technical process, but also a means to critically interpret the "nature of computation." It underscores that the major technological transitions happening at work, educational institutions, and in day-to-day life, require

---

3   John Maeda, "How I Learned What 'Digital Transformation' Truly Means after Waving to a Couple Gs," *Medium* (blog), December 24, 2020, https://johnmaeda.medium.com/how-i-learned-what-digital-transformation-truly-means-after-waving-to-a-couple-gs-3be62c4cef7a.

4   Maeda.

5   Behnam Tabrizi, Ed Lam, Kirk Girard, and Vernon Irvin, "Digital Transformation Is Not about Technology," *Harvard Business Review*, March 13, 2019, https://hbr.org/2019/03/digital-transformation-is-not-about-technology.

6   Maeda, "How I Learned What 'Digital Transformation' Truly Means after Waving to a Couple Gs."

7   Liz Stinson, "How to Speak 'Computer' While Still Speaking 'Human'—According to John Maeda," *Adobe XD Ideas* (blog), December 7, 2019, https://xd.adobe.com/ideas/perspectives/leadership-insights/john-maeda-how-to-speak-machine.

a deeper look. It is urgent to consider how digital technologies can be used for social good while also mediating and preventing "unintended consequences."[8] This interview explores the multidimensional definition of digital transformation, while also examining some of the possible educational and economic implications.

Interview

Dr. Laura Scherling: Can you share some of your thoughts about the meaning and importance of digital transformation today, particularly in design and creative work?

Dr. John Maeda: Today, we are dealing with the fact that many standard business models are shifting. One of my favorite "aha" moments about the field of graphic design is that so many staples, like print, are no longer staples anymore.

There is a statute that strongly recommends—maybe mandates—having a printed annual report. Someone's got to design that report, and printers used to be able to print them. It was not credited often. And when you think about digital transformation this way, it is interesting, isn't it? Here's a required multi-page document. It was a job for many elite design companies in New York. Today's staple is a website that always needs more work. I used to think that it was great to have the annual report industry, but websites are great, too. Once, the agencies made it all by printing it out and gluing things together. Then they got computers. They were able to do it on a computer and start publishing digitally.

As the years change, technology changes. Digital transformation means that these changes are happening. The transformation in the design world means we are adapting to changing tools and business models. But today, it is hard to figure out what you are supposed to do in a world where there is so much stock photography and so many design templates. This is a question that is going to arise continually. Digital transformation means moving from non-digital to digital, and now going toward *pure* digital. This can lead to the question: How much of it do we need humans to participate in?

---

8   Stinson.

On the education side, there will always be people who want to skill up and follow a dream. However, the business model of education is changing and unfortunately, the price of education can exceed what normal humans can afford.

LS: Is there a disconnect between education and the design profession? Many young people are now entering a situation that is largely "digital."

JM: Both "sides" are going to have a problem because of digital transformation. The job market itself is going to be transformed. Education is going to transform as well. In many instances, transformation is happening rapidly outside education walls. On some days, I wonder what's wrong with making something classic like taking a piece of wood, and carving it down, and making a stand. Maybe these timeless approaches can withstand time. When I took a class recently, I loved it. It was all about digital transformation.

We need more transformed educational experiences. Today, we need more educational services that persist after you finish and help you continue transforming what you are doing; so there is no exact "end." When you have an interaction with your students or your teachers, it *starts* and *ends*. But imagine if you had to talk to them forever? In theory, though, digital experiences are those that you should be able to keep a part of and continue a conversation past the end of the course. Education should help the busy person and not just expect all this information to have been implanted. A truly digitally transformed experience would know how to operate like that.

LS: In your research, you write about some of the "unintended consequences" of digital transformation. How can we mitigate or prevent such consequences of unethical tech use?

JM: To foster ethical tech, we need people who are diverse and "different." People running or managing something together tend to be similar-minded. Whether you are in a university or an agency or company of any size, when you interview someone, you think that if they are like you—if they are one of us—they are going to fit. And because we like "culture fit," organizations tend to be biased towards it. When you create a bias about what culture fit is or should look like, you make it harder for different kinds of people to feel safe and comfortable with new technologies, selecting like-minded, similar-minded people. So the best way to address biases is to ask yourself; how many kinds of people do you have in your company or in whatever you are doing? And that tends to change the outcome because, number one, you'll hear things you aren't used to hearing.

For example, you can have a team with 18 men and one woman, and someone will say, "Wow, we have a woman here who can represent her opinions; that is great." But what if there were more women in tech? They might have a stronger voice. If you do not consider the importance of diversity and different kinds of thinking, it will not be good enough.

LS: There is a risk of creating homogenous cultures in design.

JM: When you consider the Bauhaus, many people have trouble naming a famous female Bauhausler. In our lives, we can fail to prevent these unintended consequences of tech by not thinking, knowing, caring, etc. Once you create a more diverse group of people around you, there are gradients of diversity that people can identify with, and being able to embrace diversity and complexity is an advantage. It takes a lot of energy, but it is worth it.

It is also helpful to count the visible differences, and then to also count the *invisible* differences. You can then ask yourself how much bias is built around you.

LS: It's an interesting part of a designer's education where there is a debate about what to fit into four years.[9]

JM: We have been in the four-year model probably since the establishment of normal schools. The design field exists because of various business aspects. The Bauhaus was created by the German economic ministry, who competed with the British. In the mid-19th Century, the British had a department of science and art, and they funded the Victoria & Albert Museum (V&A) and the Royal College of Art because they were in competition with the French. Therefore, the V&A was made to educate people about how to make products, the Royal College of Art was created to accelerate industry.

LS: What you are talking about is a form of competition ...

---

9 Michael W. Meyer and Don Norman, "Changing Design Education for the 21st Century," *She Ji: The Journal of Design, Economics, and Innovation*, Design Education. Part I, 6, no. 1 (March 1, 2020): 13–49, https://doi.org/10.1016/j.sheji.2019.12.002.

JM: It has been an economic play. You could also argue that in a digital transformation era—which is interesting—if you tell a computer to do something, it never gets tired. It is mental labor that you do not need to pay for, and it is hyper-efficient.

LS: It is hyper-efficient. What do you think it looks like when designers feel empowered to use new technologies?

JM: Digitally trained people do not necessarily digitally transform because it impacts people's jobs and lives. Maybe the "customer" is super happy, but the toll on an organization is great. Some institutions are extremely hard to transform because of the rules of engagement. When you shake the system and try to transform it, and it shakes back at you, do not be surprised—number one. Number two, industries behave in different ways.

I was a digital transformer. When you first replace a system, you can imagine how unhappy people can be. After I did that, people forgot it happened, and they are collaborating easily at a global scale. I am telling this story because every time I transformed something, nobody was happy because I was interrupting people's jobs.

Sometimes, we forget that an organization is made of people and when you digitally transform it, the people in it have to be ready. When I was talking to other people who were doing this, I heard about a summer program at a university where the university hired students to teach the faculty about how to use different technologies. I thought it was the most brilliant thing because it created a "buddy system." It compensated the younger person and enabled them to see that even though someone may not use technology, they are quite intelligent, and they know a lot. If we had more of these programs, we could learn much faster. It is two-way versus one-way, and then everyone can benefit. If someone gets technology and the other person gets wiser faster, it is a win-win.

LS: Two-way tech mentoring in schools and organizations seems more intergenerational.

JM: We can use concrete examples to institute at a policy-level and let people build, test, learn, and try them out. The design space that can be very tool-driven ... I also once thought it'd be great to have a design school that froze all the versions of software and computers for years so that no changes could occur. This would then force everyone to become good at whatever was out there at the moment. That would be interesting.

LS: Like a constraint ... in that case a student could master exactly what they were doing rather than fall behind the latest update.

JM: Yes. Another idea I had was that we should remove all desktop computers and do everything on mobile. Everything would be handled on mobile ... I felt like those constraints, unless you have a specific vision, would not deliver a quantum leap. I learned so much. But one thing I remembered was that the traditional ways are interesting because they aren't storable on the Internet easily. It is important that we understand this generational gap so that we can preserve some of these ideas.

LS: Design often requires an incredible amount of precision, and the use of some tools could become obsolete.

JM: Obsolescence can also mean something "special", "diverse", and "different." It is a way to balance the scale where all this old stuff is still really cool, and all this new stuff is super relevant and cool, too. I always found that balance is difficult to forge no matter who you are. Why is this valuable? It is valuable because as "digital" gets faster, slow seems even slower. Let me give an example; I take my slow knowledge of the creative world and I bring it to a fast business world.

Recently, I found a way to be very calm. I work in this space of crisis management and all kinds of calamitous things, so the space I am in is just fascinating. I realized there are three factors to why you do not need to worry about things anymore. You cannot control them.

The first one is super important; the Earth revolves around the Sun. Depending upon where it is, you are either cold—far away—or if it is summer—you are nearby. And depending upon the orientation, you'll get hotter or colder by default. It is a basic pattern; that is number one.

Number two, in school, they say the Earth is covered by a lot of oceans. We learn that about 70 percent of Earth's surface is covered by water. We learn that the moon rotates around the Earth and attracts the ocean. Gravity changes the wave patterns and the weather patterns and we only see that Moon once in a while doing all kinds of stuff on the Earth; that is number two.

Number three, Earth is hurtling through space at about 1000 miles per hour, and its molten core is extremely hot. It causes volcanoes and earthquakes, and what I like about it is that I cannot change the molten core of the Earth. I cannot change the Moon's rotation around the Earth and I cannot change the Earth's rotation around the Sun.

That it is wonderfully humbling because if I can't do all that, then what can I do? I have crossed different digital ages. I find that my function now is using my digital knowledge to preserve the past, and diverge the present so it is less calcified, and then provide paths for others who will come after me who are divergent themselves. These are little pieces to consider on your journey.

No Back to Normal: Studio Forward at California College of the Arts
An Interview with Cristina Gaitán and Juan Carlos Rodriguez Rivera[1]

Rachel Berger[2]

> The unimaginable disruptions of 2020 radically altered our worlds while amplifying our digital connectedness across time and space. Recognizing that there is no "back to normal," design educators and students are embracing new pedagogical approaches to ensure that the designers of tomorrow are prepared to design into the future. Futures literacy, a skill that builds on the innate human capacity to imagine the future and addresses the problem of poverty-of-the-imagination, is a crucial capability for the next generation of designers.
> — *Rachel Berger, US*

---

1 California College of the Arts, US. Rodriguez Rivera is now Assistant Professor at Wayne State University, US.
2 California College of the Arts, US.

Kate Yang (front) and Morgan Wash (back) installing The Restorative Machine, CCA Hubbell Street Galleries, 2021. Photo by Rachel Berger. The Restorative Machine, created by Studio Forward students Melinda Kreuser, Morgan Wash, and Kate Yang, was a machine, composed of native plants and moss, that guided spectators through a sensorial meditative practice to address climate grief.[3]

This transcribed interview with Cristina Gaitán and Juan Carlos Rodriguez Rivera, design professors at California College of the Arts (CCA), presents a case study of transformational pedagogy in progress. In Fall 2021, Gaitán and Rodriguez Rivera co-taught the first semester of Studio Forward, a year-long sponsored course bringing together multi-disciplinary teams of graduate and undergraduate design students. The topic for Studio Forward's inaugural year was the Future of Belonging, and the course was offered in partnership with Google.

Gaitán and Rodriguez Rivera centered their curricular and pedagogical approach on "futures literacy," a UNESCO-developed competency that "allows people to better understand the role of the future in what they see and do."[4] Since 2012, UNESCO's Global Futures Literacy Network has hosted

---

3 Rachel Berger, photograph of *The Restorative Machine*, 2021.
4 UNESCO, Futures Literacy, https://en.unesco.org/futuresliteracy/about.

Futures Literacy Labs on topics such as climate justice, peace, and wellbeing. According to Gaitán, in Studio Forward, futures literacy was treated as, "a set of skills—conceptual, research, and technical—that one can learn to not just talk about the future but to also design *into* the future, to design new futures." Studio Forward students practiced futures literacy using design tools to engage in speculation, worldbuilding, and storytelling. Their outputs included artifacts, electronic prototypes, speculative mock-ups, written narratives, videos, interactions, tools, experiences, and environments—whatever they believed it would take to collectively envision (and build) the world they wanted to live in.

Demonstration of augmented reality digital social experience in Food for Thought Cafe, CCA Hubbell Street Galleries, 2021. Food for Thought Cafe, created by Studio Forward students Apurva Chinta, Leah Kallen, Valerie Liu, and Krystle Reynolds, was a tangible cafe table with an overlaid AR experience, critiquing our tendency to let remote relationships distract us from the people in front of us.[5]

---

5   Cristina Gaitán, photograph of *Food for Thought Café*, 2021.

In their conversation with Rachel Berger, Project Director for Studio Forward, Gaitán and Rodriguez Rivera reflect on their pedagogy and describe how they tried to create the conditions for students to imagine possible futures and create prototypes to inspire change. Over the course of the interview, three themes emerge: the challenge of experimental education in the Covid-impacted classroom, misconceptions about the role of technology in designing futures, and collaboration as a key capability for tomorrow's designer.

In Fall 2021, after more than a year of fully remote instruction, CCA started transitioning back to in-person classes. Initially, Gaitán and Rodriguez Rivera planned to focus the Studio Forward curriculum on belonging as a topic and speculative design and "futuring" as methodologies. To give the students agency, they deliberately left the course unstructured and the assignments open-ended. However, they soon realized they had underestimated Covid's impact on their class. The students needed much more structure than they had before the pandemic. Before they felt ready to experiment, their sense of self and community needed to be rebuilt, and their definition of design needed to be expanded.

Digital technologies are certainly fundamental to designers, but Gaitán and Rodriguez Rivera caution against equating the use of advanced technology with designing futures. Technology is a tool, one of many ways of looking at culture and understanding the larger context for design. The original topic for Studio Forward was the Future of Digital Belonging. Early on, to keep the students from automatically assuming they would be using high-tech applications like augmented reality and the blockchain in their projects, the instructors removed the word "digital" from the topic.

The first semester of Studio Forward became about collaboration above all else—between co-instructors, amongst instructors and students, within student teams, and between a school and a sponsor. Gaitán and Rodriguez Rivera cleared a lot of space in the class to focus on helping the teams learn how to work together successfully. They believed that teaching the students to collaborate would be a more important and enduring skill than any technical training or application they might offer. Their methods included pushing students to develop a shared understanding of the language they were using and the disciplines they were practicing, facilitating feedback conversations with the class, and incorporating reflection rituals to help students articulate what they were doing, making, and learning. Throughout, the instructors held themselves accountable for creating an authentic sense of belonging in a class about the future of belonging.

Interview

Rachel Berger: What is Studio Forward?

Cristina Gaitán: Studio Forward is a multi-disciplinary year-long exploratory studio. It is an incubator around this idea of the future of belonging. For me, it is about students from multiple disciplines coming together and figuring out how to collaborate and learn from each other regarding their different disciplines, practices, processes, tools, and materials.

Juan Carlos Rodriguez Rivera: What I expected Studio Forward would be and what it actually became are really different. At the beginning, there was this whole plan: interdisciplinary students would be experimenting together, exploring all these topics. That was what I thought it would be, and then the reality was that it was about collaboration: with the students, amongst the students, with Cristina, with Google, and with the department. To me, all aspects of the class were about collaborating in different contexts and with different people.

CG: I totally agree. Originally, it was also about this idea of futures literacy, which is a set of skills—conceptual, research, and technical—that one can learn to not just talk about the future but to also design *into* the future, to design new futures. For most of last semester, the students did not seem to respond to that, but we just reconvened for the spring term, and several students brought up futures literacy as the most exciting part of the last semester's work. I was excited to hear that they *did* retain it; they *were* thinking about it. Maybe they just did not know how to talk about it at the end of last semester. So, it is a thread that is still alive in what they are doing.

RB: I am working on a project with middle school students where I asked them to imagine the future, and at least half of them brought up "flying cars." Somehow, the future still equals flying cars, which I find surprising. How do you see the relationship between futuring and technology? How did you talk about and teach about technology in the course?

JCRR: I get disappointed when "future" means flying cars and advanced technology. To me, futuring and speculative design are less about having fancy technology and more about creating futures that are not oppressive. For example, how do we design these systems so we do not destroy the planet?

CG: Technology is a tool. In class, we approach it as just one of myriad ways of looking at culture and contextual information around the future, the present, or the past. Throwing the word "technology" around is also a bit ridiculous because people have different understandings of what it is. An early stone tool was a piece of technology.

JCRR: The original topic of the course was "The Future of Digital Belonging," and last year, I thought, "Oh, that sounds cool!" But "future," "digital," and "belonging" are three loaded words. Now, when I look at those three words together, I realize that is a lot to unpack in one semester.

CG: Right. We started by taking the word "digital" out because the students were too distracted by it. They had assumptions about what that meant, where they were going, and what they were supposed to create based on that one word.

We also talked about how technology has a history. What do we mean by that? What is a machine? What is a tool, and what has it been through time? Technology is just one artifact in a larger system, so we tried to deconstruct that for them in different ways and have them think about what they were making in those ways. It is hard to ask people to unlearn that kind of thing.

RB: Can you talk about some of your teaching methods and the exercises you had the students do to try to shake them out of this mindset?

CG: We pushed the students to define the terms in their statements of interest and in the questions they were asking. "This is your group's statement," we would say, "but what do each of these things mean? You are assuming you all have the same intention and understanding around this topic, and you probably do not. And even if you do, you have to get used to explaining what you mean to other people who are new to your work and new to your project."

JCRR: When the students' proposals included words that were trendy, we asked them to unpack those words in relation to their project and their group. One example was a team that used words like "healing," "collective," and "community." We asked them, "What is the collective? What is a community?

What is healing, and how does that relate to this idea of belonging?" They would say, "Community means community!" And we would say, "No. What does community actually mean to you?"

CG: This happened a lot with the last project, which was about creating machines. When we told a group, "Go make a machine," they said, "I do not know what that means." To expand their understanding, we talked about a machine historically and beyond the context of a tool or a technology. When you Google the definition of "machine," one of the definitions is a group of people doing a particular thing together. So, we taught them different ways of being conscientious about their language and what it means for them.

JCRR: Another approach we used at the beginning was to ask the students to consider who *they* are in this work. Before we can start speculating about the future in a responsible way, we need to ask, "Who am I in relation to nature, the world, or the classroom? Who am I in relation to all these moments in history and the present?" When I say it, it makes total sense—we started the students with introspection, then human-centered design, and then forecasting methodologies and practices. But in the classroom, it was challenging for the students to understand why we were asking this.

RB: Do you think that is a result of their previous training as designers where they might be discouraged from asking, "Who am I?"

JCRR: Yes, definitely. They were eager to start doing something without going deep into their relationship to what they were doing or its context. They said, "We are going to create a product! About whatever! In the future! Let's do it!" It is related to designing obsolete objects without thinking about the broader context and histories. This was hard for them to comprehend, and a lot of it was due to the baggage that everyone had.

RB: What other baggage or assumptions did people bring to the class?

CG: We did not anticipate the unlearning moment that was going to have to happen to free the students up to be on the ride with us. Because of the effects of the pandemic, we are all in this weird reality right now, and that was literally affecting the way students came to class, whether they came to class, and what they were open and available to do.

Everyone was a bit in survival mode, and I did not realize that. So, on top of the subject matter and the methodologies we were teaching, we had to think about how to be humans together. Juan and I needed to put a ton of attention into that, but I had no idea. No one had any idea, and that is still an important part of learning and collaborating with each other. It is what the class turned into.

One practical thing I realize now is that I had created a mental model of the student body we had and the different disciplines they were coming from, and that is how I was organizing them thematically in the class. That is the information I was operating on in terms of how we constructed an assignment and what we talked about. That is all important, but for some of the graduate students, it was their first semester in design school. They did not come with a design lexicon or background. They were dipping their toe into what they assumed design was.

This goes back to the question of how to create a community of totally diverse people. How do I create belonging in this class that is talking about the future of belonging? We tried out a lot of different things, and we are still working on that.

JCRR: Most of the assumptions the students came in with had to do with language. Going back to "the future of digital belonging," students assumed that meant augmented reality and virtual reality, and it was hard to move them away from that. I said, "It is good that you have this strong point of view, but let's be a little bit more open about this."

And then, when it comes to instructions, a word like "render" means completely different things for an illustrator, an MFA design student, and an industrial designer. The words we were using came with different assumptions based on each student's background. That was interesting, and we did not expect it.

RB: What was the partnership with Google like? Did you feel like you had to engage with technology in a particular way?

JCRR:

It was a weird moment to be doing all this during the pandemic. The students were expecting to be at Google, to go to the offices and the campus, but that was not possible. When they did not see it, many students felt disappointed, so we were also working through that disappointment and building something out of it.

CG: The relationship with Google was like an early-stage experimental incubator, where it felt like no one had specific expectations about where we were going. I assumed that Google would want us to be talking about the technological piece. My reaction to that is always, "Yeah, we will get there, but first, we are going to do other things that will allow us to get there in a way that has integrity." I was ready for pushback, ready to talk about why this was the right way to go, but I never had to.

It is related to what I tell graduate students when they think they need to design screens and apps to get a job. I say, "You need to do what is interesting to you. You need to figure out new ways of exploring and approaching design, and these companies will figure out how to make money off of you because that is what they do."

JCRR: The people that visited the class from Google echoed that. They said, "Google hired me because of my passion for research, not because I do beautiful UX and screen design." To me, it was so powerful to hear these people who are working at Google share their journey with the students and explain that all journeys are different and sometimes take you to unexpected places.

You learn a lot from someone telling you their story. There is a lot of knowledge there that you can apply to your own practice and life. If I could go back in time, I would love to explain that to the students more clearly and give them tools so that when someone is telling their journey story, it can feel like more of a knowledge exchange moment for the students.

CG: Early on, the students had an aversion to anecdotal information, even qualitative information, because they perceived it as not facts, not the right or the most important information. If you are really stressed out about what you think you are supposed to be doing, and there is someone coming in and talking about their story, and it doesn't feel like it is helping you get to what you are supposed to be doing, I can imagine some internal freak outs are happening.

RB: Some of the ways Studio Forward has been described sound hard to actualize in the classroom. For example, we say it is an "experimental open-ended course" and "up for questioning everything." What does this mean to you? Is that about being experimental in how you teach or about encouraging students to make experimental work? So much about traditional teaching is not about open-endedness. It is about definition and structure and making things more clear. Constant questioning could be destabilizing for a student looking for validation that they are going in the right direction. On the other hand, is stability overrated? Instability can be painful, but it is the reality we live in.

JCRR: It was experimental across many dimensions—in the class, with the assignments, and with Cristina and me, in the way we were designing the curriculum, in our ways of teaching and interacting with the students. That was a challenge, unpacking what experimental means and the value of experimentation. For some, the assumption was that to be experimental is to try three things and be done, which misses the value in the experiments themselves.

This is connected to many designers' obsession with the final form. We saw their desks. Next to what they were presenting to us, they would have everything they were trying out. However, they would not include those things in their presentations because they were only ready to show the final thing. Many students were not comfortable saying, "This is all the process that I am making. I am trying all these things, so let's see where it takes me." They were doing it, but they just were not showing it, which is weird.

The class was open-ended in the sense of how much we were constantly changing it in reaction to what was happening, not only in the classroom but also around us. There were all these evolutions where we had to sit down and rethink why this project is going in this direction, why we should push it in the other direction, and why the students are feeling this way or the other way.

We asked ourselves how to build some structure into this "open-ended" course, not a hierarchical structure but one that is more lateral. That was a challenge, and I do not think we ever got to that point. If a hierarchy is a pyramid, our structure goes like this. [Forms a triangle with his hands, then tips it over.] It is still a pyramid! It never became lateral. We tried things to make that happen, like spending a class meeting doing an aligning exercise with the students and us. We also had meetings just to listen to the students and ask, "What are you feeling? What do you want to see?" We gave space to listen to the students and talk with them about how we move forward with this. Those were specific moments where the open-ended idea became a reality.

CG: Initially, I assumed that the students would be really self-driven within their fields and show up as outspoken advocates of their disciplines. I imagined them coming together in teams and an industrial design student saying, "I love rendering! I will take these concepts and render them and print them and make them real," and a graphic design student saying, "I am really into this particular aesthetic, and I am going to make the publication!"

Instead, because this open-ended thing was open in all directions—from the deliverables they had to make to the process they might use to how we related to them in class—there were too many open ends, and it did not allow them the confidence to show up in that way. I also think my assumptions did not account for the difference between undergraduate and graduate students. I can imagine that some of the undergrads felt intimidated. They were rock stars, but they seemed to take a backseat to the louder voices in the room, which happened for the most part to be grad students. That really impacted the conversation in the class, what the groups were making, and how they related to each other.

Maybe this is my survival reaction, but the way that my pendulum swung was to create a little more structure. There needed to be some scaffolding. We did not need to line the entire building, but we needed more than half a wall. That is important because it frees them up to do something. Our colleague Saraleah Fordyce taught our students and us some simple methods for reflection, so we had these little moments, these little stepping stones, even in a super ambiguous space, to pause and think about what we are doing, what we have made, and what we have learned. The students did that for themselves and for each other. It was so important because the students might go, live, do whatever they are going to do for the next year, and then have this moment where they realize, "Oh! That is what we were doing back then." You can't always immediately articulate what you are learning and what you are doing. It takes time.

So yes, having some structure is important, but that can look many different ways. You can create structure by having two weeks of "unlearning" where you create a common foundation for all disciplines, or by being super specific about all the deliverables. The structure should always be in service of open-endedness.

JCRR: In general, stability is overrated, but right now, it is really necessary. Last semester, everything was unstable. We were online and then in-person and then online, and then someone got Covid-19, so we went online again. Then there were no printers, and then there was no Internet. The whole world was unstable, and we were proposing this class where we said, "Do whatever you want! The final form can be anything!" And the students said, "Whoa. We need one thing in this whole equation that is more stable." It was a good learning experience for me.

RB: I am interested in the tension between what students were learning about what it means to be a designer in their other classes and what you asked of them. In Meredith Davis's design futures research, she describes the "new mindsets, knowledge, and skills that traditionally trained designers must acquire to transition successfully to the aspects of professional work that are likely to dominate the field in the future." She continues, "College faculty must be cautious not to overload curricula with content of temporary relevance at the expense of more enduring knowledge that transcends a rapidly changing context."[6] Do you agree with her assessment? What are the mindsets, knowledge, and skills that designers should be acquiring?

JCRR: Yes, to both quotes. There were two cores of the Studio Forward class: futures literacy and collaboration. These are things that designers need to learn to transition into professional work, no matter what that means for them. Unfortunately, this was also where a discrepancy happened because students were asking us to teach them tools like VR and AR to give them steps on speculation. However, we did not want to overload the curriculum with technical how-to's. Trying to balance that was hard, but I believe that to be a good and responsible designer, it is more important for a student to learn collaboration than focusing the entire semester on whatever is trendy right now, such as bitcoins, NFTs, and memes.

CG: First, students need to learn about the ethical dilemmas of design and a designer's responsibilities. In my education as a designer, I was never directly taught this or made to answer for it. When I teach interaction design, it is in the very first material that we talk about. What are you making and why? What are its implications on other people, places, and animals?

Second, we tried to teach the students that they can use design processes to look at anything in the world, including things that people do not think of when they think of design. We can design and redesign government, for example. Students can use the tools that design teaches them to be more active people in the world, in whatever ways they are interested in.

---

6   Meredith Davis, "Introduction to Design Futures," AIGA, 2019, https://www.aiga.org/aiga-design-futures/introduction-to-design-futures.

JCRR: One other thing we were trying to do when defining design with them was that design is more than your discipline. Design is a bigger concept. Design is how the world is designed. It was hard for them to get out of the mindset that design for me is graphic design because that is what I do. Design for me is interaction design because that is what I do. I do not think we were able to get them all the way out of that bubble, that design is what my discipline is. That is a little disappointing, but it is real. It is really hard for people to understand that design is all of this!

RB: When you think of the students who were most successful in the class, what mindset did they bring or develop?

CG: I immediately think of two students who ended up collaborating closely. Their mindsets were pretty different, but they worked very well together. One is super multi-disciplinary. He has a background in performance. He came to school without any hard design skills, but he was open to looking at the world, objects, and environments through design. He understands design and that everything is and can be designed. He is also not afraid to take risks. When he gets inspired by something, he keeps following it and playing around with it, and he does not need to know what it is going to be in the end.

The other student really knows what she is passionate about. When I hear her speak about what she did last semester and what she wants to do, it is all about accessibility. She is very dedicated to that topic, and she figures out how to keep plugging along at it mostly through the medium of graphic design. They are both very dedicated to their development and their practice.

JCRR: They were also successful because they were really good at collaborating and negotiating and making decisions together. Another group was successful because their topic was important to all of them. They wanted to work with global warming. We asked, "How do we bring it to a smaller scale? How do we bring it into your passion?" And they were able to figure that out. That group was successful because their shared focus was the topic they chose and how to be critical about it.

CG: That is right. I like the example of the second group because they each brought different things to that project. One had a background in writing and research. She felt a little less secure about the making aspect but was still totally able to be involved in everything. Another brought graphic design into it. Another was an industrial designer. It was a really well-balanced, multi-disciplinary group, and they found a way to say, "This is my thing. I can help the group with my thing." They supported each other with their strengths.

RB: What advice do you have for designers who want to integrate more futuring and speculative design into their practice?

CG: First, understand the history. It is easy to look at the outputs of speculative design, even historically, and assume these are weird sculptural things, so learning the history is key.

Next, try to separate the allure of a word like "technology" from tools. Learn to divorce how you might react to the forms you see in speculative design from your understanding of the ways of working within it and the power of that. Understand the power of stories in design and between people. In class last week, my colleague Mathew Kneebone said, "An object is nothing without a story." Implicitly, we learn it in design, but we are not always given the tools or the time to develop the way we tell stories, and that can be very powerful.

In class, I often frame futuring in opposition to human-centered design. When Ari Melenciano visited us, she asked why we are still talking about human-centered design.[7] She challenged us to think about all sentient beings and how we relate to the world, humans just happening to be one part of it. Futuring can also be really accessible. You do not have to be trained as a designer. You do not need particular skills to be able to speculate. For example, with a very simple prompt, I can start to imagine what my life would be like in twenty years if I did not have water.

There are so many different ways in which speculation, foresight, or futuring are used in both art and industry, and it is important to understand that those things come from the same place. It might seem like a weird art thing, but giant companies use it all the time to do real things like making products. Speculative design is nothing new, and people are doing it all the time, so go for it.

JCRR: I am going to get political and philosophical. The political part is that it is really important to know the history of how futuring has been used for

---

7   California College of the Arts, *Ari Melenciano: Speculating Futures through Omni-Specialized Design*, YouTube video, 2021, https://www.youtube.com/watch?v=Fcx6QFmJTKU

terrible things. When we look at genocides and colonizations these people were thinking about creating futures. They were futuring, but that came with genocide and killing and destruction. Thus, when thinking about the future, there has to be a lot of responsibility in how we think about it, what we want to create, and for who and why. There are a lot of ideas and speculation about the future that bring oppression and destruction along with them. On the flip side, there is no conversation about the future without Afrofuturism, which is imagining the future from some of the most oppressed people on the planet. The discipline of speculative design has so much to learn from movements like Afrofuturism.

The philosophical part is that we have to understand time differently when thinking about the future. When we create something, it is probably going to live longer than us. We were thinking about the future while we were creating it, but we did not think about the full lifetime of that creation—not just our time, but the time of the objects and the projects we are creating, and what story and what legacy they are going to keep in the future, beyond our time, and beyond the person that designed it.

Those two things are really important: understanding the histories that come with futuring and understanding the different temporalities of futuring.

An Archaeology of Digital Architecture

Kai Franz[1]

Computer-aided design (CAD) originated as a translation that extended technical drafting into the digital sphere. Alongside the use of computers to aid in the creation and design came new methods of modifications, analyses, and optimizations. The immaterial condition of information as the new basis of digital design and its computational architecture gave birth to parametric design. Today, this digital architecture complex co-describes and ingrains most design practices, processes, and products. It is simply everywhere, and yet remains elusive. This case study explores research, works and phenomena in the area of digital architecture and computational design. This is exemplified in the plopper (dual axis precision deposition system), a low-res 3D printer that drives computation towards its periphery by combining its determinism with elements of chance and chaos. It is a machine that translates vectors, bits, numbers, points, lines, and algorithms into the opaque realm of matter and materiality. Post-digital in nature, the machine-made artifacts fabricated in this process never leave their digital origin entirely behind. Instead, we are asked to read them as traces or relics in an archaeology of digital architecture.
— *Kai Franz, US/Germany*

---

1 Rhode Island School of Design, US/Germany.

What is digital architecture? Antoine Picon discusses this question in his book *Digital Culture in Architecture*. He asks if the sheer assistance of computers in the design process allows for this classification, or if the probing of the machine's capacities to be more than a drawing tool is needed. Picon reveals that "in order to distinguish the term [digital architecture] from the rapidly increasing use of computer-aided design [...], there has been a tendency to confuse digital and experimental."[2] Furthermore, Picon observed that numerous contemporary practitioners respond to the question of what constitutes digital architecture. But their positions, contributions and models of practice diverge enormously. In the case of Frank Gehry, Picon noticed the heavy use of parametric modeling to achieve complex innovative geometries, despite the top-down authorship model of the practice. In the case of the architecture of Herzog & de Meuron, it is a new emphasis on surface and ornamentation that must be read in relation to digital culture. Finally, Picon observes what he calls "frozen fluidity," capturing the rise of a new formalism rooted in fluidity and gradual variability.[3] All of these concepts and manifestations have their part in digital architecture. They speak to the influence digital culture and computational methods and thinking had on the discipline.

Computational design—another protagonist in the digital architecture complex—is a term that refers to the use of computational methodologies in the design process. Antoni Gaudi's Sagrada Familia in Barcelona, Spain, famously one of the earliest examples with its highly complex and intricate rule-based design, incorporates many computational design techniques. Today, parametric modeling with algorithmic optimization falls into the category of computational design. The Bird's Nest (the Beijing National Stadium in China), a project emblematic of this problem-solving side of the equation, utilized computational design methods for the purpose of advanced digital modeling and simulation to optimize the complex structural design. Computational design also refers to procedural and generative explorations, where practitioners utilize computational approaches more experimentally. An example would be the generative form-finding studies of Gregg Lynn that I will discuss later. These radically experimental practitioners and their search for a new formal language has often overshadowed the algorithmic optimization of parametric modeling and again we get another glimpse at the

---

2   Antoine Picon, *Digital Culture in Architecture: An Introduction for the Design Professions* (Basel: Birkhäuser GmbH, 2010), 60.
3   Picon, 60.

confusion of "digital" and "experimental" that Picon pointed out. How do we reconcile these differences and their transformational impact on architecture and design? Today, this digital architecture complex co-describes and ingrains most design practices, processes, and products.

Arguably, it is precisely this wide range of meanings – and not mere vagueness – that defines the *digital* in digital architectural theory and practice. Simply, digital architecture also includes the actual tools and software used to create digital models, plans, and environments. And the aesthetics of these emergent forms and processes are hardly neutral. Indeed, this capaciousness, the messy oscillation of digital culture, shifting computational methodologies and tools, and the atomization of the architectural object informs my own engagement with computer-aided design.

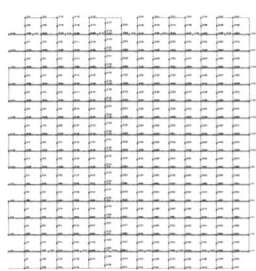 

CAD Seed for Reset (left) and Reset (right), 2017, CAD drawing, CNC-code, CAM-software, plopper (dual-axis precision deposition system), polyurethane, sand, 36" × 36" × 3"[4]

---

4   © Kai Franz, 2017.

CRTL+A/+C/+V/+Z

The digital turn in architecture began when computers were integrated into the design process. Computer-aided design (CAD) originated as a translation that extended technical drafting into the digital sphere. The use of computers to aid the creation of an architectural drawing was initially intended to increase productivity and efficiency, but—as with most transformations from analog to digital—it had far wider implications for the discipline of architecture than these early promises suggested. The basis for this digital turn is rooted in the conception of *disegno*,[5] the principal method that produced the foundation of architecture and the fine arts during the Renaissance. *Disegno* signified the key intellectual element in the visual arts, validating its elevation from craft. Central to *disegno* was the use of drawings as the basic components to construct a finished composition. The blank ground of the drawing facilitated the space for invention, the capacity for designing the whole. Imaginative and intellectual at its core, this drawing process gave *disegno* its philosophical gravitas and ultimately gave birth to a concept of design as we know it today.

Arguably, much of what separates *disegno* from colorito or the mere skill of drawing from observation also marks the shift from manual drafting to CAD and the application of new technologies in drafting. Let us examine what this shift entailed by closely reading the two techniques, methods, and modes of drafting against each other. Most commonly, CAD software uses vector-based graphics to depict the objects of traditional drafting. Yet, these objects are more than just shapes. Already in the traditions of manual drafting (for example, in technical architectural or engineering drawings), the drawing is always already more than the drawing. It conveys information about processes, materials, dimensions, and tolerances in accordance with discipline-specific conventions. The same is true for the digital CAD drawing—it maintains these conventions of holding additional information, where a line is not just a line. Moreover, the digital line is never an actual line but itself already pure information. As a mathematical vector equation, the line itself becomes information, rendered visible only to the human eye. It starts to float and becomes light, malleable, smart, and fast.

As with other transitions of analog media, however, digitalization produces a profound transformative shift: the immaterial condition of a digital

---

5   Disegno is the Italian word for drawing or design. It describes the total concept that constitutes the design in a work of art.

drawing gives rise to a new kind of editability, and it dissolves the singularity of the original drawing—"same, same, but different."[6] Together, these new conditions have established the foundation for digital architecture and allowed for a new set of design methodologies that would change architecture and its practice. Later, this new state of digital drawing would also be the basis for networked capabilities, creating new forms of collaboration, circulation, and exchange. When editability was established, the line became an informational object in the form of an equation, thus becoming computable. It can now be automated.

As a result, the proliferation of object-oriented programming (OOP), starting in the 2000s, caused new tools to emerge and required different skills, giving rise to parametric projects in architecture and design. Simultaneously, it is indeed the same binary core that set up the basis for the integration of digital fabrication technologies and the possibility of mass customization. Seemingly seamless, digitization in architecture penetrated architecture and the discipline as a whole.

Plans, drawings, and architectural models have played a critical role in shaping the discipline of architecture. These were never just bare artifacts of technical necessity; they acted more like a medium. One has to only think back to the countless examples of designs and buildings in competitions that were never realized but have been influential in effect. The same might be true for digital architecture, including all digital artifacts—be it CAD drawings, renderings, 2D/3D models, building information models (BIMs), or computer numerical control (CNC) technologies. Additionally, when we account for the computational end of things, the list should include information architecture with all its scripts, data structures, for-loops, and algorithms, all of which might be of equal importance, as they might bear the same potential: to reveal and trace their capacity for change.

---

6   Oliver Laric, *Versions*, online video, 2010, https://vimeo.com/17805188. In this essayistic film, Laric establishes the concept of objects as "versions" that permute through time and history, challenging the modernist dichotomy of copy and original. The work superimposes an audio essay with a visual essay combining animation and found footage from historical references, pop culture, memes and original digital media content to build its theory of version.

216   Part 2: Case Studies and Interviews on Educational Processes and Practices

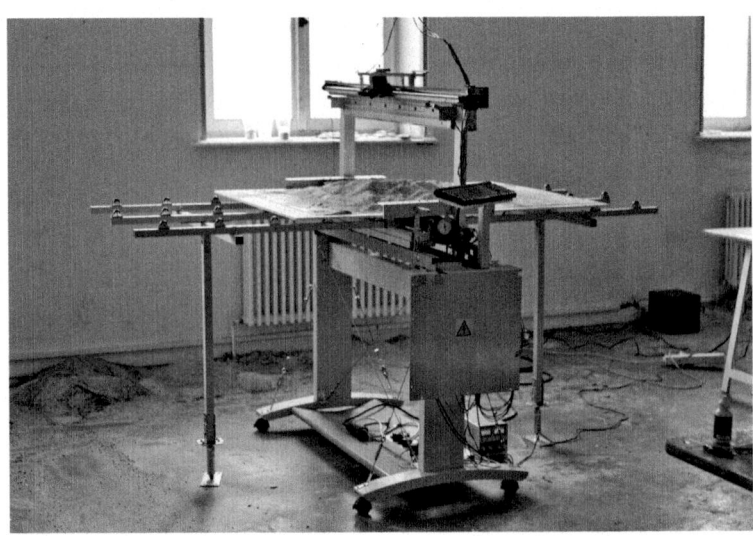

Plopper (Dual-Axis Precision Deposition System), CNC machine, hacked plotter, custom software and gcode, 4' × 7' × 5', Stuttgart, Akademie Schloss Solitude.[7]

My research and work have intersected the areas of architecture, computational design, and art through the plopper, a machine built to critically and playfully engage with pressing issues in the field of digital design. The plopper, a hacked architectural plotter, first deposits sand, then drops resin onto the landscape of sand, building up sculptural/architectural artifacts from the digital domain, layer by layer. In doing so, the machine translates the seemingly high-res from the digital condition into the impervious realm of matter and material.

The plopper is something like a low-res 3D printer. The machine and process are designed to critique contemporary fabrication technology for its premature relationship of the physical to the digital, of virtuality to actuality, and of matter to materiality. It drives computation towards its periphery by combining its determinism with chance and chaos. While the plopper's inputs—virtual 3D-models and CAD-drawings—are regulated by control, precision, and perfection, the machine utilizes chance, imperfection, and the will of matter in an effort to overcome determination. Post-digital in nature,

---

7   © Kai Franz, 2011–ongoing.

the machine-made artifacts fabricated in this process never leave their digital origin entirely behind. Instead, the objects can be read as traces or relics in an archaeology of digital architecture.

The plopper primarily fabricates artifacts that might read as sculptures or architecture, but occasionally, it also produces prints, drawings, and films. The artifacts begin as digital drawings created with computer-aided-design (CAD) software and are then fabricated through a custom computer-aided manufacturing (CAM) process. This additive process starts with the deposition of loose sand onto a wooden board, creating what could be characterized as a serialized landscape—serialized because, unlike natural entropic land formations, the underlying forces at play with this machine are driven by the logic of computation. Factors such as increment, scale, and resolution become substitutes for the weather, and the geology of the terrain is sterile like the monochrome grain of sieved play sand, the kind that we might purchase at a construction store.

In a second run, the machine then drops polyurethane onto this landscape. When the resin hits the sand, it sinks in and freezes the form. When a saturation point is reached, it flows at the contours and along the valleys, leaving the CAD drawing behind, following a new inner logic across the path of least resistance. This moment of adherence defines the point when the CAD drawing is converted into an artifact, when it is translated from a virtual digital drawing into a post-digital medium condition, when it ossifies in matter. Here, the plopps become readable, not just as if the drawing is rendered in a different mode.

In computation, the term serialization refers to the process of translating data structures or object states into a format that can be stored (for example, in a file or memory data buffer) or transmitted (for example, over a network) and reconstructed at a later moment in time. Can we use this concept to decipher the workings behind the plopper? It literally applies because information is translated into machine movement when the digital drawing is interpreted, decrypted by the computer, and transmitted to the machine to be executed. However, serialization might also serve as a conceptual framework to understand the nature of the process and help us unpack the workings and questions behind the machine. Eventually, we might view the constructed artifacts that the machine produces analogous to a file—as information stored in sand. While it might not be possible to reconstruct the original data states from these objects perfectly, this concept introduces a temporal dimension because stored means to be used later and/or otherwise, and equally that there was indeed a past set of operations that have been recorded. The potential for reading these digital artifacts implies that we are at a distant moment of pause. They are readable in an archeological sense.

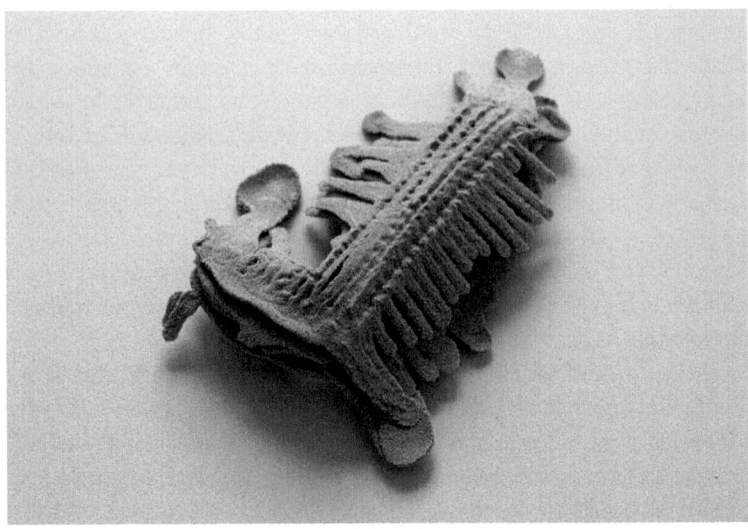

Untitled Plopp No. 36, CAD drawing, CNC-code, CAM-software, plopper (dual-axis precision deposition system), polyurethane, sand, 6" × 12" × 4".[8]

Was ist das? Was willst du von mir?[9]

Aesthetically, when I started to work with this process, the initial plopps gave me pause. The works seemed as concrete as they were abstract. Their indeterminacy was something that was striking. The objects exhibited an underlying serial nature irrespective of their formlessness. Together, these qualities read almost absurd or surreal. Yet, this surrealism was also immediately nullified by their concreteness, not to mention their superficial origin.

---

8   © Kai Franz, 2011.
9   English translation: What is that? What do you want from me?

At the time, it was important to me to stay with this technique. I did not want to invent another machine at risk of fetishizing the spectacle of the invention or, even worse, the inventor. I thought it would be more challenging to stay with what was in front of me and figure out what was at stake, conceptually and aesthetically. It was the first step to conceive of these works as artifacts in an archeology of digital architecture, which has become a methodology of my creative practice for over ten years.

There is a discrepancy of the work in its virtual vis-à-vis its physical state. All of the little fingers and arms seen in image 3 are not actually part of the drawing. These only emerge in the fabrication process. I classify the early works that were created by the machine as calibration pieces as they were designed to probe the internal mechanics and manifestations of the process/technique. The guiding questions for creating the CAD input, the seed drawings, were simple: What is the difference in mark between a horizontal, a vertical, and a diagonal line? When does a grid turn into a surface? Later works manufactured total abstractions, where the complexity did not allow reading the machine language as clearly. The impetus then became an inquiry aimed at exposing the differences between the analog and the digital states of the work: What happens when the same drawing is produced twice?

Möbius-Wurst[10]

In the studio classes I teach at the Rhode Island School of Design, I integrate technology into my courses in unorthodox ways so that students immediately question and challenge the meaning and use of a particular software or technology. For instance, when I introduce my students to Rhino, a 3D-modeling software, I usually give a brief fifteen-minute introduction to the

---

10   "Möbius-Wurst" does not directly refer to the author's artwork of the same title. Said work, a hand-made small-scale sculpture also formed out of sand and polyurethane resin, parallel in material to the plopps yet inversely to their forces, external not internal, was 3D scanned which resulted in a 3D model full of triangles; like a hollow shell the triangulation stood against the original form, a formless sausage-like figure, whose upward facing motion, the tilt and lift of the head, with its spiraling torso, could only be interpreted as though the thing was stretching into a Möbius-strip or maybe becoming a Möbius-strip; but cast with that web of mathematically secure triangles, it oscillated between completely fixed geometric definition and loose formlessness, a Wurst-like thing, a digitally processed Wurst, a triangulated Möbius-Wurst.

user interface and the program's functionality. I then bring in a nude model and continue with "3D-modeling from observation" and give instructions that sit somewhere between a software tutorial and a classical live drawing session. For example, "Create a new layer, and use the polyline tool only to draw the contour of the figure" or "Draw a random shape and use the copy tool to work out the shading by duplicating this curve." This playful—and in certain ways impossible—task that the students are confronted with instantaneously challenges the underlying mathematical bones of the software and its working environment. It also confronts the difference of virtuality, and the diagrammatic nature of space in CAD environments, as opposed to the actuality of physical space in real life, an inquiry that is central to the entire studio, my practice and the work presented here.

Sometimes, I think of the plopps as alien spit–a reference to their serial nature, futuristic characteristics, and loose geometric qualities. Simultaneously, the works also read as remnants of some long-deceased civilization, as archeological relics, or as artifacts retrieved from the bottom of an ocean. The title for my recent solo exhibition at the Bell Gallery at Brown University "While Still Before Us After All" was an attempt to highlight and foreground this contradictory temporal dimension of the work. It was also an effort to render the body of work visible as an acceleration of today–as a dark residue of our current culture and technologically determined existence.

In 2014, it had gotten to a point where I was frustrated with the fact that I would create the initial drawings, the input for the machine. The larger project was conceived to question notions of authorship in an age of computational production. For a human subject to create the "seed" it was operating in opposition to this, as the subject would remain the author throughout. It also seemed old-fashioned, because the work would follow a lineage from idea, over sketch (or drawing), and making, to object (or plopp). Several attempts followed, aimed to question the authority of the drawing.

CAD compositions for one piece were appropriated from test patterns and structural compositions from common 3D printing paths. In another attempt to undermine the deterministic weight of the drawing, the CAD drawing was exposed to virtual gravity in a computer simulation, prior to the fabrication. This intervention was inspired by the process itself. If before the work stayed clean, computed, and perfect in its diagrammatic state (namely the digital drawing), and things only turned messy in the physical realm, then here the attempt was to break these distinctions and hierarchies.

Kai Franz: An Archaeology of Digital Architecture 221

Perlin Grid, 2017, Perlin noise algorithm, CAD drawing, CNC-code, CAM-software, plopper (dual-axis precision deposition system), polyurethane, sand, 65" × 105" × 25", David Winton Bell Gallery Brown University, Providence, USA.[11]

---

11 © Kai Franz, 2017.

Almost in a kind of for-loop fashion or recursive gesture, it was aimed to replicate what is happening in the physical state of the work in the digital condition using the same logic for its distortion-gravitational force and material behaviors. At other times the drawings were generated mathematically, through probability and randomness, or algorithmically determined, as with the following work.

Sand to Noise

The formation of the sand landscape in *Perlin Grid (2017)* is determined by a Perlin algorithm, a noise algorithm that is commonly used to simulate natural phenomena in computer graphics. In *Perlin Grid*, this digital procedure, which is used to emulate nature in CGI (computer-generated imagery), was returned to the physical realm. Perlin noise, invented by Ken Perlin in the 1980s, produces textural gradient noise that is used to increase the appearance of realism in computer graphics. Synthetic textures using Perlin noise are found in CGI to make computer-generated visual elements appear more natural, by imitating the controlled random appearance of textures in nature[12]–objects of application span from the ephemeral to the complex, they include "representations of clouds, fire, water, stars, marble, wood, rock, soap films and crystal,"[13] but also terrain and vegetation. By now, these images have become ubiquitous, in certain ways they are the very grain of computations' idea of nature.

Emergence

During the second half of the twentieth century, computer science and the natural sciences experienced a revolution, when bottom-up thinking and design challenged its basic methodologies–away from hypothesis, that rests in approval and disapproval–towards the study of the effects of emergence. Cellular automata are an example of this shift and "while studied by some

---

[12] "Perlin Noise," in *Wikipedia*, accessed May 31, 2022, https://en.wikipedia.org/w/index.php?title=Perlin_noise&oldid=1090721154.

[13] Ken Perlin, "An Image Synthesizer," *ACM SIGGRAPH Computer Graphics* 19, no. 3 (July 1, 1985), 287, https://doi.org/10.1145/325165.325247.

throughout the 1950s and 1960s, it was not until the 1970s and Conway's *Game of Life*, a two-dimensional cellular automaton, that interest in the subject expanded beyond academia"[14]. In the 1980s, Stephen Wolfram developed expansive research of one-dimensional cellular automata, the simplest type of a cellular automaton, a binary, nearest-neighbor, one-dimensional automaton that culminated in the publication of his book *A New Kind of Science* (2002).

Cellular automata are just one example of a generative system that produces emergence. In essence, these systems produce unpredictable phenomena and a high degree of complexity in behavior based on a simple generative logic, such as deterministic rules and parameters. Synonymous to such generative design strategies are agent-based design systems and particle simulations, L-systems, and evolutionary or genetic algorithms, these are computational procedures and models which have been instrumentalized and celebrated by architects over the last two decades as novel methodologies in design.

A common denominator of these generative design processes is that they do not produce a single outcome, but instead output a class of images or results. Greg Lynn, as one of the earliest–and among the most ambitious–practitioners to experiment and theorize digital architecture calls these resulting arrays "families of forms." Lynn's *Embryological House (1997–2001)*, often seen as a pivotal work in the discourse of digital architecture, was a conceptual project, aimed to rethink the house typology beyond the modernist doctrines of simplicity, linearity, modularity, and repetition. His concept was based on an organic prototype that is at once genetic and generic, from this generative prototype or system an infinite number of iterations could be generated[15]. The project was never built, in fact it was conceived as a conceptual work occupying and remaining exclusively in the digital sphere. Moreover, aesthetically and formally, the project embraced the utopian belief in the digital as a paradigm shift and new ground, typical for the 1990s and 2000s.

---

14 "Cellular Automaton," in *Wikipedia*, accessed June 14, 2022, https://en.wikipedia.org/w/index.php?title=Cellular_automaton&oldid=1093143614.
15 The Canadian Centre for Architecture, "Greg Lynn's Embryological House: Case Study in the Preservation of Digital Architecture," accessed July 2, 2022, https://www.docam.ca/conservation/embryological-house/GL3ArchSig.html.

Keep Smiling, Game of Life cellular automaton, instructional PDF, house paint on wooden board, 48″ × 48″ × 9″.[16]

In my own work, I have explored themes of emergence and the relationship of encoded information and rules-based systems intensely. In a series of algorithmic paintings, I literally re-enacted the *Game of Life* following the instructions of the computer simulation of Conway's 1970 *Game of Life*. The act of painting here is dumbed down: Deprived of human agency in the execution of this work, I drop spoonfuls of paint onto a wooden board. The *Game of Life* consists of a two-dimensional grid, where cells can either be on or off, dead or alive. The initial start composition, the states of all cells at the beginning, is called generation zero. It is determined externally, either by the "player" or through randomness–all cells are either dead or alive. What follows is the

---

16   © Kai Franz, 2015–16.

application of a simple set of three rules relative to the states of the neighboring cells for each cell on the grid: (1) Any live cell with two or three live neighbors will be reborn. (2) Any dead cell with exactly three neighbors that are alive will be newborn. (3) All other live cells die or remain dead. These rules are applied to each cell to compute the following generation(s). In my re-enactment of the *Game of Life*, for every cell that is alive, I drop one spoon of house paint. When the generation is complete, the paint dries. Afterwards, the next generation will be completed. What takes seconds to compute in the simulation, takes many months to execute. To paint via this process means to manage paint. The question is no longer "what", or "how to paint", but maybe how to cope with paint. But paint is only one part of the equation.

Between 2015 and 2016, I created four works as parts of a series of algorithmic paintings in this manner. All four are re-enactments of the *Game of Life* again, all four have the same initial starting condition at the beginning, their diagrams are identical. However, the boards were orientated on different angles in space. This was an effort to acknowledge and simultaneously overcome gravity as a totalizing force or condition. The series took about 18 months to complete. Is it too far to say, duration and the impact on everyday life mirror computational ubiquity and determinism today? The titles of these works indicate the vector of the surface normal of the grid or plane, in other words its orientation in space during the making. One exception, "Keep Smiling", was chosen with a bit of black humor and alludes to the endurance of the work. It was also a silly way to entertain myself, or maintain sanity. I chose this particular pattern or cumulative composition at least in part, because I noticed and liked the grotesque clown-like smiling face in the negative space of the work. It is also somewhat of a friendly smile at many of the modulations that the parametric project in architecture has produced. My critique: While said to reject the homogenization (serial repetition) of modernism and pure difference (agglomeration of unrelated elements) of post-modernism in favor of differentiation and correlation as key compositional values, it seems merely to produce a gradient of form, and it does this across the grid and still within it.

In 2018–19, I created another series of *Game of Life* paintings. This time they were matte black. A decision that seemed at first somewhat counterintuitive. It felt like a digital move, like changing the fill color on a shape in Illustrator. It was a step sideways and not forward. Imagining the black and the white paintings next to each other, it was indeed also a wink at the binary determinism that inspired me to make this work.

 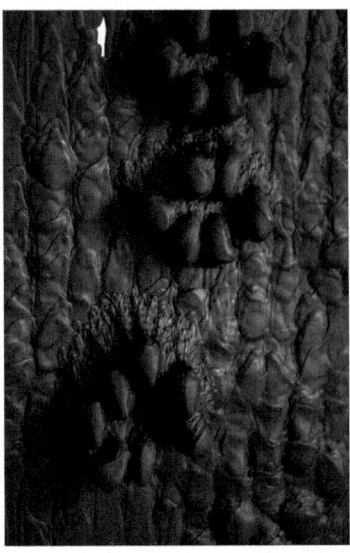

Life (-0.14, -0.51, 0.85), 2018–19, Game of Life cellular automaton, instructional PDF, house paint on wooden board, 48" × 48" × 10".[17]

Failure/Infinity

If *disegno* drew its emancipatory power, the facility for intervention and design, from the possibility of the blank ground or the infinity of the whiteboard, then it seems that with digital architecture such affinities for infinity newly appear. Only now they lie within the object itself, namely in the fluid dynamism of architectural form, behind the infinite class of objects.

Earlier, I used the concept of serialization as a metaphorical vehicle to introduce the idea of readability in the plopps. The truth is however, that these artifacts will never be legible to a machine. They are simply incomputable, because the works absorbed actual randomness and chance when they came to life. Any attempt to accurately reconstruct from these artifacts would fail. This point of non-return is indeed a conscious part of the design, aimed to break the all too often linear chain of optimization and computational

---

17   © Kai Franz, 2018–19.

over-determinism that habitually wants to rest in the pure optimism of digital design. Computational prediction and simulation still fail at the level of individual grains of sand, no matter how banal the parameters of our pseudo-rationality might be. Why do we dare to bring them to life? At best, the dynamism in these digital methodologies presents us with an animated diagram of *disegno*, where all the iterations morph into an endlessly malleable figure. It seems that the captivating allure of this brightly shining figure in the moving image still fascinates us, maybe even blinds us. But this is precisely why judgment should come with urgency. For, if *disegno* is still *design*, the question of quality is still an open one. All too often it seems to be a forgotten one. I am inclined to say it is still a human one.

Designing Games for Social Change
An Interview with Colleen Macklin[1]

Laura Scherling[2]

"Play has the potential to reveal new things about books, music, culture itself, and the material world. The idea is that play lets us take something and *stretch it, push it, and play with it*. We take it from its original form and try new things with it. Play is ultimately at the core of what it means to be human. We learn about the world by playing with it. When we were little babies, we were constantly touching things, throwing things, and playing with things to understand how the world works. We have to continue retaining that playful spirit, especially today in the world of complex systems. In a world where we are dealing with climate change and other humanitarian emergencies, to understand things through play is to get beneath the surface and understand them a bit more deeply."
— Colleen Macklin, US

---

1   Parsons School of Design, US.
2   Columbia University, US.

Games have long played a role in shaping societies and belief systems. Ancient Olympic games were designed to honor Zeus, and the mancala game, popular in Western Africa, is one of the oldest two-player strategy board games in the world. Games have the power to educate, entertain, and to interpret existing cultures, reinvent them, and make them more playful. More recently, social impact game design has contributed to helping communities to solve complex problems, from disaster preparedness to urban renewal. Games that tackle social issues have been at the center of Colleen Macklin's work.

In this interview, Macklin describes her experiences as a game designer and as a professor at Parsons School of Design. Macklin has observed that designers and creative professionals are increasingly positioned to have a positive social impact and that games function as an "active literacy for the 21st Century." In her 2017 TedXCambridge talk, for instance, she described that, "Games help us understand concepts and systems better than many other approaches to learning. Game design might be key to modeling some of our most complex systems, including climate, finance, and politics."

Throughout her career, Macklin has engaged with organizations, students, and her close collaborators at Local No. 12 to create positive social change and to ask challenging questions about "what it means to be human in the 21st century" and how to "make design more equitable," departing from the more traditional or fundamental roles that games have frequently played. In this interview, Macklin recalls her work designing Dear Reader (a game of literary wordplay), her work for the American Red Cross, and her recent experimentations with using artificial intelligence in game design and development.

Interview

Dr. Laura Scherling: Can you tell me about your work as a designer and educator?

Professor Colleen Macklin: I teach at Parsons School of Design and have been teaching there since the mid-90s. I started teaching interaction design and began to transition into game design, which was a return to something I loved doing when I was a kid. When I was nine years old, I designed video games and programmed them in Basic, so you could say it was a full circle for me. I also run a research lab called PetLab, which stands for Prototyping Education and Technology Lab at Parsons. We create games in the social interest. We have worked with partners such as the Red Cross, the U.S. Holocaust Memorial Museum, the Boys and Girls Club, and many others, creating interactive and game-based learning and approaching difficult subjects with the notion of play and games.

LS: I saw your app Dear Reader, a game of literary wordplay. Can you tell me about Dear Reader?

CM: Dear Reader was released on Apple Arcade in September 2019, and we continue to be an exclusive game on the Arcade platform, a subscription-based service. The idea behind the game came when my colleagues Peter Berry, John Sharp and Eric Zimmerman—the four of us who comprise the company Local No. 12—were thinking about how we might create a game that you could play using a text-based application. In particular, we were looking at how to make a game you can play on Twitter. Of course, we have moved far away from that initial idea, but over time, when we were first prototyping, we wondered what texts we should use for this word puzzle idea. We thought we might pull something from Project Gutenberg or open-source libraries of different kinds of literature.

We picked up Alice in Wonderland and started to use sentences from the book as the basis for these word puzzles. We quickly realized that the exciting thing about this project is not so much the puzzles, although I think we did a nice job with the different word puzzles and gameplay we have in the game. Instead, it is about rediscovering this amazing literature that is out and available in the public domain. Dear Reader has over a hundred books, from a diversity of perspectives and genres, from Pride and Prejudice to the poetry of Phillis Wheatley Peters. We highlight not only European and American "classics" that people are most familiar with in the English-speaking world, but also a wide range of literature from around the world, as well as works by indigenous authors, authors of color, and writing from queer and feminist perspectives.

The gameplay is essentially taking different snippets from these texts and putting them back together so that you can remake the book. It is as if someone jumbled everything up, and you have to go through and make sense of everything. There are over twenty different word puzzle types in the game. Some puzzles scramble words up, some turn words into anagrams or ask you to find words within words, and some work at a paragraph-level where you try to put sentences back into order. Ultimately, one of the goals of the game for us was to develop a deeper appreciation of these amazing works of literature and the beauty of language itself. Local No.12's primary goal is to take existing culture and make it playful. There is plenty of learning that can be had when you are looking at some of these books and revisiting them. You can enjoy the craft of these beautiful sentences, the meaning of the texts themselves, and being playful with language and literature.

LS: The suggested age is twelve and above. Who is playing the game?

CM: We have a great audience and some really dedicated players. In fact, we even have some folks who have almost finished all 100 books, which is a major task. That means playing Dear Reader for hundreds of hours! Nonetheless, the majority of our players are those who like word puzzle games and are interested in reading. They might not necessarily be what you would consider " gamers," but they are fascinated with literature and word puzzles, and they like to keep their minds moving. Many of our players are super dedicated and reach out to us and speak to us directly with suggestions for books to add and some really great design ideas. In addition, we have players from all over the world. Some players are from nonEnglish-speaking backgrounds; they might be learning English, and they are using the game as an opportunity to practice English.

LS: When you update Dear Reader, do you add some additional books?

CM: We add new books to Dear Reader all the time, as well as new design features – again often inspired by what we hear from our players. In addition, every year new books go into the public domain, which means that we get to choose which ones to add.

LS: Do you do the design work? Do you work with a studio?

CM: We are a small team of about seven at the moment. Everyone has a say in the overall game design, and most of us work on adding the books and editing the content into bite-sized chapters, which is incredibly labor-intensive. We also have our specialties. Karina Popp is our lead book curator, she helps us decide what to add and does the lion's share of adding books to the game. Peter Berry is the lead programmer, John Sharp is our lead visual designer, Diego Garcia does visual design and animation, Alexander King does a lot of game balancing and analytics, Eric Zimmerman is lead game designer and puzzle-crafter, and I focus primarily on player experience and user interface. That is a simplified rundown, however – we all wear many hats!

LS: Can you talk about the importance of literary apps?

CM: Play has the potential to reveal new things about books, music, culture itself, and the material world. The idea is that play lets us take something and stretch it, push it, and play with it. We take it from its original form and try new things with it.

Play is ultimately at the core of what it means to be human. We learn about the world by playing with it. When we were little babies, we were constantly touching things, throwing things, and playing with things to understand how the world works. We have to continue retaining that playful spirit, especially today in the world of complex systems. In a world where we are dealing with climate change and other humanitarian emergencies, to understand things through play is to get beneath the surface and understand them more deeply. At least that is my opinion.

Therefore, when we are talking about literature, that is one aspect. However, play can be applied to all kinds of things in the world to get us to think in new ways about the form of things.

LS: You have had a lot of experience with these systems in your work for the Red Cross. I would like to hear more about this work.

CM: My work with the Red Cross started with the Red Cross/Red Crescent Climate Centre, and then expanded to other Red Cross branches, including the American Red Cross and their affiliates around the world. They were primarily dealing with the impacts of climate change and resilience in the face of flooding, drought, and natural disasters. Our work together spanned about nine years, between 2009–2018. The funny thing about it is that we designed ourselves out of the project by the end. We created a training framework in games and co-design that enabled the Red Cross to facilitate the program on their own. Therefore, our work is still used in the Red Cross, but we are not as actively involved.

When I started working with the Red Cross, the first project was meant to facilitate conversations between meteorologists and those involved in the climate science side of things, people who live in places hardest hit by climate change related events, and logistics people at the Red Cross. We created this game to bring all these folks together to talk about the challenges and knowing what kind of response to take when a forecast comes out. For instance, flooding. If you get a forecast that has a lot of rain, how do you know when it is important to evacuate to higher ground?

The game was meant to show how difficult it is to make that call, and discuss how to work together to be more resilient. It did not necessarily teach you what to do; it just revealed difficulties and was a place to have a conversation. I developed the game with several of my design students at Parsons after meeting with some great people from the Red Cross, and we designed it quickly. It only took about three weeks to design the initial prototype, which I, along with local and international Red Cross members brought to Senegal to an island called Doune Baba Dieye, a fishing village and an island off the coast of Saint-Louis. We designed this game to "playtest" there.

When I visited, I was immediately struck by the fact that play was a universal language. We made a card game that was simple, translated it to French, and tried it out. That also created the opportunity to talk about shared experiences. That was the main takeaway with this project: you could have folks whose profession is fishing—people in a village where fishing was the main economy—and climate scientists and people from the international aid community working together by playing together. From these different perspectives, the game created common ground and a shared experience that prompted incredible conversations.

The gameplay was simple, similar to Apples to Apples or Cards Against Humanity, but with a very different deck of cards and purpose! One player deals out a series of weather forecasts with different time-horizons, and everyone else plays a response. One response might be to evacuate, whereas the other might be a longer-term response such as creating communication networks or putting a go-bag together. We also included blank cards for players to write-in a response. These were shuffled into the deck to be played by others. We ended up learning what local communities were doing and the game became a way for different communities to share knowledge. For example, one intervention included replacing chickens with ducks for communities prone to seasonal flooding because ducks float, whereas chickens do not! This "crowd-sourced" deck of cards sparked conversation and new ideas about how communities could mitigate climate risks.

Three years later, the island of Doune Baba Dièye, where we first playtested the game, disappeared underwater. The villagers had to be relocated to a very different place from the island they lived on. Their whole way of life was upended, a tragedy in the deepest sense. Of course, no game can stop a flood, and even if we're better prepared after playing one, the magnitude and complexity of the world can't be matched in even the most realistic simulations. However, games can help us talk about the problems we have on a shared basis. Games can't replicate reality, but they can help us practice the skills needed to deal with it. Climate-related disasters are increasing in Senegal and around the world. A game will not necessarily give us the answer to how we deal with that, but it could get us talking about it; thinking about it, and hopefully also forming social ties and bonds to be more resilient because it is going to take everyone working together.

LS: As an outsider working with the residents of Doune Baba Dieye, what did you need to learn or do in order to join the community while working with them?

CM: I studied international affairs at the graduate level, so I learned how one might work in an international context, which was somewhat helpful. I also taught abroad for several years, which was a humbling learning experience. However, the key thing is that we got things wrong several times; and in order to learn, you need to own and learn from your failures. In those early years working with communities outside the US, what we did wrong is that we designed games based on the ones we play here. While play may be a universal language, games are cultural – they reflect the cultures in which they're played. I would advise a designer joining another community to go without even designing anything at all first and learn the games that community plays. That's what we ended up doing, and as a result, we ended up learning the games people played in different places around the world.

In Uganda, we learned probably fifteen different versions of mancala (and lost each game!) We learned different playground games and other games that children were playing. We also learned the games the adults were playing and ended up co-designing games together. Therefore, you have to go in without anything. With hands empty, go learn from the community that is there. The other benefit to playing local games is that when we arrived, we were outsiders. But as soon as we started playing games with people and failing or falling down literally—we were learning a jump rope game, and my colleague John had a big wipeout. Once we made sure he was ok, it was an exciting moment because everyone laughed in a kind of celebration of our shared fallibilities as humans.

Playing with each other is a great way to start designing with each other, and that was ultimately the takeaway.

LS: In our current situation with the Covid-19 pandemic, how do "games" and "play" help us?

CM: If anything, games have more of a place in helping us connect to each other at a moment where it feels like we are all in our little bubbles. I've been playing games with friends online and at home. There are more hours in the day now that we are not commuting as much as we used to, and games are a great way to fill that time while also finding ways to connect. I am not talking about video games only but also traditional tabletop games that have been converted to online games to enable remote play.

LS: Have you seen anything interesting happening with board game design during this crisis?

CM: Board games are experiencing an incredible renaissance right now! I would say that board games, video games, and tools become more accessible as people realize that you can make a game yourself. We are experiencing a time where more and more hobbyists and independent designers are in the space making games and getting them out there. People are realizing that there is a real value to the connection that games can create. There's a resurgence in tabletop role-playing games like Dungeons and Dragons as a social alternative to single-player games. And of course, video games do not have to be only single-player; there are many online multiplayer games.

LS: A lot has changed with digital transformation in design. We have a lot of variety! How do you personally view the development of digital technologies in design today?

CM: Designers are increasingly becoming public figures. Whether you are on Twitter writing short things or online writing a medium post, there is much more writing about design and the design process today than there was twenty years ago. This is a great development because it provides more of a sense of community practice. That is one thing I have seen change, which is funny. Writing is not high-tech; it's ancient, but with social media and online platforms there is more of it out there now about how games and other designed technologies are made.

I think that designers need to increasingly partner with scientists and engineers, especially to understand the impacts of what they are making in the world. And that could be anything from something physical—like the computer mouse and its impact in terms of material and lifecycle—or some computer code and understanding how the user interface impacts people. Accessibility is incredibly important. Therefore, the increasing use of technology in everyday life necessitates more thoughtful and ethical design, placing designers in a position of great responsibility to ensure that their products are sustainable, accessible, and not creating evil in the world.

LS: When you think about young designers being in this position of responsibility, is there anything particular you would tell them?

CM: Everyone makes mistakes! Try to make your mistakes early in the process, prototype, and test your designs. In game design, we call it playtesting. Everything has externalities. Everything you make has an impact. Just think about it, and learn from failure. Try to make things better in this world, but experiment, explore, and talk to people from different fields, practices and life-experiences. An important sense for designers to cultivate aside from seeing, hearing, and touching, is empathy—knowing how what you make impacts others, and playtesting is a good method for figuring that out. Be humble, and do not be fooled. If somebody says they like something, look at their expression and body language. If things don't go the way you intended, accept failure, learn from it, and integrate it into your practice.

LS: This is an important piece of advice! When it comes to products, especially digital products that are not tactile, it can be especially challenging to grasp these impacts. Is there anything else you would like to share about the work and research you have been doing?

CM: My interests have expanded! Lately, I have been looking at artificial intelligence and what it means to interface with other forms of intelligence other than our own. I am far more interested in what the creative potentials of these alternate viewpoints are in the world and what happens when AI stops working and starts playing. Therefore, I am doing a project called "Cloud Theory," a simple little game where you can talk to an AI about the shapes they see in clouds. I'm using these tiny, very rudimentary language models that say funny and often nonsensical things about the clouds. Just like we see shapes in clouds, we can find meaning in the strange strings of words these little language models put together. This, to me, is more interesting than the state of the art research in making large language models that replicate human intelligence.

LS: When you are in a dialogue with an AI, what do you learn from these conversations and from some of your other research?

CM: The game works by talking to a very small and early GPT-based language model that I train with the public domain writing of different authors and thinkers. Therefore, you can have a conversation with a fictional character that sounds kind of like Alice from Alice in Wonderland. Alternatively, you can have a conversation with the philosopher Bertrand Russell about what they see in the clouds. However, as I've been working on this project, I have started to feed the outputs of the models back into themselves, which is kind of like copying something with a Xerox Machine so many times that it becomes something else. Each time you play, you have a different "artificial friend" to talk to.

I am also interested in how we can make games differently. In other words, in addition to making games for social change, how can we change how we think about game design? Most games are based on core mechanics and genres that are pretty well-trodden. There is the first-person shooter, the platformer, racing and sports games, and other common design patterns and narrative tropes that players expect.

I am interested in how games can explore other spaces. For example, can we create experiences that help us understand non-human ways of being? Games can do this – they can help us think about systems, and experience new worlds, and forms of agency. With the climate crisis, with inequalities in the world, to ensure that we survive and thrive and that everyone has an opportunity for a good life, we need to be able to think differently.

Games are a reflection of culture, society, and our desires as humans. Therefore, they can also reflect the less desirable aspects of humanity. Games can reinforce a belief in ideas like the meritocracy that does not exist because we live in an unequal world. Therefore, games are part of both the problem and the solution. This is where my latest interests regarding change for games come from; we need to be thinking about not only what a game is about but also what it does and what it reinforces under the surface.

We are at a time when algorithms define much of how we live and the information we get, and they are applied unequally. Algorithmic bias is a well-researched and existing thing in the world. Games are the original algorithms. They are rules-based systems with a great deal to reveal about rules and laws and algorithms in real life. My hope for the field of game design is that we continue developing new ways for games to connect us, to reveal the workings of the world and that helps us think about what the future might be. I believe in striving for utopia. I am an optimist. I feel like games can give us a space where we playfully try things out, where we can connect and have shared experiences to build a baseline for making the world a better place.

LS: That should always be the goal, making the world a better place!

Digital Transformation and Service Design Practice in Public Sector

Sahar Nikzad[1] and Paulina Porten[2]

The digital transformation wave is impacting municipal administration structures and strategies. Governments and cities are aiming to digitize their internal systems and communications with residents, and given the rapid pace of digitalization in all aspects of society, the public sector is expected to follow suit. However, e-government throughout the world has proven that this transformation is far from simple. Some practices, such as those in service design, may promote and support the issues by encouraging and facilitating a different way of thinking and doing things. This enrichment is explained and examined in the service design project "MeinungsMobil," which was carried out in collaboration with the City of Cologne. MeinungsMobil is a citizen participation project that promotes engagement with city decision-making and is usable for all departments in the city. During the development phase, the project's goals were to address the inclusion of citizen engagement, which was both physical and digital, and to provide individuals the freedom to select how they wanted to interact with the city based on their circumstances. To understand municipal administration digital transformation, a lot can be learned from the problems and restrictions encountered during the process, such as the transfer of design prototypes to realized service, and the service design methodology used to discover solutions based on present facilities.
— *Sahar Nikzad, Iran/Germany, and Paulina Porten, Germany*

---

1   Köln International School of Design, Iran/Germany.
2   Köln International School of Design, Germany.

How Digital Transformation and Service Design in the Public Sector are Related

The discipline of service design has been around for more than twenty-five years and has gone through various phases of experimentation, framing, and expansion. It is a field that is constantly growing. Service design is an evolving organism that adapts to people and their needs. The UK Design Council aptly described the discipline as "all about making the service you deliver useful, usable, efficient, effective and desirable."[3] Service design roles can differ slightly in different fields. Manuela Aguirre, lead systemic designer at Designit believes that, "service design is a vehicle to reduce inequalities in the public sector, to work across organizational silos, to enable a culture of collaboration and to enable participation of citizens."[4] Aguirre also claimed that collaboration, participation, and human-centeredness are the values embedded in a service design approach. Service design is about finding out what customers need and adapting processes and products to meet those needs. Service design in the public sector needs to consider both parties: the city's possibilities and conditions, and the citizens' needs and wants.

Digital transformation, on the other hand, is often about digitizing existing processes and products, thus making them more efficient. Anastasia Bondar, a service designer in the City of Cologne, illustrated why service design and digital transformation could benefit each other by referring to the administration project Einfache Leistungen für Eltern (ELFE), meaning Simple Benefits for Parents. The administration project was about the digitalization of child benefit applications and has aimed to relieve parents of the bureaucracy in the time around becoming a parent. According to Bondar, "digitizing this process without service design would result in exactly the same amount of work for parents. Using service design, the bureaucratic steps are analyzed, reconsidered, and reduced as much as possible in order to give parents more time for their newborn." This example demonstrated that with service design, digital transformation is about rethinking and re-inventing

---

3   Marc Stickdorn, Markus Edgar Hormess, Adam Lawrence, and Jakob Schneider, *This Is Service Design Doing: Applying Service Design Thinking in the Real World*, (Sebastopol: O'Reilly Media, 2018), 53.
4   Majid Iqbal, Stephan Jenniskens, and Dounia Ouchene, "Service Design Impact Report: Public Sector" (Service Design Network, October 2016), 24, https://www.service-desig n-network.org/uploads/sdn-impact-report_public-sector.pdf.

services in a holistic user- and system-centered way. Service *design thinking* can make a fundamental contribution to digital transformation and has proven indispensable for transferring services into the online world. At the same time, digitalization also greatly influenced the service design discipline as it brought up new questions, tools, and possibilities for solving problems.

Governments across the world are digitizing transactions and services to improve governing bodies' contracts with the general public. A growing number of nations, including Brazil, Ireland, Greece, and the United Kingdom, are exploring strategies for the design and delivery of services that streamline the user experience and consolidate their public sector web estates into a single government domain.[5] E-governance is intended to save money by shifting channels and providing more efficient services. An initial wave of digitization has benefited individuals and the government, but much work still needs to be done. If a service has fundamental faults, merely shifting it to a digital channel will not improve the services. To make services useful to users, they must be developed with people—and entire communities—in mind from the start. This entails examining policy, design, and service delivery, as well as bringing together the many diverse government sectors involved. A tool that may be used for this is service design.[6] Citizens' evaluations of their service experiences are heavily influenced by the service design features of e-government services, and this has significant implications for outcomes like perceived service quality and citizen satisfaction with e-government[7].

In order to fully understand these new challenges, this chapter is focuses on the case study "MeinungsMobil" (which translates to "mobile for opinions"), a service design project in the public sector. Birgit Mager, President of the Service Design Network (SDN), emphasized that service design increasingly contributes to the public sector, especially when it comes to digitalization

---

5   OECD, "Digital Government Review of Slovenia: Leading the Digital Transformation of the Public Sector," (Paris: OECD Digital Government Studies, 2021), https://doi.org/10.1787/954b0e74-en.
6   Majid Iqbal, Stephen Jenniskens and Dounie Ouchene, "Service Design Impact Report: Public Sector," 85.
7   Frank K.Y. Chan, James Y. L. Thong, Susan A. Brown, Venkatesh, Viswanath. "Service Design and Citizen Satisfaction with E-Government Services: A Multidimensional Perspective." *Public Administration Review* Volume, 81. Issue 5 (September/October 2021), 874–894, https://doi.org/10.1111/puar.13308.

and innovation.[8] This case study investigates how to create a balance between customer needs and digitalization, and how service designers can use digital change to their advantage, including which questions and challenges still need to be solved.

MeinungsMobil: Service Design for the City Administration

Strategic designer Caroline Paulick-Thiel, who does consulting and facilitation of digital transformation projects and promotes new governance models, pointed out the power of service design in public systems. Across the design disciplines, there are many tools to reach out and engage the citizens appropriately.[9] It is clear to many governments now that the most effective work for creating a better society is going far beyond traditional stakeholder hearings and internal meetings. It is about applying participatory approaches, involving diverse groups of people, and connecting end-users and stakeholders in the entire creative process (depending on the project). Therefore, the question is not whether to let the public participate but how to *design* participation processes most efficiently.

MeinungsMobil was a service design project of Köln International School of Design (KISD) in collaboration with the City of Cologne. The seven-month-long project dealt with the topic of mobile public citizen participation and service design thinking and aimed to directly approach citizens as users of municipal services. MeinungsMobil was designed as a bicycle trailer that can be driven to the location of the planned participation. This enabled co-creative work, which was necessary to find holistic solutions that met citizens' needs, including in the context of digital transformation within a city's administration. Through a modular set of participation and service design methods integrated into the MeinungsMobil, three designated levels of participation were explored: information, consultation, and co-creation. The project was an outcome of a larger program with the City of Cologne and the German government, which dealt with digitalization in the city administration with the help of service design. In order to understand how MeinungsMobil

---

8   Birgit Mager, "The Future of Service Design," in *The Future of Service Design*, ed. Birgit Mager (Köln: KISD, TH Köln, 2020), 17.

9   Yushi Chen and Sara Lucia Arbelaez Llano, "Service Design and Government," in *The Future of Service Design*, ed. Birgit Mager (Köln: KISD, TH Köln, 2020), 40.

came about and what requirements were placed on the project, it is necessary to take a look at the legislation in Germany regarding digital transformation.

Germany, like many countries, remains in need of development in terms of e-government. The public sector still has a lot of catching up to do regarding the digital transformation of government services. Therefore, it participated in the Online Access Act (OZG),[10] which has aimed to make public administration more accessible by translating forms and documents from analog formats into user-friendly digital formats, making the application process for government services and benefits easier.[11] By 2023, it is expected to provide 575 types of digital administration services, enabling citizens and businesses to use these services from anywhere at any time with just one account. Since businesses will be able to make requests and notifications to authorities more efficiently, the administrative load on businesses should be reduced. Investing in digital transformation is ensuring that people are informed and have the essential insights into which government entities store and access data. The implementation process is aiming to be transparent, participatory, and user-centric. Other programs in Germany that have set out to accomplish digital transformation in government and society at large are including support for digital education infrastructure in schools, digital education programs for the elderly, support for digital cultural projects, and funding of more human-technology interaction (HTI)[12] innovations to empower and educate people.

Public participation and involvement, as well as the digital transformation of states and society, are two key components of Germany's Open Government implementation. Since North Rhine-Westphalia has an Open Government Pact, it has open government activities and networks. Cologne, which is located within this state, has an innovation office that is responsible for city administration transformation initiatives. The City of Cologne is currently working on 182 innovation projects, and thirty-four of these are digitization-focused. They are aspiring to design future administration

---

10 The Organization for Economic Co-operation and Development (OECD) defines open government as a culture of governance based on innovative and sustainable public policies inspired by the principles of transparency, accountability, and participation. Germany has been a participant in the OZG since December 2016.
11 "What Is the Online Access Act?," Federal Ministry of the Interior and Community, accessed June 29, 2022, https://www.onlinezugangsgesetz.de/Webs/OZG/EN/home/home-node.html;jsessionid=D4FFF25C8D3CC04D36BD25F57F051048.2_cid364.
12 HTI is about studying people's interactions with technology in order to better understand and enhance technology's fit with its users.

that has digital transformation capabilities and expedites and simplifies citizen-administration interactions. They have also created new services for individuals and have digitized and modernized the organization. These initiatives involve digitizing city department files, construction, urban cleaning, online registration, and communications, as well as virtual communication and online counseling for citizens.

The City of Cologne recognized the importance of service design in establishing successful services, and the innovation office approached Birgit Mager to support them using service design practices. They signed a three-year contract with KISD, which involved a six- to eight-week project every semester and enabled students to work on projects with the city focusing on innovation in the public sector. As part of these projects, students are focusing on consulting and assisting the City of Cologne in changing its structures and working methods. MeinungsMobil was a result of this collaboration's medium-term project.

MeinungsMobil: Challenges for Service Design Practice

In order to understand the impact of digital transformation in service design practice in detail, the design process of MeinungsMobil can be considered. It is best described using the common service design thinking model "Double Diamond." The whole process began with this challenge. While the first step (or "diamond") was dedicated to information gathering and ideation to clarify a defined problem, the second diamond is emphasizing on iterative design, conceptualization, and information processing. This process ends with a design solution. At MeinungsMobil, the first diamond, "Discover and Define," and the first part, "Develop," of the second diamond, were implemented from April to June 2021 as a mid-term project at KISD in collaboration with the city of Cologne and twenty-three students.[13] The second diamond, "Develop and Deliver," was developed between July and October 2021 by a team of six

---

13 Participating students: Michael Möckel, Christoph Laszig, Theresa Tropschuh, André Freiha, Julius Walsch, Tim Walta, Duane Carlos Meurer, Giulia Barone, Mariana Taveira, Paulina Porten, Jihee Hwang, Lilli Koskinen, Ying-Yu Chiang, Jiye Kim, Cora Gläser, Christian Wild von Hohenborn, Ben Simon Schrieber, David Stoffel, Johanna Pirwitz, Sahar Nikzad, Giulia Senni, Franciska Lucas Dias. Project supervisor: Prof. Birgit Mager, Janina Rösch, Anastasia Bondar. City administration: Maik Dick, Anastasia Bondar, Paul Wehner, Maria Knaup, Jennifer Stehr, Leonie Firmenich.

KISD student designers.[14] The development phase was conducted iteratively. The following section explains and analyzes the work process based on these two phases.

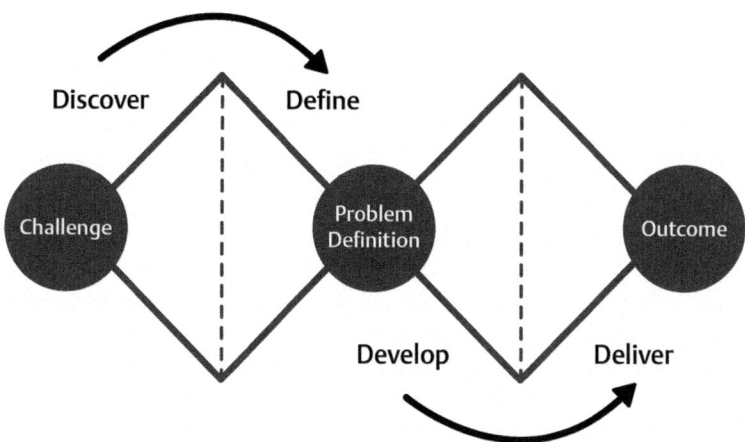

Double Diamond: a design process model popularized by the British Design Council in 2005.[15]

Discover, Define, and Develop

The "Discover, Define, and Develop" phases involved research, conducting interviews, co-design workshops with stakeholders, prototyping, and testing. The project's starting point was the question, "How can we design a participation process and tools for the City of Cologne resulting in the most benefits?"

During the "Discover" phase, digital tools such as Zoom, Miro, and Conceptboard were particularly enriching to the service design practice. They enabled conducting interviews with an international and diverse spectrum of experts from the industry, such as FutureGov from the UK, GovLabAustria,

---

14   Team members: Theresa Tropschuh, Julius Walsch, Paulina Porten, Johanna Pirwitz, Janina Rösch, and Anastasia Bondar.
15   Sahar Nikzad and Paulina Porten, Graphic, 2021.

and the Center Cork County Council & Snook from Ireland.[16] These interviews aimed to discover these organizations' approaches to service design and their methods of engaging citizens to participate in city projects. The experts shared their daily experiences with working in the public sector. Moreover, partners from the city administration of Cologne and participation experts from Germany collaborated simultaneously, co-creatively, and remotely during an online co-creation workshop. The workshop focused on answering the question: "How can the City of Cologne involve citizens in city planning processes?" For the workshop, the participants were given four use cases in which citizen participation needed to be improved. During the "Discover" phase, the design practice benefited significantly from digital facilities as it provided flexible communication with customers and experts, access to research resources, and enabling low-threshold collaboration and co-creation.

This first phase led to the "Define" phase, where main insights about what was needed for successful participation and service design thinking in the context of public space and digitalization were collected. These requirements can be considered as a result of the discovery and focus on the question of how to design participation resulting in the most benefits:

1. Quick and active public involvement.
2. Multiple opportunities for the public to communicate their ideas.
3. The power of physical spaces.
4. The importance of digital public collaboration, and
5. The combination of analog and digital tools to reach all citizens.

With these in mind, the first iteration of the development process was conducted with the final outcome of three prototypes related to mobile participation and service design thinking. The prototypes included:

---

16   A total of nine interviews were conducted with: Future Gov (UK), Scottish Government (Scotland), Tech4 Germany (Germany), Cork County Council & Snook (Ireland), GovLab (Austria), CityLAB Berlin (Germany), Verschwörhaus Ulm (Germany), and UpLab (Germany).

- A physical cart that was easy to transport around the city.
- Service design thinking methods (digital and analog ways to engage citizens through participation).[17]
- Two digital platforms including an app for the citizens to contribute digitally via their mobile phones, and an app for city staff that supported the physical service and mobile application.

In summary, the main focus of the prototypes was to combine analog and digital ways of engagement using technologies like augmented reality and artificial intelligence based on the insights gained in the "Discovery" phase. The design challenge was building a trustworthy relationship between the city and the citizens of Cologne. This entailed a careful balance between modern solutions and adapting to the future of digitization while still being relatable for all citizens. The key was to combine simple participatory methods with an appealing physical brand identity, using digitization as a bridge between citizens and the city. For a public service design tool like MeinungsMobil that is aiming to engage all kinds of users, the right balance between the increasingly digital world and the physical space was particularly important.

Develop and Deliver

In order to understand how to optimally balance digital and analog engagement and the challenges that service design practice was facing, the final implementation of MeinungsMobil in the city administration must be considered. This is described as the "Develop and Deliver" phase, which included iterative feedback sessions with the city administration, the development of prototypes, testing, and the final implementation of MeinungsMobil as a participation and service design tool in the City of Cologne.

---

17   The developed methods are: MeinungAR, MeinungsStimme and MeinungsRöhren. MeinungAR is an interactive augmented reality-driven solution for image-based voting processes. MeinungsStimme is a voice and artificial intelligence-aided concept for an easy and direct way of leaving opinions. MeinungsRöhren is a rather traditional voting poll attached to the MeinungsMobil. It is a common and effective way of asking the citizens' opinion.

Testing the final implemented service, MeinungsMobil, with Cologne citizens, 2021.[18]

The second project section started with a workshop with city administration where previous prototypes were reconsidered and revised in the form of requirement analysis. This analysis pointed out that the previous advanced digital approaches did not match the facilities and needs of the city administration and citizens. While thinking outside the box and coming up with new perspectives is needed for a successful digital transformation, service design practices also need to react to community needs and consider their point of view concerning digital technologies. As the prototypes had an advanced technical approach, using technologies like augmented reality and artificial intelligence, future users would need detailed onboarding to be able to implement and evaluate the methods adequately. However, MeinungsMobil aimed for quick and accessible participation and co-design, the reason why the methods had to be rethought in iterative feedback sessions with the city administration. Compared to the first phase, the second phase mainly focused on the right balance between analog and digital components regarding the needs of the city administrations and citizens. The outcome of the requirement analysis covered the following aspects:

---

18   Theresa Tropschuh, Photograph of MeinungsMobil, 2021.

1. MeinungsMobil should expand the existing participation possibilities of the City of Cologne through more innovative methods. The existing co-creation tools should become mobile.
2. MeinungsMobil is supposed to enhance the dialogue with and between citizens by creating a mobile/temporary meeting and information places in a public space.
3. MeinungsMobil should link digital and analog participation (e.g., with the municipal participation website "Meinung für Köln"[19] tablet and Internet access).
4. MeinungsMobil should function in a cross-project and modular way.
5. The documented results/evaluations of participation should be able to flow into further planning processes.

Veedels Check project for MeinungsMobil.[20]

---

19 "Meinung für Köln" is a digital participation platform that the City of Cologne uses to gather citizens' opinions and comments on projects, accessed June 30, 2022, https://www.meinungfuer.koeln.
20 "Hey Köln!," Beteiligungsportal der Stadt Köln, accessed June 29, 2022, https://meinungfuer.koeln/hey-koeln.

During the development phase, several challenges arose. First of all, the implementation involved planning and constructing a bike trailer that fit traffic regulations, which led to various structural challenges. MeinungsMobil was designed in detail in 3D software and manufactured using computer-controlled production techniques. These digital tools made it possible to precisely translate the prototype into the final product. Additionally, the digital platform and methods were adjusted to the needs of the city administration and citizens trying to find a more accessible way of combining digital and analog engagement. Instead of creating new participation services from scratch, the city administration's existing participation tools were considered. Compared to the earlier prototypes, the final implemented methods were more aligned with the city administration's existing structure and way of engaging citizens by, for example, linking to the municipal participation website "Meinung für Köln" (Opinions for Cologne) onsite.

The final MeinungsMobil design included a bike trailer and a series of participation and service design methods. The broad selection of integrated methods would enable them to be used in all levels of city administration. There was an information stand set up with the possibility to display flyers and attach posters and plans, and citizens could easily be informed about projects. Quantitative opinion polls could be conducted with integrated opinion tubes. Whiteboards provided a basis for short co-creation workshops to develop ideas together on site. Moreover, audio-visual content could be incorporated thanks to an integrated laptop (convertible). An integrated router offered the possibility to conduct hybrid formats and, for example, to connect speakers via live stream. The city began utilizing MeinungsMobil in March 2022 as a tool to involve residents in co-creative decision-making in various initiatives. Veedels Check was the first initiative that encouraged young citizens (12+ years old) to link to a digital map and mark locations they liked or disliked. MeinungsMobil remained in Mülheim, one of the city's key districts, to inform people about the program, encourage them to participate, and create improvements in Cologne based on young people's ideas.

Conclusion

All in all, the service design project MeinungsMobil case study underlined that digital transformation in city administration can be challenging. It is particularly important for the service design practice to find the right balance between innovation and community needs and facilities. We observed that a digital solution might solve many problems quickly and efficiently, but might not be easily applicable to all users. As service designers, it is important to be aware of this gap and to figure out: "How many changes can I make without it being overwhelming and losing users along the way?" In the context of digital transformation and service design in city administrations, one of the biggest challenges was finding the right balance between expanding the space for technical tools and the citizens' needs.

In German city administration, there is still room for improvement in terms of digital transformation. It is particularly important to understand that it is necessary to co-creatively work on digital transformation in order to get holistic solutions that meet the needs of the citizens. Even if MeinungsMobil had to compromise on its original digital approach, it can still be seen as a contribution to digitalization. It is enabling the City of Cologne to approach the citizens in the public space and ask for feedback. Engagement within this process is particularly important to meet the users' needs.

Despite large-scale increases in IT spending, the German public's utilization of current digital services has been slowly dropping in recent years. Being one of the world's most significant economies, Germany has frequently been rated in the low-to-mid-range digital government rankings.[21] Although the German government has begun a large-scale reform of its public service delivery model, one of the biggest challenges confronting the German public sector in undertaking this transformation journey is the country's federal system, which leaves each state to devise its own digitalization strategies.[22] On the other hand, citizens do not utilize many online public services and administrative applications because they are unavailable or require additional technology to be associated with the electronic identification and a personal service account.

These accessibility challenges require a high level of administrative literacy that many individuals do not need for their otherwise private online

---

21 Ines Mergel, "Digital Transformation of the German State," in Public Administration in Germany, ed. Sabine Kuhlmann et al., Governance and Public Management (Cham: Springer International Publishing, 2021), 331–55, https://doi.org/10.1007/978-3-030-53697-8_19.

22 Harry Baldock, "Digitally Transforming the German Public Sector: The Path to a Smarter Society," Totaltelecom, January 20, 2022, https://www.totaltele.com/512217/Digitally-transforming-the-German-public-sector-The-path-to-a-smarter-society.

interactions. Of course, this is not the only reason why individuals are hesitant to use government services. German citizens and people in many countries around the world have a long history of being worried about handing over data to the government out of fear of becoming "transparent citizens."[23]

Five main areas where service design may help with innovation in the public sector include policy-making, cultural and organizational reform, training, capacity building, and civic engagement. One of the most essential ways for the public sector to re-invent its services is through digitalization, which has become one of the primary interfaces between public service providers and citizens.[24] As Birgit Mager emphasized: "Digital transformation is something that every sector and service is facing. This transformation also affects the public sector and its services which need to transform into digital in order to be accessible to the public. Service design contributes here by zooming out and seeing the bigger picture by integrating the different stakeholders and by working co-creatively on solutions that bring real value for the users."

---

23   Baldock.
24   Iqbal, Jenniskens, and Ouchene, "Service Design Impact Report: Public Sector," 8.

In Support of Design Students
An Interview with Ellen Lupton[1]

Laura Scherling[2]

"For many years I taught graphic design history, and I continue to teach Design Theory. With history, you have to go back. The crisis is not so much about 'digital' but also comes from issues of globalization and the need for decolonization. There is also the question of who owns design history and defines the design practice."
— Ellen Lupton, US

---

1   Maryland Institute College of Art (MICA), USA.
2   Columbia University, US.

This interview and provocation with designer, educator, and curator Ellen Lupton explores general trends in design education related to digital technology change. In contemporary design education and work settings, young designers must contend with a variety of issues in order to lead successful practices. Challenges like accessing health support services and paying for college can create major anxiety points for designers. Design students are, for example, also learning to use new tools, develop skills in coding, conduct research, and to think critically about design theory and history, which can be enriching and overwhelming. This interview considers some of the varied education-related issues that design students face, and provides a snapshot of how design education has changed, and examines some of the roles that schools and employers can take in support of design students.

Interview

Laura Scherling: Can you tell me a little about your work as a designer, writer, and educator? What do your days look like?

Ellen Lupton: I am a faculty member at Maryland Institute College of Art, MICA, and I was the senior curator of contemporary design at Cooper Hewitt, Smithsonian Design Museum. I've been at MICA since 1997. I get up early, take care of my dogs, and then work for a while. I work at home a lot.

LS: Can you talk about what it was like entering the design profession?

EL: College was very enriching. I went to Cooper Union, an incredible place and very open in terms of how design was experienced and practiced by students there. Then after graduating, I joined an art history Ph.D. program for a couple of years, where I worked with Rosalind Krauss and Rosemarie Haag Bletter, who are possibly the most brilliant art theorist and the most brilliant architectural historian, respectively. Those were very enriching experiences.

I have always been into education and learning things. Therefore, I took a bunch of technology-oriented classes early on. First, there was the switch to digital production from traditional print production. We used Quark and Photoshop, preparing files digitally for print. That was the early 90s. Then, in the mid-90s, there was the Internet. There were new outcomes, new places for design to be, and new ways for people to interact with design.

I have also taken a lot of writing classes more recently. Of course, working is extremely educational when you are a writer and a teacher, because you have to learn all these things. You learn so many things just from working. School is intellectual and exposes you to what design is, what the world is, what critical theory is, and a kind of realm of ideas. By the time I was working as a designer, everything was different.

We are creators of our time. I wish I was 20 years younger and starting out now as a designer. I went to school at a certain time that is different from the time we are living now. Nonetheless, I have learned a lot and stayed engaged in thinking about what design is and how it functions and, in a way, have done so continuously. I started to be a writer and a critic when I graduated from school. I did that right after graduating, and I have been really consistent. What we write, teach, and think about has certainly changed—it is not a solid state. Thus, perhaps the focus of my career is a continuous focus on an object that is shifting and unstable.

LS: How do you stay informed of the most recent developments in design?

EL: As a curator, I stay up-to-date by reading blogs and news media. As a teacher, I pay attention to what the students are doing and bring visiting artists to do things in our program. This requires paying attention to what's going on and what people are doing, which means being aware of who's doing things in graphic design in particular. I also organize the conference *Typographics* at The Cooper Union. I am also at the point in my career where I do a lot of writing and public speaking.

LS: How are you responding to the digital transformation of design in your work?

EL: For many years I taught graphic design history, and I continue to teach Design Theory. With history, you have to go back. The crisis is not so much about "digital" but also comes from issues of globalization and the need for decolonization. There is also the question of who owns design history and defines the design practice.

We certainly talk about digital transformation as a chapter in design history. In the theory class, we incorporate studies of user experience, behavior, experience design, design thinking, and service design as a phenomenon—which is very much a "post-object" way of looking at design for better or worse. The notion of digital practice is woven into that course.

When I teach graduate students and advise them on their thesis work, many of them do digitally-based work, while some of them are more interested in objects and print or typeface design, which is also software-related, but we would not think of it as "digital design" per se.

Many of my students are digital designers. Many are into coding, interactive media, virtual reality, and technology-based work. This is what they are interested in and what they are creating. If you are in graduate school, you have to create work that prepares you for what you are going to do next. Some of them do digital design, and some came to graduate school to make unique things that I am not going to do, such as printmaking. In grad school, there is a lot of agency.

LS: How can we cope with the number of digital technologies we need?

EL: There has to be a lot of self-education because there are many different skills that designers can learn and can apply to their work. We have specific classes that are very tech-oriented where students learn particular software like After Effects or Cinema 4D—these things are fascinating. Students also want to learn specific things that relate to their projects, and you can't necessarily take a whole class on that. Therefore, all of us have to do a lot of self-learning.

Furthermore, not everybody would agree that history is important—I think it is. There is a huge industry that employs people who aren't interested in foundations or the history of anything. However, people who want to get a master's in design are usually interested in the discourse of design as a global conversation.

LS: How do you think young design students can be better supported with all these changes happening?

EL: There is a difference between a boutique studio in Brooklyn and a big corporation like Google or even a big consultancy like Frog Design. Thus, those different organizations have different abilities to support designers. A lot of people end up working in tech because the pay is so much better.

Designers also need better-paid family leave and permanent contracts as opposed to everybody being a freelancer forever. We need pay equity. We need better support for designers seeking visas, and better support in general for immigrant students. Designers who are moving to the US from elsewhere and want to work here permanently require a lot of support from employers. Many employers want to avoid having permanent employees in favor of temporary workers, and it is not just little studios that are doing it.

There is a rise in the "gig mentality." The nature of work will change so quickly that it is scary to commit to anyone because who knows which design skills they will need to know in five years? It can be very uncertain and stressful.

We also need affordable schools. Students have to pay for a program that is not subsidized heavily by taxpayers. That can be very limiting. It limits who can participate, which is a problem for many students who do not realistically assess that. The finances can be a source of anxiety for students, and that gets in the way of learning.

Anxiety also gets in the way. You are probably familiar with epidemic levels of mental health distress among students worldwide, not just in the US. It's very challenging. What is the role of the school in healing students at that level? It's a big challenge.

LS: Do you have any other thoughts on the relationship between mental healthcare in the visual arts and design?

EL: In an ideal world, they would have more access to high-quality psychotherapy. Not specific to art school or the visual arts—it is just something that people need and where the demand outstrips the supply of available care. It is something that schools, in particular, can solve.

Designing and Digital Storytelling for Climate Change Education

Gege Dong, Mir Sana Ullah Khan, and Andrea Orellana[1]

> Digital technology has made rapid advancements in knowledge sharing and communication. As one of the most effective methods in enhancing social connections, digital storytelling offers an opportunity to take on perspectives different from our own and empathize with the challenges, dreams, disappointments, and accomplishments of others. Although storytelling is not a new concept, digital storytelling is still new in the context of climate change education. As one of the most popular tools in education, it offers enormous potential for achieving climate change education goals to realize this global fightback. The application of digital storytelling in climate change education is particularly critical for youth who are among those most at risk from the global climate crisis. In addition to providing a sense of personal agency and empowerment to young people, digital storytelling in climate change education can have a significant impact on both major and minor decision-making. Digital storytelling could help weave engaging, positive, and action-oriented narratives. Yet, it could easily create narratives of displacement, exclusion, and extremism. Designing an interactive digital storytelling curriculum that transitions from predominantly negative to a more balanced spectrum has been concerning for educators. In accordance with this premise, researchers aim to provide examples of digital storytelling as a medium for climate change education curriculum design.
>
> — *Gege Dong, China, Mir Sana Ullah Khan, Pakistan, Andrea Orellana, US*

---

1 Teachers College, Columbia University, US.

Digital technology has transformed the way we share stories. In recent years, interactive design techniques and tools have opened new avenues for creative expression. In particular, the storytelling medium can break free from traditional media by leveraging visually dynamic digital elements,[2] such as video, illustrations, 3D objects, and animations. Designers and educators working with the storytelling medium may come from varied backgrounds in media design, motion graphics, user experience design, or additionally have hybrid roles as designer/filmmaker or in design research. Digital stories are not required to be static, linear affairs consisting of fixed text and image blocks – they need not even follow a traditional content format. This allows audiences to engage with the stories. In the education field, storytelling is the original form of teaching. By crafting storylines, teachers help students make sense of the complex and chaotic world around them.[3] Using digital storytelling as a pedagogical design can engage students in more profound, more meaningful learning experiences.[4] Compelling, emotionally engaging formats that combine story-making and story distribution services to prioritize the power of individual perspectives make digital storytelling an effective tool in the classroom.[5]

In climate change education, storytelling can introduce hard concepts,[6] bringing a human element to a discipline often perceived as sterile.[7] Climate change education could use stories for different purposes: connecting to students, creating "interweaving" between problematic situations, and explaining or asking questions. The key is to bring out the student's perspective

---

2   Yogesh K. Dwivedi et al., "Setting the Future of Digital and Social Media Marketing Research: Perspectives and Research Propositions," *International Journal of Information Management* 59 (2021), https://doi.org/10.1016/j.ijinfomgt.2020.102168.

3   Bernard R. Robin, "Digital storytelling: A powerful technology tool for the 21st century classroom." *Theory into practice* 47, no. 3 (2008), 221.

4   Najat Smeda, Eva Dakich, and Nalin Sharda, "The Effectiveness of Digital Storytelling in the Classrooms: A Comprehensive Study," *Smart Learning Environments* 1, no. 1 (December 2014), https://doi.org/10.1186/s40561-014-0006-3.

5   Bernard R. Robin, "The Power of Digital Storytelling to Support Teaching and Learning," *Digital Education Review* 30 (December 1, 2016): 19, https://eric.ed.gov/?id=EJ1125504.

6   Miranda Jeanne Marie Iossifidis and Lisa Garforth, "Reimagining Climate Futures: Reading Annihilation," *Geoforum*, December 2021, https://doi.org/10.1016/j.geoforum.2021.12.001.

7   Bryan R. Warnick and Campbell F. Scribner, "Discipline, Punishment, and the Moral Community of Schools," *Theory and Research in Education* 18, no. 1 (February 10, 2020): 147787852090494, https://doi.org/10.1177/1477878520904943.

on the matter and how climate change affects their lives. For instance, students coming from under-resourced backgrounds may be struggling with accessing a balanced diet. Digital stories can help students understand how food insecurity is connected with climate change and the actions that could be taken to counter them. In the 2019 film, *The Boy who harnessed the Wind*, a fourteen-year-old in Malawi living in a drought-struck village decided to use his knowledge of physics to design and build a wind turbine to help his village deal with the crisis.[8] The story, inspired by the real achievements of William Kamkwamba, presents themes of drive, resilience, and most importantly, hope. The power of such stories lies in their ability to make a boy in New York relate to a boy in Malawi, facing the same set of issues albeit on a different scale.

Digital Storytelling Design Development and Elements

The "Digital Storytelling Movement" originated at the StoryCenter, and traces its roots to the artistic and cultural ferment of the 1970s and 1980s in the US. An experienced theater producer Joe Lambert founded the StoryCenter in Berkeley, California as a non-profit community arts organization. Lambert developed seven elements comprising digital storytelling theory, including: self-revelation, personal or the first-person voice, live experiences, the use of photos more than moving images, soundtracks, length and design, and intentions.[9]

Additionally, Lambert discussed the seven steps of digital storytelling in story circles, including having insight, "catching the moment," seeing, hearing, assembling, and sharing their stories.[10] According to Bernard R. Robin's theory, educators need 12 elements to complete the design of a digital storytelling project. It is important to note that the script development process consists of 12 steps, including selecting a topic, conducting research, writing the first draft, receiving feedback on the script, revising the script, finding, creating, and adding images, respecting copyright, creating a

---

8   Jan-Erik Leonhardt et al., "Glocal Perspectives in Film-Based Foreign Language Education: Teaching about Sustainability with 'the Boy Who Harnessed the Wind' (2019)," *Global Education Review 8*, no. 2–3 (September 13, 2021), 48, https://ger.mercy.edu/index.php/ger/article/view/602.
9   Joe Lambert, Digital Storytelling Cookbook (Digital Diner Press, 2010), 9.
10 Ibid.

storyboard, recording audio narration, adding background music (optional), and building the digital story.[11] Schuck and Kearney argue that additional digital storytelling steps, also involved in developing the idea, are: capturing the pedagogical frame, structuring the storyboard, arranging the storyboard, preparing the video, recording the video, arranging the video, presenting the video to a small group, presenting the video to a large audience/classroom, and disseminating the video.[12]

Compared to the traditional lectures, digital storytelling combines storytelling and digital components including texts, pictures, recorded audio narrations, music, and videos in the curriculum.[13] The use of digital storytelling in the classroom serves as an effective educational tool when designers and educators produce historical documentaries and instructional videos that provide students with an understanding of an important concept or practice.[14] The video or documentary they make combines the language of the words to evoke the audience's empathy directly. In other words, digital storytelling is a passport to connect the fundamentals of human communication and interaction, as oral tradition has contributed to the transfer of knowledge, skills, attitudes, and values since the birth of language.[15] Hence, the relationship between digital storytelling and education is inextricably linked. With climate change education, students already come across plenty of first-hand experiences with their environment making digital

---

11   Robin, "The Power of Digital Storytelling to Support Teaching and Learning," 22.

12   Sandra Schuck, "Classroom-Based Use of Two Educational Technologies: A Socio-Cultural Perspective," January 1, 2008, https://www.academia.edu/79048310/Classroom_based_use_of_two_educational_technologies_A_socio_cultural_perspective.

13   Rita Mojtahedzadeh et al., "How Digital Storytelling Applied in Health Profession Education: A Systematized Review," *Journal of Advances in Medical Education & Professionalism* 9, no. 2 (2021): 63–78, https://doi.org/10.30476/jamp.2021.87856.1326.

14   Bernard R. Robin, "Digital Storytelling: A Powerful Technology Tool for the 21st Century Classroom," *Theory into Practice* 47, no. 3 (July 11, 2008): 221, https://doi.org/10.1080/00405840802153916.

15   Jan-Erik Leonhardt et al., "Glocal Perspectives in Film-Based Foreign Language Education: Teaching about Sustainability with 'the Boy Who Harnessed the Wind' (2019)," *Global Education Review* 8, no. 2–3 (September 13, 2021), https://ger.mercy.edu/index.php/ger/article/view/602.

storytelling an effective tool to connect their experiences to the broader global challenges.[16]

Digital Storytelling Forms

Designing the storytelling process in the classroom is critical to achieving learning objectives. The goal is to achieve a shift in narratives, attitudes, and levels of knowledge after going through a storytelling exercise. Consider the following forms of storytelling techniques that educators could use in the classroom.

Personal Narratives are stories based on personal experiences – a powerful tool for building emotional connections.[17] For instance, a personal narrative could be about a farmer in Pakistan, describing his struggling to grow crops because of extreme weather patterns. The story could dive into the farmer's experience dealing with floods, droughts, and other events and how it has impacted their life, finances, and relationship with the community around them. Personal narratives like these help educators connect students with climate change issues by evoking empathy. While effective in reaching students who might otherwise not take climate change as seriously, this is also a limitation to personal narratives because they can risk narrowing the scope of complex issues leading to climate change. In this instance, issues like systemic barriers to stop carbon emissions, and government reluctance to policies that prioritize the environment over profits may not be apparent from the personal narrative of a farmer.

Visual Storytelling uses images, videos, graphics, and other visual elements to tell a story or convey a message. In the context of climate change education, visual storytelling could be used to communicate complex information about climate science, the impacts of climate change, and potential solutions in an engaging way. Visual storytelling can help to make information more memorable and easier to understand. Research has shown that people are

---

16 Ya-Ting C. Yang and Wan-Chi I. Wu, "Digital Storytelling for Enhancing Student Academic Achievement, Critical Thinking, and Learning Motivation: A Year-Long Experimental Study," in Cas.columbia.edu, 2012, 350, www-sciencedirect-com.ezproxy.cul.columbia.edu/science/article/pii/S0360131511003289.

17 Ana Roeschley and Jeonghyun Kim, "'Something That Feels like a Community': The Role of Personal Stories in Building Community-Based Participatory Archives," *Archival Science* 19, no. 1 (February 7, 2019), 29, https://doi.org/10.1007/s10502-019-09302-2.

more likely to remember information when it is presented in a visual format. That visuals can help to simplify complex information by breaking it down into smaller, more digestible pieces.[18] Movies, documentaries, and short videos are effective visual storytelling media. With the rise of short video platforms like TikTok among young people, the medium presents an enormous opportunity for educators to level with their students and meet them where they are comfortable. For instance, the Drawdown Stories Project focused on climate justice and reimagined climate storytelling using underrepresented climate heroes to amplify individual voices and reimagine climate storytelling.[19]

Interactive storytelling is a type of storytelling that allows the audience to participate in the story and shape its outcome. In the context of climate change education, interactive storytelling can be used to engage students and help them to understand complex issues related to climate science, impacts, and solutions. It also can take many forms, from choose-your-own-adventure style narratives to role-playing games, simulations, and virtual reality experiences.[20] Interactive storytelling aims to create an immersive and engaging experience that allows students to explore different perspectives and outcomes related to climate change.[21] Interactive storytelling can help to increase engagement and motivation among students. Allowing students to take an active role in the story makes them more likely to be emotionally invested in the outcome and retain the information presented. Therefore, interactive storytelling can help to develop critical thinking skills and encourage collaboration and communication. When students are presented with choices and consequences, they must analyze the information presented and make decisions based on their understanding of the topic. This can lead to discussions and debates, which can help students to refine their thinking and learn from one another. Examples include online simulations that allow students to explore different scenarios related to climate science and policy, role-playing games that simulate the impact of climate change

---

18 Eliza Bobek and Barbara Tversky, "Creating Visual Explanations Improves Learning," *Cognitive Research: Principles and Implications* 1, no. 27 (December 2016), https://doi.org/10.1186/s41235-016-0031-6.

19 "Drawdown Stories," Project Drawdown, January 20, 2022, https://drawdown.org/stories.

20 See note 18 above.

21 Mark Owen Riedl and Vadim Bulitko, "Interactive Narrative: An Intelligent Systems Approach," *AI Magazine* 34, no. 1 (December 6, 2012): 67, https://doi.org/10.1609/aimag.v34i1.2449.

on communities and ecosystems, and virtual reality experiences that allow students to experience the effects of climate change firsthand.

Green Game Jam, for instance, is a video game studio that incorporates green activation by including environmentally themed features and messages and educating its users on environmental issues. Besides increasing the entertainment, this game story engages students in an interactive discussion about climate change and human activities. Currently, there are more than a billion players who have participated in the 2021 game campaign, and over 60,000 pledges have been signed for the UN campaigns, as well as $800,000 donated to various charities working on environmental issues.[22]

Future scenarios are a type of storytelling that involve imagining possible futures based on different projections and assumptions related to climate change.[23] In the context of climate change education, future scenarios can help students understand the potential impacts of climate change, strategies for mitigating and adapting to its effects. Future scenarios typically involve creating narratives that describe possible worlds based on different scenarios related to climate science, policy, and technology.[24] These narratives can be presented in various formats, from written stories to visual media such as videos or infographics. The goal is to create a compelling and realistic future vision that students can engage with and explore.

Engaging students in a future scenario exercise can help develop their critical thinking skills and encourage them to think creatively about solutions to climate change. Students are encouraged to analyze and evaluate the presented information by presenting different scenarios and outcomes and considering the potential consequences of other choices and actions. In addition, by presenting a compelling and realistic vision of the future, students are more likely to be emotionally invested in the topic and to feel a sense of urgency about taking action to address climate change. Examples include narratives that describe possible future worlds based on different levels of greenhouse gas emissions, population growth, and technological advances.

---

22 UN News, "Video Games for Climate Action: Winning Solutions for the Planet," May 31, 2022, https://news.un.org/en/story/2022/05/1119292.

23 Emma Frances Bloomfield and Chris Manktelow, "Climate Communication and Storytelling," *Climatic Change* 167, no. 34 (August 2021), https://doi.org/10.1007/s10584-021-03199-6.

24 Antonia Liguori et al., "Towards 'creative participatory science': exploring future scenarios through specialist drought science and community storytelling," *Frontiers in Environmental Science* 8 (2021).

These narratives can be presented in various formats, from written stories to visual media such as videos or infographics.

Mythological narratives are a powerful tool for storytelling in climate change education. They draw on ancient myths and legends to create compelling stories that connect contemporary audiences with timeless themes and universal human experiences. In the context of climate change education, mythological narratives can be used to explore the complex relationships between humans and nature and to inspire people to take action to address the urgent environmental challenges we face. It also provides a rich and diverse source of stories and archetypes that can help engage a broad audience range. These stories are often deeply ingrained in cultural traditions and passed down through generations, making them a powerful and familiar reference point for many people. Mythological narratives can also help to connect people with the natural world and to inspire a sense of reverence and awe for it. Many myths and legends feature gods, goddesses, and other mythical beings intimately connected with the natural world and embody its power and beauty. By drawing on these stories, educators can help students appreciate nature's wonders and develop a deeper connection with the natural world.

Examples of mythological narratives in climate change education include stories that explore themes such as the balance between human needs and the needs of the natural world, the consequences of human actions on the environment, and the power of human ingenuity and cooperation to address environmental challenges. These stories can be presented in various formats, from written reports to visual media such as videos or art installations.

Effectiveness of Digital Storytelling in Climate Change

Integrating climate crisis problems within a real or imaginary story, such as environmental justice, is crucial to climate change education. This approach facilitates the process of problem-solving by engaging students in a meaningful and relatable manner. However, as with any form of information exchange in digital media, there are potential downsides. The inundation of overwhelming or inaccurate information can influence individuals to make uninformed decisions.[25] The improper or excessive use of digital media

---

25   Daniela Acquadro Maran and Tatiana Begotti, "Media Exposure to Climate Change, Anxiety, and Efficacy Beliefs in a Sample of Italian University Students," *International*

stories can also lead to mental health issues such as depression, anxiety, and addiction.[26] Therefore, it is imperative to ensure that digital storytelling projects are designed thoughtfully, portraying a sense of hope and connection in communities nationwide that are actively working towards implementing climate solutions. A well-designed digital storytelling project can inspire students to participate actively in the fight against climate change while promoting mental well-being through positive and uplifting narratives.

Zan Rosetta identified narrative fractures in the story-problem formulation, where breakpoints exist between the mathematical structure and the narrative dimension.[27] In the context of climate change education, it is crucial to establish a strong connection between the question structure and the narrative dimension to avoid such fractures. This connection allows students to build strong community relationships and relate to climate problems described in digital storytelling representations. Conversely, the story may obstruct the solution process when climate problems do not arise spontaneously from the context or the narrative information does not relate to the problematic situation.

If the narrative part dominates the climate problems, students may become too engrossed in the story and pay attention to the consistency of climate change education. For instance, when a tale prioritizes entertainment and engagement over education and action, the purpose of climate change education could be lost. For example, a digital story about a fantastical, post-apocalyptic world affected by climate change may be visually stunning and engaging. Still, it could leave the viewer with a sense of hopelessness or apathy and may have few lessons in climate change education. Similarly, storytelling that focuses solely on individual experiences and emotions without providing a broader context or scientific information may not effectively convey the urgency and severity of the climate crisis.

Storytelling also runs the risk of reinforcing existing biases and perpetuating harmful stereotypes. For example, a digital story about a

---

Journal of Environmental Research and Public Health 18, no. 17 (September 4, 2021), https://doi.org/10.3390/ijerph18179358.

26 Elena Bozzola et al., "The Use of Social Media in Children and Adolescents: Scoping Review on the Potential Risks," *International Journal of Environmental Research and Public Health 19*, no. 16 (August 12, 2022), https://doi.org/10.3390/ijerph19169960.

27 Rosetta Zan, "The Crucial Role of Narrative Thought in Understanding Story Problems," no. 2 (2017), https://doi.org/10.33683/ddm.17.2.3.

climate activist portrayed as a radical or extremist could discourage viewers from taking action or lead them to dismiss the importance of climate activism. Similarly, digital stories that focus on individuals in wealthy or developed countries may need to address the disproportionate impact of climate change on vulnerable populations in less developed areas.

It is essential to approach storytelling with a clear purpose and message to avoid these pitfalls and ensure that digital storytelling effectively engages and educates audiences about climate change. Similarly, it is essential to incite empathy through digital storytelling to introduce the best way for individuals to express their story and evoke emotion from their audience, making the entire experience more authentic and three-dimensional. An excellent digital storytelling project presents a collection of stories that portray a sense of hope and connection in communities working to bring climate solutions to fruition while avoiding overwhelming or inaccurate information that can negatively impact mental health.

Two Case Studies in Digital Storytelling for Climate Change

The connections between digital storytelling design and climate change education are apparent in light of the overview above. The following section presents two case studies of applied projects designed to examine how climate change movements utilize digital storytelling to organize student activities, coordinate community members, and raise public awareness. The first case study is from Global Oneness Project, a free multimedia education platform providing stories and lessons for growing minds.[28] The climate change digital storytelling project from Global Oneness Project aims to transform students' experience through digital tools to make connections between themselves and the globalized world. The second case study comes from Love&Future, a non-profit organization in the US that supports youth to be change agents through inspirational digital storytelling. Love&Future's digital storytelling project proposed a hands-on journey in utilizing artificial intelligence technology applications in storytelling curricula. In both projects, digital tools are used for storytelling to foster compassion, interconnectedness, and awareness regarding the impact of human activities on the planet.

---

28 "Featured," Global Oneness Project (GlobalOnenessProject.org, 2020), https://www.globalonenessproject.org.

Using Digital Storytelling to Interpret Climate Impact

Founded in 2006 as an initiative of Kalliopeia Foundation, the Global Oneness Project aims to sow the seeds of empathy, resilience, and a sacred relationship with the planet. They achieve this by utilizing stories as a pedagogical tool for growing minds and bringing the world's cultures to life in classrooms. Committed to exploring cultural, environmental, and social issues, the project offers a vast library of multimedia stories, including award-winning films, photo essays, and written essays, along with companion curriculum and discussion guides.[29]

Their mission is to connect the local human experience to global issues such as climate change, water scarcity, food insecurity, poverty, endangered cultures, migration, and sustainability through stories. By featuring individuals and communities impacted by these issues, the stories and lessons offer opportunities to examine universal themes such as identity, diversity, hope, resilience, imagination, adversity, empathy, love, responsibility, and our common humanity. The project's interdisciplinary approach to learning promotes the development of critical thinking, inquiry, empathy, and listening skills. The resources are available in both English and Spanish and are aligned with National and Common Core Standards. The Global Oneness project was built on collaboration with young people to explore their hopes and fears for the future through digital technology. According to Bowman, as young people look toward an uncertain future, their imaginations flourish.[30] The project addressed the growing interest in climate activism among young people, especially as it is shaped by their perceptions of the future.

As a complement to narrative theory, the Global Oneness Project allowed students to develop universal human values and respect for the living environment through personal narratives, visual storytelling, digital films, and photo essays. Stories serve many purposes, including challenging people to

---

29 Global Oneness Project, "About Us," accessed April 8, 2023, https://www.globalonenessproject.org/about-project.

30 Benjamin Bowman, "Imagining future worlds alongside young climate activists: a new framework for research." *Fennia-International Journal of Geography* 197, no. 2 (2019), 297.

consider their contributions to the world in which they live.[31] As a result of stories, students' perspectives are expanded, and they are introduced to worlds they may not have imagined. For instance, one of the most touching films from the project named *Lost World* illustrates how climate change impacts individuals, communities, and ecosystems across the globe. From a woman's perspective from Cambodia, the film allowed the audience to learn how indigenous communities are losing their subsistence lifestyles and land due to changes in temperatures and rainfall, among other factors.[32] While most of the stock footage is *show-and-tell* type that directly relates to the script, producer Mam Kalyanee in *Lost World* also used many visual metaphors. For example, the film compared landscapes of natural beauty and industrial production pollution. Through the digital image impact, students reflected on the changes associated with the visual perception of the landscape due to human activities. Using this film story as a resource, students became aware of the world they live in without having to understand another language, thus creating a sense of empathy and allowing them to reflect on a world suffering from the same challenge everywhere i.e., climate change.

Digital storytelling for the Global Oneness Project, therefore, served as a new language, a democratic literacy, that everyone (including students and educators) can use to demonstrate their proficiency as climate change agents designing a sustainable future. Students, especially those with marginal status, can exhibit knowledge and skills typically suppressed in traditional teaching methods when they use digital storytelling.

To date, the Global Oneness Project has contributed to developing students' critical thinking, inquiry, empathy, listening skills, and an interdisciplinary approach to the learning process.[33] Several international media outlets have featured their films and lessons, including *National Geographic*, PBS, *The Atlantic*, *The New York Times*, *The New Yorker*, TED-Ed, and the Smithsonian.[34] Their educational resources are being used in a wide range of settings, from

---

31 Athriyana S. Pattiwael, "Literature for Developing Student's Humanity Awareness," *Journal International Seminar on Languages, Literature, Arts, and Education (ISLLAE)* 1, no. 1 (2019), 80.

32 Kalyanee Man, "Lost World," Global Oneness Project, accessed April 2nd, 2023, https://www.globalonenessproject.org/library/films/lost-world.

33 Kalyanee Man.

34 Grateful.org, "Grateful Changemakers: Global Oneness Project," July 25, 2019, https://grateful.org/grateful-changemakers/grateful-changemakers-global-oneness-project.

public schools to independent schools, both internationally and nationally.[35] In 2018, Common Sense Media selected the Global Oneness Project as one of its top picks for learning, stating that the project offered "captivating, cross-curricular stories to increase cultural awareness."[36]

Visualizing the Imagination of Climate Future through Artificial Intelligence

Love&Future, a US-based non-profit working on issues of climate change and sustainability, organized an online workshop in January 2023 to delve into the potential of artificial intelligence and digital art in climate change education. The workshop targeted high school students and aimed to harness their digital skills to inspire positive action and optimism towards sustainability. The central objective of this workshop was to help students envision potential climate futures and empower them to express themselves more effectively.

The emergence of artificial intelligence has revolutionized the means by which individuals communicate and produce material. Canva AI is an artificial intelligence-powered story generator that turns open-ended text into actionable knowledge.[37] Furthermore, MidJourney is a tool that uses artificial intelligence algorithms to create visual artwork, providing users with the ability to quickly generate visuals for digital storytelling. Despite the abstract and elusive nature of climate change's impact, the potential offered by artificial intelligence tools like Canva AI and MidJourney is limitless. The use of artificial intelligence in climate change education has not been widely researched. This section looks at the use of MidJourney as a promising tool in climate change education by Love&Future that demonstrates how artificial intelligence can convert text into digital images that can be utilized in climate change education. Incorporating artificial intelligence images into curriculum development allows students to gain a better understanding of the impacts of climate change and explore the possibilities of technology in addressing these

---

35 Global Oneness Project, March 29, 2017, https://hundred.org/en/innovations/global-oneness-project.
36 Global Oneness Project, March 23, 2021, https://en.wikipedia.org/wiki/Global_Oneness_Project.
37 "AI Story and Plot Generator," accessed March 23, 2023, https://www.canva.com/ai-image-generator.

challenges. Such an approach bridges the gap between human creativity and technology in designing an effective climate change curriculum.

Hicks and Holden argued that incorporating probable and preferable futures, scenarios, and envisioning in the classroom can be beneficial in developing a futures perspective in environmental and sustainability education.[38] They advocated for future literacy as an essential aspect of such education. Using MidJourney enhances the engagement among a younger generation and supports them to drive equality, create inclusiveness, and build relationships. Andrea Orellana, the Digital Storytelling Manager, has designed a captivating digital storytelling image for her workshop participants called Today and Tomorrow. This digital illustration shows global warming and environmental degradation in 2023 versus 2050.

"Today and Tomorrow" is a digital story that masterfully combines future scenarios and visually captivating elements to convey a powerful message about the consequences of global warming and pollution. The story aims to raise awareness and encourage consideration for the world around us by highlighting the fragility of the environment and the devastating impact of human activities on climate change. At its core, the piece represents a powerful intersection between storytelling and education, using a stunning digital image to bring to life the complex relationship between humans and the earth.

Over the course of two weeks, Love&Future hosted a digital storytelling workshop that engaged 35 high school students in immersive, hands-on learning experiences. According to student feedback, digital storytelling is a relatively new educational tool that is not commonly utilized in traditional classroom settings. However, students found that digital storytelling was an effective way to comprehend and share information about climate change. They also expressed that this workshop helped them to convey their vision for a sustainable future, particularly through the use of digital technology in education. Students believed that digital storytelling could effectively communicate, interact with, and shape the mindsets of others towards making sustainable choices. Through the process of designing digital content in climate change education, students could share and exchange perspectives on the three most critical aspects of sustainable living: survival, connection, and meaning.

---

38 David Hicks and Cathie Holden, "Remembering the Future: What Do Children Think?," *Environmental Education Research* 13, no. 4 (September 2007): 501–512, https://doi.org/10.1080/13504620701581596.

Digital Storytelling for a Sustainable Future

Climate change is an urgent issue that requires immediate action, and one way to raise awareness and inspire action is through storytelling. Stories have the power to inspire, inform, and change behavior. They have the power to create empathy and foster a sense of shared responsibility, helping individuals to understand the impact of their actions on the environment and encouraging them to take action to reduce their carbon footprint. Digital storytelling is an effective way to make complex issues accessible and engaging. It has the potential to create engaging and impactful stories that can reach a wider audience and inspire meaningful action.

For example, the Global Oneness Project uses digital storytelling to promote ecological sustainability and social justice by sharing stories of people who are working to create positive change in their communities. By harnessing the power of storytelling, they aim to inspire more people to take action on climate change and create a better future for ourselves and future generations. Similarly, Love&Future emphasizes the importance of empowering young people to be active agents of change in the face of climate change, rather than passive observers. Another organization that uses digital storytelling is the Climate Museum, a New York-based museum that aims to inspire and empower visitors to take action on climate change. The museum's exhibits feature immersive experiences and interactive displays that use storytelling to communicate the impacts of climate change and the urgent need for action. By creating an emotional connection with visitors, the Climate Museum is helping to build a sense of shared responsibility and inspire action on climate change. From the Global Oneness Project to Love&Future to the Climate Museum, there are numerous examples of organizations that are using storytelling to raise awareness and inspire action on climate change.

To succeed in a world facing the great challenge of climate change, it is imperative to embrace the shift towards digital technology especially for educators who have to prepare young people for the world they live in. The mere mention of "climate change" on a screen is insufficient; to captivate and motivate students, educators must make digital storytelling compelling, stirring, and action-oriented. They must strive to cultivate vital skills like listening, sharing, healing, and persuasion – much as oral and written storytelling have for centuries.

To prepare for including digital storytelling in education, educators should familiarize themselves with the various digital tools and platforms available for storytelling, such as social media, podcasts, videos, and interactive media. They should also explore different formats and styles of digital storytelling, from short-form social media stories to long-form documentaries. They must consider the audience they are trying to reach and tailor their storytelling accordingly. For example, if the target audience is younger students, educators may want to focus on more visual and interactive storytelling formats, while for older students or adults, more in-depth and data-driven storytelling may be more effective.

In addition, educators should collaborate with other stakeholders, such as designers, media specialists, and environmental experts, to ensure that the digital storytelling content is not only engaging but also accurate and effective in communicating the urgency of climate change. Lastly, educators should prioritize ethical considerations in digital storytelling, including data privacy, representation and inclusivity, and responsible use of digital tools. Through a little effort, educators can effectively integrate digital storytelling into their teaching practices, fostering critical thinking and inspiring action towards climate change mitigation and adaptation.

Navigating the Transformative Potential of Technologies in Design
A Conclusion

Laura Scherling

The essays, case studies, and interviews in this edited collection explore the increasingly interconnected processes and practices across the design disciplines, brought together by digital transformation. As human interaction with emergent technologies deepens, navigating the transformative potential of digital products, tools, graphics, and artifacts, is an exciting yet urgent call to action. These chapters emphasized the importance of thinking about technology change critically, equitably, and imaginatively.

In our expanding "human-technology entanglement" there are still many "unknowns" around mass adoption of technologies, digitization, "algorithmization" and the automation of tasks, along with the ethical, economic, and social challenges that can occur after a digital transformation is initiated through a design.[1] Examining these new and "unknown" digital landscapes, educator and researcher, Amarolinda Zanela Klein wrote that challenges related to digital transformation are plentiful, including the role of AI in decision making and the "indiscriminate use of personal information."[2] Lieselot Danneels and Stijn Viaene, professors who research digital transformation in the public and private sectors, highlighted that the "disruptive potential of digital technologies" demands organizational change and requires more ways of understanding tensions related to digital transformation.[3] As we negotiate with the exciting, yet disruptive use

---

1 Amarolinda Zanela Klein, "Ethical Issues of Digital Transformation," *Organizações & Sociedade* 29 (2022), 444.
2 Amarolinda Zanela Klein, "Ethical Issues of Digital Transformation," 444.
3 Danneels, Lieselot, and Stijn Viaene. "Identifying Digital Transformation Paradoxes: A Design Perspective." *Business & Information Systems Engineering* (2022): 499.

technologies, it's also clear that technology brings us together in numerous ways.

In Kai Franz's case study "An Archaeology of Digital Architecture," he reflected on the conception of *disegno*, an Italian word that carries complex meaning beyond the simple translation to a design or drawing. Disegno involves the making of a design or drawing but also embodies "the intellectual capacity to invent the design."[4] Is there such a word today that can capture the myriad of ways that technology-driven designs are fundamentally "omnipresent" in much of society and "more consequential than ever"?[5] Do words like "transdisciplinary," "immersive," or "interactive," capture the depth of the shared and complicated experience of digital transformation in design?

It may once have been challenging to envision there would be a shared vocabulary among designers and their peers on the use of software, hardware and sensors, cloud computing, big data, machine learning, and artificial intelligence. This vocabulary about technologies is expressed among product designers, graphic designers, architects, textile designers, service designers, game designers, artists, and creative technologists alike. In Dr. Serena Cangiano's case study, "Design for Future Skills: Three Case Studies on the Role of Design in Shaping the Narrative of Technology Education," she recalled that computational artists and designers in the past decades have created new tools and methods for teaching technology to communities of users, but it wasn't merely about developing a skill. It precipitated "global movements of change makers in technology education", and sparked the creation of new ways of interacting with the machines.[6] These interactions play out in versatile design and technology spaces, seen throughout this collection in examples like FabLab

---

4   The National Gallery, "Disegno," accessed on August 10, 2023, https://www.nationalgallery.org.uk/paintings/glossary/disegno.
5   Anne Quito, "SVA Design Leaders on Their Ever-Changing Field," School of Visual Arts, February 28, 2023, https://sva.edu/features/sva-design-leaders-on-their-ever-changing-field.
6   See Serena Cangiano, "Design for Future Skills: Three Case Studies on the Role of Design in Shaping the Narrative of Technology Education."

SUPSI,⁷ PETLab,⁸ GovLabAustria,⁹ the plopps,¹⁰ Studio Forward.¹¹ At Studio Forward, which was directed by Rachel Berger at the California College of the Arts, students practiced "futures literacy" and created electronic prototypes, written narratives, videos, artifacts, and speculative mockups to envision the world they "wanted to live in."

In these rapidly evolving spaces for design and technology, new possibilities are forged. Designs can scale beyond the lab and the classroom to entire societies. The digital transformation of communications and information, healthcare, education, government, financial services, fashion, entertainment, manufacturing and consumer goods was once difficult to imagine, yet it is rapidly infusing into our everyday lives. In a 1991 publication, *Computers in Society*, edited by Kathryn Schellenberg, the contributing authors wrote about the coming of a "data superhighway," "mass customization," "electronic democracy," "adaptive technology," " virtual reality", and the "computer you can talk to."¹² Decades later, many seek out and rely on digital systems, which the authors of this book have so conscientiously explored. In their case study "Digital Transformation and Service Design Practice in Public Sector" Sahar Nikzad and Paulina Porten argued for the importance of municipal administration digital transformation, and took an active role in cultivating citizen participation in e-government with their service design project "MeinungsMobil." In her essay on "Crafted Identities: Technological Transformations in Textile Design," Nishra Ranpura observed that novel means of fabrication and e-textiles are reframing "values of crafting" while driving innovation in wellness and health industries.¹³ In their case study "Designing and Digital Storytelling for Climate Change Education," Gege Dong, China, Mir Sana Ullah Khan, and Andrea Orellana examined how

---

7   See "Design for Future Skills: Three Case Studies on the Role of Design in Shaping the Narrative of Technology Education."
8   See Laura Scherling and Colleen Macklin, "Designing Games for Social Change."
9   Sahar Nikzad and Paulina Porten, "Digital Transformation and Service Design Practice in Public Sector."
10   Kai Franz, "An Archaeology of Digital Architecture."
11   Rachel Berger, "No Back to Normal: Studio Forward at California College of the Arts."
12   Kathryn Schellenberg, Computers in Society, Guilford: Duskin Publishing Group, 1994: 6–10, https://archive.org/details/computersinsocieooooounse_x9y9/page/n9/mode/2up.
13   See Nishra Ranpura, "Crafted Identities: Technological Transformations in Textile Design."

different design and storytelling approaches can promote critical thinking about "climate change, food insecurity, water scarcity, poverty, endangered cultures, and migration." Additionally, "NFTs between Art and Design: A Story of Digital Transformation" by Lucilla Grossi and Luca Guerrini, analyzed how "NFT provenance" has had an unprecedented impact on digital design and art communities. Without the capacity to create new designs, the aforementioned transformations would not wholly exist.

Returning to some of the risks, it is evident that along with a shared vocabulary of design and technology there are also shared concerns. In an interview for this book, Dr. John Maeda described that "transformation in the design world means we are adapting to changing tools and business models" while we are also doing the difficult work to mitigate bias and "foster ethical tech."[14] To reiterate, a bunch of sensors or an algorithm design alone simply cannot make the world a more equitable place. From mass layoffs in big tech to ethical concerns about AI, the blockchain and cryptocurrencies, and data profiling, recent developments have shown us that even an exemplary design with sound user experience is not infallible. Design critic and journalist, Anne Quito, observed there is a developing awareness among creative practitioners and the public that "decisions made at the drafting table can have immense and unintended consequences."[15]

The authors explored how a number of these inequities play out. In Dr. Jeffrey Chan's essay, "Digital Design for Trust and Trustworthiness", he called attention to the fact that "discussions on trust remain anemic in design studies."[16] At a time when cybersecurity attacks run rampant, he challenged us to contend with how digitization projects can depart from their original aims, and erode or undermine trust. In his essay "Delegated Power: The Ethics of Nudging in Building More Equitable Product Experiences", Timothy Bardlavens asked, "Where do we begin?" "How do we think about building more equitable products?"[17] In the essay "DialecTikTok: The Dynamic Semiotics of Amateur Visual Trends on TikTok," Sarah Edmands Martin delved into "trend" languages and investigated how social media platforms can enlighten,

---

14   See Laura Scherling and John Maeda, "Reflections on Digital Transformation in Design."
15   Anne Quito, "SVA Design Leaders on Their Ever-Changing Field."
16   See Jeffrey Chan, "Digital Design for Trust and Trustworthiness."
17   See Timothy Bardlavens, "Delegated Power: The Ethics of Nudging in Building More Equitable Product Experiences."

empower, censor, shame, and even "cancel" its users. Looking at the power dynamics in gaming communities, Dr. Zhenzhen Qi acknowledged that procedural rules in virtual environments can also "shape the identity of real players embodied in that world."[18]

Empowered by a shared repertoire on design, technology, and digital transformation, it would appear that we are in a more informed place to identify and address the inequities before us. In an interconnected world, it is the endeavor to achieve more good in the world than harm. With our expanding capabilities we can do things like create "responsive" digital typography that can support "readers who are neurodiverse", "older in age", or have "low vision."[19] We can design "community-owned Internet infrastructure" and improve Internet access.[20] We can design games to impart positive social change, improve EV car sharing, address "gender equality and bodily autonomy" in digital health apps,[21] and support childrens' development with STEM/STEAM educational tools.

Ideally what you discovered in our collection provided an exhaustive sample about the potential of digital technologies in design. As conventional design forms, materials, and modes of communication undergo digital transformation, we must stop to consider the social, economic, and ethical impacts. Is it accessible? Is it secure? Does this do more good than harm? In her essay, Sarah Edmands Martin concludes that if design is about "the health and care of people, then perhaps more oversight on the set of machines and algorithms in our virtual agoras"[22] would produce a kinder and more equitable experience.

---

18   See Zhenzhen Qi, "Design of Virtual Worlds."
19   See Thomas Jockin, "Equality of Fit in Digital Typography."
20   See Laura Scherling, "Equitable Digital Access in an Era of Uncertainty."
21   See Catalina Alzate, "Learning from FemTech to Inform the Design of Healthcare Technologies."
22   See Chapter 3, Sarah Edmands Martin, "DialecTikTok: The Dynamic Semiotics of Amateur Visual Trends on TikTok."

Contributing Authors

Dr. Laura S. Scherling is a designer, researcher, and educator. She works as a director and faculty at Columbia University. Her research interests include emerging technologies, ethics, and sustainability topics. Scherling completed her doctorate at Columbia University Teachers College. She is the co-editor of the edited collection Ethics in Design and Communication: Critical Perspectives (Bloomsbury Academic). Her work has been published in Brookings Metro, Design Observer, Design and Culture, Spark Journal, Interiors: Design/Architecture/Culture, the Futures Worth Preserving Cultural Constructions of Nostalgia and Sustainability, and the Urban Activist. Her design and publication portfolio can be viewed at laurascherling.info, and her Instagram account is @laura.skierling.

Catalina Alzate (she/her) is a Colombian designer, researcher and educator working at the intersection of cultural studies, technology activism and community healthcare. She is an Assistant Professor in the School of Art & Design at The University of Illinois at Urbana-Champaign. In the past, she served as an advisor for the Feminist Internet Research Network, a collaborative organization that supports research on gender, digital rights and internet policy. Previously as faculty at the Srishti Manipal Institute of Art Design and Technology, Bangalore, India she engaged in teaching and research involving service design in the context of community healthcare and technology design.

Timothy Bardlavens is chaotic good in its purest form. He is a Gay, Black man from the Carolinas, the youngest son of a single mother; he is everything that institutional trauma and oppression said he could not be or become. Timothy is a Product Executive, a Cultural Strategist, Diversity, Equity & Justice expert, a Co-Founder, a Writer and International Speaker & Facilitator. For over a decade, he has also built and scaled product teams, set product vision and product strategy for companies like Meta (formerly Facebook), Microsoft, and Adobe. Timothy Bardlavens is also a pioneer in the development of Product Equity as a practice.

Rachel Berger is the Director of Studio Forward and Associate Professor of Graphic Design at California College of the Arts. Her writing on education, design, and culture has been published by Bloomsbury, MIT Press, AIGA Eye on Design, and Works That Work.

Dr. Serena Cangiano is the Head of FabLab SUPSI and a teacher at MA in Interaction design SUPSI. Since 2009, she has worked on designing educational formats combining design and technology through prototyping. As a researcher, Cangiano carries out applied research projects and programs on design and innovation with an open and social impact. She co-founded the edtech project Ethafa, a kit to teach electronics through stories.

Dr. Jeffrey Chan is a designer, researcher, and educator, currently an Assistant Professor at Singapore University of Technology and Design. Chan completed a Ph.D. with the University of California, Berkeley, and has published his research with the California Management Review, Landscape and Urban Planning, Design Studies, and Space and Culture.

Gege Dong is a sustainability researcher and graduate student at Columbia University, Teachers College, majoring in political science. She graduated from Seton Hall University with a Bachelor of Science in Finance. As an educator and researcher, she is interested in exploring the role of multi-stakeholder collaborations in promoting education for sustainability and integrating sustainability strategies within higher education institutions. She is the CEO of the U.S.-based NGO, Love&Future, working on education for sustainability.

Kai Franz is an Associate Professor of Spatial Dynamics in the Division of Experimental and Foundation Studies at the Rhode Island School of Design. His artistic research practice centers on the intersection of digital media, architecture, and design. Franz received fellowships from MacDowell and the Akademie Schloss Solitude. In 2015, Edition Solitude published Serial Nature, a book that critically examines Franz's practice and work (Franz & Stubbs, 2014).

His work has been exhibited in numerous exhibitions in Europe and the US, most recently in a solo exhibition at the David Winton Bell Gallery at Brown University.

Lucilla Grossi is a spatial designer whose research focuses on the evolution of artistic languages and their interaction with space. She is interested in contemporary art, exhibit design, and anthropology of architecture, focusing on the possible evolutions of the social system in psychologically and environmentally sustainable ways. She currently collaborates with the Design Department of Politecnico di Milano and is a teaching fellow. Aside from the academic environment, Grossi collaborates with cultural institutions and carries out spatial research with independent groups such as Studio di Margine where she is a co-creator.

Luca Guerrini is an associate professor in the Department of Design at Politecnico di Milano where he has worked since 1993. A trained architect, he has carried out applied research and projects in transportation and environmental design, interior and spatial design, and cultural heritage design. His studies focus on the concept and perception of space in the relationship between design and the arts. He teaches Interior Design and Arts and Languages of the Present at the School of Design. Since 1999 he has been a faculty member of several Ph.D. programs and is a former Director (2015–2017) of the Ph.D. program in design. He is in charge of the joint Politecnico di Milano and Tsinghua University, Beijing degree program in design. Since 2018 he has been the Dean's delegate for the admission test of the School of design. He has lectured on M.A. and Ph.D. Courses in Italy and abroad.

Thomas Jockin is a typographic designer and educator. His work has been featured by AIGA Eye on Design, I Love Typography, and Typography Served. Jockin is the founder of TypeThursday, a global superfamily that converges monthly to help one another improve letterforms over drinks. Jockin is a Lecturer at the University of North Georgia. He has previously taught at the City University of New York, Queens College, City College, and State University of New York Fashion Institute of Technology.

Mir Sana Ullah Khan is a Fulbright Scholar with a Master's in Curriculum and Teaching from Columbia University, Teachers College. He belongs to Khyber Pakhtunkhwa, Pakistan. Previously, he graduated with a bachelor's in economics from Lahore University of Management Sciences as a National Outreach Program Scholar. Mir has a strong foundation in research, data analysis, writing, and communication. He is interested in social justice issues in education, climate change, and public service design. He is the COO of a U.S.-based NGO, Love&Future, working on education for sustainability.

Sarah Edmands Martin is an Assistant Professor of Visual Communication Design at the University of Notre Dame. Her work reimagines the ways social and civic systems distribute and exercise power within contemporary, mediated spaces. She is a 2024 Fulbright Scholar, a 2023 Design Fellow at Chicago's Writing Space, a 2021 Research Fellow at Indiana University's Institute for Digital Arts + Humanities, and a 2020 Design Incubation Fellow in New York City.

Sahar Nikzad is an experience and service designer, and graduated with a Master's degree in Integrated Design and "Social and Public Innovation Service Design" cluster. She has eight years of experience designing products in a variety of sectors (jewelry, fashion, furniture, and lighting). After graduating from industrial design discipline and witnessing how the world is evolving into more intangible experiences and products, she shifted her professional path to service and experience design. She is currently working as a user experience designer at Publicis Sapient and is a member of SDN Young Talent Board, leading and supervising different projects.

Andrea Orellana is a mixed race (Indigenous and European) woman from Central America, raised in Southern California. She holds her BA in English from the University of California, Irvine, and her first MA in English Literature from the Queen Mary University of London. She is an MA Candidate in the Art and Art Education department at Columbia University, Teachers College. She is the digital storytelling manager of a US-based NGO, Love&Future, working on education for sustainability.

Paulina Porten is a creative technologist, interaction and service designer, and is currently doing her Master's degree in Integrated Design with a focus on "Social and Public Innovation" at Köln International School of Design in Cologne. Since 2018, she has been intensively involved with Augmented Reality and focused on how to create social innovation and co-design with the help of this technology. In 2020, she graduated with her Bachelor's degree in communication and interaction design from the University of Applied Sciences in Hamburg. In 2022, she did a four-month research semester in the field of "Design for Social Innovation" at the DESIS Lab at Politecnico di Milano. She currently researches on "How XR technology can add value to co-creation in urban design". Besides researching and studying, Paulina Porten is working freelance as a Creative Technologist, where she creates design solutions that are strategic and conceptual. They enable people to vibrantly experience their surroundings, focusing on immersive technologies.

Dr. Zhenzhen Qi is an educator, researcher, and technologist based in Brooklyn, New York. Since 2014, she has taught courses on interactive media and web and game development at Teachers College, Columbia University, City University of New York (CUNY), among others, as an adjunct professor. She has given talks and led workshops at New York Creative Tech Week, Museum 2050, and Asia Art Archive in America among others. She is the recipient of the Creative Technology Fellowship and Macy Fellowship at Columbia University. Qi was a member of NEW INC, a culture and technology incubator at the New Museum, and a technology resident at Pioneer Works Center for Art and Innovation. She co-founded zzyw.org, an artist and research collective which produces software application, installation, and text as instruments to examine the cultural, political, and educational imprints of computation. Her computational art has been curated by leading art institutions around the world, such as Rhizome of New Museum in New York and Power Station of Art in Shanghai, China. She is the co-founder and director of NYC-based experiential production lab Power Nap Studio.

Nishra Ranpura is a designer, a researcher, and an educator from India practicing in the USA in the fields of crafts and emerging technologies. She has an MFA in Design and Technology from Parsons School of Design (The New School) in New York, USA. She gained her Bachelor's in Textile Design from the National Institute of Fashion Technology (NIFT), in Gandhinagar, India. She makes things and breaks things. Sometimes, she writes. Oftentimes, she wonders.

Selected Readings

"Open Government Deutschland: Second National Action Plan 2019–2021." Berlin, Germany: Federal Chancellery, September 30, 2021. https://www.bundesregierung.de/breg-de/service/publikationen/open-government-deutschland-second-national-action-plan-2019-2021-final-report-1997180.

Aarseth, Espen J. *Cybertext: Perspectives on Ergodic Literature*. Baltimore, MD: Johns Hopkins University Press, 1997.

Ackermann, Edith. "Piaget's Constructivism, Papert's Constructionism: What's the Difference?" *Future of Learning Group Publication* 5, no. 3 (January 1, 2001): 438.

Aizenberg, Evgeni, and Jeroen van den Hoven. "Designing for Human Rights in AI." *Big Data & Society* 7, no. 2 (July 1, 2020): 1–14. https://doi.org/10.1177/2053951720949566.

Anthropy, Anna. *Rise of the Videogame Zinesters: How Freaks, Normals, Amateurs, Artists, Dreamers, Drop-Outs, Queers, Housewives, and People Like You Are Taking Back an Art Form*. New York: Seven Stories Press, 2012.

Arditi, Aries. "Adjustable Typography: An Approach to Enhancing Low Vision Text Accessibility." *Ergonomics* 47, no. 5 (April 15, 2004): 469–82. https://doi.org/10.1080/0014013031000085680.

Auxier, Brooke, and Monica Anderson. "Social Media Use in 2021." *Pew Research Center: Internet, Science & Tech* (blog), April 7, 2021. https://www.pewresearch.org/internet/2021/04/07/social-media-use-in-2021.

Bailey, Emilia. "Play-to-Earn Gaming Sounds Too Good to Be True. It Probably Is." *The World News*, May 18, 2022. https://theworldnews.net/us-news/play-to-earn-gaming-sounds-too-good-to-be-true-it-probably-is.

Baker, Mark. *Digital Transformation*. 2nd ed. Buckingham: CreateSpace Independent Publishing Platform, 2014.

Banzi, Massimo, and Michael Shiloh. *Make: Getting Started with Arduino*. 3rd ed. Maker Media, Incorporated, 2008.

Bawden, David. "Origins and Concepts of Digital Literacy." Edited by Colin Lankshear and Michele Knobel. *Digital Literacies: Concepts, Policies and Practices* 30, no. 2008 (2008): 17–32.

Bayer, Herbert. "Towards a Universal Type." *Industrial Arts*, 1936.

Baytiyeh, Hoda, and Jay Pfaffman. "Volunteers in Wikipedia: Why the Community Matters." *Journal of Educational Technology & Society* 13, no. 2 (2010): 128–40.

Berger, John. *Ways of Seeing: Based on the BBC Television Series*. 1st edition. London: Penguin Books, 1990.

Bilyalova, A. A., D. A. Salimova, and T. I. Zelenina. "Digital Transformation in Education." In *Integrated Science in the Digital Age*, edited by Tatiana Antipova, 265–76. Lecture Notes in Networks and Systems. Cham: Springer International Publishing, 2020. https://doi.org/10.1007/978-3-030-22493-6_24.

Blascovich, Jim, and Jeremy Bailenson. *Infinite Reality: The Hidden Blueprint of Our Virtual Lives*. New York: William Morrow Paperbacks, 2012.

Bono, Edward de. *Lateral Thinking: A Textbook of Creativity*. Penguin Adult, 2010.

Bostrom, Nick. *Superintelligence: Paths, Dangers, Strategies*. Oxford University Press, 2014.

Botsman, Rachel. *Who Can You Trust?: How Technology Brought Us Together and Why It Might Drive Us Apart*. New York: PublicAffairs, 2017.

Boza-Kiss, Benigna, Shonali Pachauri, and Caroline Zimm. "Deprivations and Inequities in Cities Viewed Through a Pandemic Lens." *Frontiers in Sustainable Cities* 3 (2021). https://doi.org/10.3389/frsc.2021.645914.

Bruno, Munari. *Le macchine di Munari*. Torino, Einaudi, 1942.

Buchholz, Beth A., Jason DeHart, and Gary Moorman. "Digital Citizenship During a Global Pandemic: Moving Beyond Digital Literacy." *Journal of Adolescent & Adult Literacy* 64, no. 1 (2020): 11–17. https://doi.org/10.1002/jaal.1076.

Buchloh, Benjamin H. D. "Conceptual Art 1962–1969: From the Aesthetic of Administration to the Critique of Institutions." *October* 55 (1990): 105–43. https://doi.org/10.2307/778941.

California College of the Arts. *Ari Melenciano: Speculating Futures through Omni-Specialized Design*. YouTube Video, 2021. https://www.youtube.com/watch?v=Fcx6QFmJTKU.

Campbell, Joseph. *The Hero with a Thousand Faces*. 3rd ed. Novato, CA: New World Library, 2008.

Carroll, Antionette D. "Equity-Centered Community Design." Slow Factory. Accessed June 27, 2022. https://slowfactory.earth/courses/equity-centered-community-design/.

Carroll, Antionette D. *Design No Harm: Why Humility Is Essential in the Journey Toward Equity*. Online Video. In/Visible Talks 2020, 2020. https://vimeo.com/389018075.

Chen, Melvin. "Trust and Trust-Engineering in Artificial Intelligence Research: Theory and Praxis." *Philosophy & Technology* 34, no. 4 (December 1, 2021): 1429–47. https://doi.org/10.1007/s13347-021-00465-4.

Chen, Yushi, and Sara Lucia Arbelaez Llano. "Service Design and Government." In *The Future of Service Design*, edited by Birgit Mager, 40. Köln: KISD, TH Köln, 2020.

Chivers, Tom. *The AI Does Not Hate You: The Rationalists and Their Quest to Save the World*. Orion Publishing Group, Limited, 2019.

Conrey, Brian J. "The Riemann Hypothesis." *Notices of the American Mathematical Society* 50, no. 3 (January 1, 2003): 341–53.

Danto, Arthur C. *What Art Is*. New Haven, CT: Yale University Press, 2014.

Davis, Meredith. "Introduction to Design Futures." AIGA, 2019. https://www.aiga.org/aiga-design-futures/introduction-to-design-futures/.

Devon, Richard. "Design Ethics: The Social Ethics Paradigm." *International Journal of Engineering Education* 20, no. 3 (2004): 461–69.

Dickie, George. *Art and the Aesthetic: An Institutional Analysis*. Ithaca, N.Y: Cornell University Press, 1974.

Dijk, Jan A. G. M. van. "Digital Divide Research, Achievements and Shortcomings." *Poetics*, The digital divide in the twenty-first century, 34, no. 4 (August 1, 2006): 221–35. https://doi.org/10.1016/j.poetic.2006.05.004.

Dobres, Jonathan, Nadine Chahine, Bryan Reimer, David Gould, Bruce Mehler, and Joseph F. Coughlin. "Utilising Psychophysical Techniques to Investigate the Effects of Age, Typeface Design, Size and Display Polarity on Glance Legibility." *Ergonomics* 59, no. 10 (October 2016): 1377–91. https://doi.org/10.1080/00140139.2015.1137637.

Drees-Gross, Franz, and Pepe Zhang. "Poor Digital Access Is Holding Latin America and the Caribbean Back. Here's How to Change It." *World Bank Blogs* (blog), August 12, 2021. https://blogs.worldbank.org/latinamerica/poor-digital-access-holding-latin-america-and-caribbean-back-heres-how-change-it.

Featherstone, Mark. "The Eye of War: Images of Destruction in Virilio and Bataille." *Journal for Cultural Research* 7, no. 4 (October 1, 2003): 433–47. https://doi.org/10.1080/1479758032000165066.

Franceschet, Massimo, Giovanni Colavizza, Tai Smith, Blake Finucane, Martin Lukas Ostachowski, Sergio Scalet, Jonathan Perkins, James Morgan, and Sebastian Hernandez. "Crypto Art: A Decentralized View." arXiv, June 9, 2019. https://doi.org/10.48550/arXiv.1906.03263.

Friedman, Batya, and David G. Hendry. *Value Sensitive Design: Shaping Technology with Moral Imagination*. Cambridge, MA: The MIT Press, 2019.

Gamman, Lorraine, and Tom Fisher. "Introduction: Ways of Thinking Tricky Design." In *Tricky Design: The Ethics of Things*, edited by Tom Fisher and Lorraine Gamman. New York: Bloomsbury Visual Arts, 2020.

Gardner, Howard, and Katie Davis. *The App Generation: How Today's Youth Navigate Identity, Intimacy, and Imagination in a Digital World*. New Haven, CT: Yale University Press, 2013.

Garoian, Charles R., and Yvonne M. Gaudelius. "Cyborg Pedagogy: Performing Resistance in the Digital Age." *Studies in Art Education* 42, no. 4 (July 1, 2001): 333–47. https://doi.org/10.1080/00393541.2001.11651708.

Gooding, Sian, Yevgeni Berzak, Tony Mak, and Matt Sharifi. "Predicting Text Readability from Scrolling Interactions." In *Proceedings of the 25th Conference on Computational Natural Language Learning*, 380–90. Online: Association for Computational Linguistics, 2021. https://doi.org/10.18653/v1/2021.conll-1.30.

Goodman, Nelson. *Languages of Art: An Approach to a Theory of Symbols*. The Bobbs-Merrill Company, 1968.

Grey, Anne-Marie. "The Case for Connectivity, the New Human Right." United Nations, December 10, 2020. https://www.un.org/en/un-chronicle/case-connectivity-new-human-right.

Han, Byung-Chul. *In the Swarm: Digital Prospects*. Translated by Erik Butler. Cambridge, MA: The MIT Press, 2017.

Hardin, Russell. "Conceptions and Explanations of Trust." In *Trust in Society*, edited by Karen S. Cook. New York: Russell Sage Foundation, 2001.

Hawks, Phil. "The Relevance of Traditional Drawing in the Digital Age." In *Proceedings of the Electronic Visualisation and the Arts (EVA 2010)*. BCS Learning & Development, 2010. https://doi.org/10.14236/ewic/EVA2010.47.

Hayles, Katherine. *How We Think: Digital Media and Contemporary Technogenesis*. Chicago; London: University of Chicago Press, 2012.

Hui, Yuk. *Art and Cosmotechnics*. Minneapolis, MN: eflux Architecture, 2021.

International Telecommunication Union. "Measuring Digital Development: Facts and Figures 2021." ITU. Accessed June 25, 2022. https://www.itu.in t:443/en/ITU-D/Statistics/Pages/facts/default.aspx.

Internet Society. "Internet for Education in Africa: Helping Policy Makers to Meet the Global Education Agenda Sustainable Development Goal 4." *Internet Society* (blog), April 11, 2017. https://www.internetsociety.org/reso urces/doc/2017/internet-for-education-in-africa-helping-policy-makers-to-meet-the-global-education-agenda-sustainable-development-goal-4/.

Jacob, Ogunode Niyi, Okwelogu Izunna Somadina, Yahaya Danjuma M, and T. G. Olatunde-Aiyedun. "Deployment of ICT Facilities by Post-Basic Education and Career Development (PBECD) During Covid-19 in Nigeria: Challenges and Way Forward." *International Journal of Discoveries and Innovations in Applied Sciences* 1, no. 5 (October 6, 2021): 19–25.

Joselit, David. "NFTs, or The Readymade Reversed." *October* Winter, no. 175 (April 10, 2021): 3–4. https://doi.org/10.1162/octo_a_00419.

Jurkiewicz, Carole L. "Big Data, Big Concerns: Ethics in the Digital Age." *Public Integrity* 20, no. sup1 (January 18, 2018): S46–59. https://doi.org/10.1080/10 999922.2018.1448218.

Juul, Jesper. *Half-Real: Video Games between Real Rules and Fictional Worlds*. Cambridge, MA: The MIT Press, 2011.

Kelton, Conor, Zijun Wei, Seoyoung Ahn, Aruna Balasubramanian, Samir Das, Dimitris Samaras, and Gregory Zelinsky. "Reading Detection in Real-Time." In *Proceedings of the 11th ACM Symposium on Eye Tracking Research & Applications*, 43:1–5. ACM, 2019. https://doi.org/10.1145/3314111.3319916.

Knight Foundation. "Social Impact Games: Do They Work?" Knight Foundation, April 2012. https://knightfoundation.org/wp-content/up loads/2012/04/Knight_Games_Evaluation_Brochure.pdf.

Lades, Leonhard K., and Liam Delaney. "Nudge FORGOOD." *Behavioural Public Policy* 6, no. 1 (January 2022): 75–94. https://doi.org/10.1017/bpp.2019.53.

Lefebvre, Henri, and Gregory Elliott. *Critique of Everyday Life*. Translated by John Moore. London: Verso, 2014.

Lofgren, Eric T., and Nina H. Fefferman. "The Untapped Potential of Virtual Game Worlds to Shed Light on Real World Epidemics." *The Lancet Infectious Diseases* 7, no. 9 (September 1, 2007): 625–29. https://doi.org/10.1016/S1473 -3099(07)70212-8.

Lynch, Kevin. *The Image of the City*. Cambridge: MIT Press, 1964.

Maeda, John. "How I Learned What 'Digital Transformation' Truly Means after Waving to a Couple Gs." *Medium* (blog), December 24, 2020. https://john

maeda.medium.com/how-i-learned-what-digital-transformation-truly-means-after-waving-to-a-couple-gs-3be62c4cef7a.

Mager, Birgit. "The Future of Service Design." In *The Future of Service Design*, edited by Birgit Mager. Köln: KISD, TH Köln, 2020.

Manzini, Ezio. *Design, When Everybody Designs: An Introduction to Design for Social Innovation*. Translated by Rachel Coad. Cambridge, MA: The MIT Press, 2015.

McLeod, Saul. "Social Identity Theory." Simply Psychology, October 24, 2019. https://www.simplypsychology.org/social-identity-theory.html.

McLuhan, Marshall. *Understanding Media: The Extensions of Man*. Cambridge, MA: The MIT Press, 1964.

Mergel, Ines. "Digital Transformation of the German State." In *Public Administration in Germany*, edited by Sabine Kuhlmann, Isabella Proeller, Dieter Schimanke, and Jan Ziekow, 331–55. Governance and Public Management. Cham: Springer International Publishing, 2021. https://doi.org/10.1007/978-3-030-53697-8_19.

Munari, Alberto. "Bruno Munari The Surpriser." In *Giro Giro Tondo/ Design for children*, edited by Silvana Annicchiarico, 204–5. Milan: Mondadori Electa, 2017.

Murray, Kate M. "Digital Equity In Access To Justice." Vancouver, BC: Legal Services Society, BC, October 2021. https://legalaid.bc.ca/sites/default/files/inline-files/Murray_2021_LABC_Achieving_Digital_Equity_Final_Report_0.pdf.

Nagel, Emily van der. "'Networks That Work Too Well': Intervening in Algorithmic Connections." *Media International Australia* 168, no. 1 (August 1, 2018): 81–92. https://doi.org/10.1177/1329878X18783002.

National Digital Inclusion Alliance. "Local Government COVID-19 Digital Inclusion Response." Accessed June 26, 2022. https://www.digitalinclusion.org/local-government-covid-19-digital-inclusion-response/.

Neto, Isabel, and Michel Rogy. "Too Many Africans Cannot Access the Technology They Need. A World Bank Initiative Aims to Help Reverse That." *World Bank Blogs* (blog), September 22, 2021. https://blogs.worldbank.org/digital-development/too-many-africans-cannot-access-technology-they-need-world-bank-initiative-aims.

Nickel, Philip J. "Design for the Value of Trust." In *Handbook of Ethics, Values, and Technological Design*, edited by Jeroen van den Hoven, Pieter E. Vermaas, and Ibo van de Poel, 551–67. New York: Springer, 2015. https://link.springer.com/book/10.1007/978-94-007-6970-0.

OECD. "Understanding the Digital Divide." Paris: OECD, January 1, 2001. https://doi.org/10.1787/236405667766.
Papert, Seymour A. *Mindstorms: Children, Computers, And Powerful Ideas*. 2nd ed. New York: Basic Books, 1993.
Paul, Christiane. *Digital Art*. 3rd ed. London: Thames & Hudson, 2015.
Perkin, Neil, and Peter Abraham. *Building the Agile Business through Digital Transformation*. Kogan Page, 2017.
Pettit, Philip. "The Cunning of Trust." *Philosophy & Public Affairs* 24, no. 3 (1995): 202–25. https://doi.org/10.1111/j.1088-4963.1995.tb00029.x.
Prensky, Marc. "Digital Natives, Digital Immigrants Part 1." *On the Horizon* 9, no. 5 (January 1, 2001): 1–6. https://doi.org/10.1108/10748120110424816.
Ragnedda, Massimo. *Enhancing Digital Equity: Connecting the Digital Underclass*. Cham, Switzerland: Palgrave Macmillan, 2020.
Rangaswamy, Nimmi. "Telecenters and Internet Cafés: The Case of ICTs in Small Businesses." *Asian Journal of Communication* 18, no. 4 (December 1, 2008): 365–78. https://doi.org/10.1080/01292980802344208.
Resnick, Paul, and Richard Zeckhauser. "Trust among Strangers in Internet Transactions: Empirical Analysis of EBay's Reputation System." In *The Economics of the Internet and E-Commerce*, edited by Michael R. Baye, 11:127–57. Advances in Applied Microeconomics. Emerald Group Publishing Limited, 2002. https://doi.org/10.1016/S0278-0984(02)11030-3.
Robinson, Laura, Shelia R. Cotten, Hiroshi Ono, Anabel Quan-Haase, Gustavo Mesch, Wenhong Chen, Jeremy Schulz, Timothy M. Hale, and Michael J. Stern. "Digital Inequalities and Why They Matter." *Information, Communication & Society* 18, no. 5 (May 4, 2015): 569–82. https://doi.org/10.1080/1369118X.2015.1012532.
Rogers, David L. *The Digital Transformation Playbook: Rethink Your Business for the Digital Age*. New York: Columbia Business School Publishing, 2016.
Rosati, Luca. "How to Design Interfaces for Choice: Hick-Hyman Law and Classification for Information Architecture." In *Proceedings of the International UDC Seminar*, 125–38. The Hague, 2013.
Schaefer, Kristin E., Jessie Y. C. Chen, James L. Szalma, and P. A. Hancock. "A Meta-Analysis of Factors Influencing the Development of Trust in Automation: Implications for Understanding Autonomy in Future Systems." *Human Factors* 58, no. 3 (May 1, 2016): 377–400. https://doi.org/10.1177/0018720816634228.

Scherling, Laura S. *Learning During a Digital Transformation in Communication Design: Faculty, Professional, and Student Views on Changing Pedagogical Practices*. New York: Teachers College, Columbia University, 2020.

Scherling, Laura, and Andrew DeRosa, eds. *Ethics in Design and Communication: Critical Perspectives*. Bloomsbury Publishing, 2020.

Schmidt, Andreas T., and Bart Engelen. "The Ethics of Nudging: An Overview." *Philosophy Compass* 15, no. 4 (2020): e12658. https://doi.org/10.1111/phc3.12658.

Service, Owain, Michael Hallsworth, David Halpern, Felicity Algate, Rory Gallagher, and Sam Nguyen. "EAST: Four Simple Ways to Apply Behavioural Insights." Behavioural Insights Team, July 2015. https://www.bi.team/publications/east-four-simple-ways-to-apply-behavioural-insights/.

Servon, Lisa. "Four Myths about the Digital Divide." *Planning Theory & Practice* 3, no. 2 (January 1, 2002): 222–27. https://doi.org/10.1080/14649350220150080.

Shuhaiber, Ahmed, and Ibrahim Mashal. "Understanding Users' Acceptance of Smart Homes." *Technology in Society* 58 (August 1, 2019): 101110. https://doi.org/10.1016/j.techsoc.2019.01.003.

Steyerl, Hito. *Duty Free Art: Art in the Age of Planetary Civil War*. London: Verso, 2017.

Stickdorn, Marc, Markus Hormess, Adam Lawrence, and Jakob Schneider. *This Is Service Design Doing: Applying Service Design Thinking in the Real World*. Sebastopol (CA): O'Reilly Media, 2018.

Suárez-Guerrero, Cristóbal, Carmen Lloret-Catala, and Santiago Mengual-Andres. "Teachers' Perceptions of the Digital Transformation of the Classroom through the Use of Tablets: A Study in Spain." *Comunicar* 24, no. 49 (July 1, 2016). https://doi.org/10.3916/C49-2016-08.

Sugarman, Julie, and Melissa Lazarín. "Educating English Learners during the COVID-19 Pandemic: Policy Ideas for States and School Districts." Policy Brief. Migration Policy Institute, 2020. https://www.migrationpolicy.org/sites/default/files/publications/mpi-english-learners-covid-19-final.pdf.

Tanni, Valentina. *Memestetica: Il settembre eterno dell'arte*. Roma: Nero Edizioni, 2020.

Tapscott, Don. *The Digital Economy: Promise and Peril In The Age of Networked Intelligence*. New York: McGraw-Hill, 1997.

Thaler, Richard H., and Cass R. Sunstein. *Nudge: Improving Decisions about Health, Wealth, and Happiness*. Revised & Expanded edition. New York: Penguin Books, 2009.

Tinker, M. A. "Experimental Study of Reading." *Psychological Bulletin* 31, no. 2 (1934): 98–110. https://doi.org/10.1037/h0074040.

Turkle, Sherry. "Always-On/Always-On-You: The Tethered Self." In the *Handbook of Mobile Communication Studies*. The MIT Press, 2008. https://doi.org/10.7551/mitpress/9780262113120.003.0010.

Vermaas, Pieter E., Yao-Hua Tan, Jeroen van den Hoven, Brigitte Burgemeestre, and Joris Hulstijn. "Designing for Trust: A Case of Value-Sensitive Design." *Knowledge, Technology & Policy* 23, no. 3 (December 1, 2010): 491–505. https://doi.org/10.1007/s12130-010-9130-8.

Werbach, Kevin. *The Blockchain and the New Architecture of Trust*. Cambridge, MA: The MIT Press, 2018.

Youngblood, Michael, Benjamin J. Chesluk, and Nadeem Haidary. *Rethinking Users: The Design Guide to User Ecosystem Thinking*. Amsterdam: Laurence King Publishing, 2021.

Zacharia, Zacharias C., Tasos Hovardas, Nikoletta Xenofontos, Ivoni Pavlou, and Maria Irakleous. "Education and Employment of Women in Science, Technology and the Digital Economy, Including AI and Its Influence on Gender Equality." European Parliament, April 15, 2020. https://www.europarl.europa.eu/thinktank/en/document/IPOL_STU(2020)651042.

Zengotita, Thomas de. *Mediated: How the Media Shapes Your World and the Way You Live in It*. Bloomsbury, USA: Baker & Taylor, 2010.

Zhou, Shao-Na, Hui Zeng, Shao-Rui Xu, Lu-Chang Chen, and Hua Xiao. "Exploring Changes In Primary Students' Attitudes Towards Science, Technology, Engineering And Mathematics (STEM) Across Genders And Grade Levels." *Journal of Baltic Science Education* 18, no. 3 (2019): 466–80. https://doi.org/10.33225/jbse/19.18.466.

Zorzi, Marco, Chiara Barbiero, Andrea Facoetti, Isabella Lonciari, Marco Carrozzi, Marcella Montico, Laura Bravar, Florence George, Catherine Pech-Georgel, and Johannes C. Ziegler. "Extra-Large Letter Spacing Improves Reading in Dyslexia." *Proceedings of the National Academy of Sciences of the United States of America* 109, no. 28 (July 10, 2012): 11455–59. https://doi.org/10.1073/pnas.1205566109.

Zuboff, Shoshana. *The Age of Surveillance Capitalism: The Fight for a Human Future at the New Frontier of Power*. New York, NY: PublicAffairs, 2019.